A JUDGE'S JOURNEY

John Dyson is one of the leading lawyers of his generation. After a career at the Bar, he rose to become a Justice of the Supreme Court and Master of the Rolls. In this compelling memoir, he describes his life and career with disarming candour and gives real insights into the challenges of judging. He also gives a fascinating account of his immigrant background, the impact of the Holocaust on his family and his journey from the Jewish community in Leeds in the 1950s to the top of his profession. Although he may be perceived as being a member of the Establishment, this arresting story shows how he continues to be influenced by his Jewish and European roots.

A Judge's Journey

John Dyson

·HART·

OXFORD · LONDON · NEW YORK · NEW DELHI · SYDNEY

HART PUBLISHING

Bloomsbury Publishing Plc

Kemp House, Chawley Park, Cumnor Hill, Oxford, OX2 9PH, UK

HART PUBLISHING, the Hart/Stag logo, BLOOMSBURY and the Diana logo are
trademarks of Bloomsbury Publishing Plc

First published in Great Britain 2019

Reprinted 2019

Copyright © John Dyson, 2019

John Dyson has asserted his right under the Copyright, Designs and Patents
Act 1988 to be identified as Author of this work.

All rights reserved. No part of this publication may be reproduced or transmitted in any form or by any
means, electronic or mechanical, including photocopying, recording, or any information storage
or retrieval system, without prior permission in writing from the publishers.

While every care has been taken to ensure the accuracy of this work, no responsibility for
loss or damage occasioned to any person acting or refraining from action as a result of any
statement in it can be accepted by the authors, editors or publishers.

All UK Government legislation and other public sector information used in the work is
Crown Copyright ©. All House of Lords and House of Commons information used in
the work is Parliamentary Copyright ©. This information is reused under the terms
of the Open Government Licence v3.0 (http://www.nationalarchives.gov.uk/doc/
open-government-licence/version/3) except where otherwise stated.

All Eur-lex material used in the work is © European Union,
http://eur-lex.europa.eu/, 1998–2019.

A catalogue record for this book is available from the British Library.

Library of Congress Cataloging-in-Publication data

Names: Dyson, John, Lord, 1943-, author.

Title: A judge's journey / John Dyson.

Description: Chicago : Hart Publishing, 2019.

Identifiers: LCCN 2019021087 (print) | LCCN 2019021904 (ebook) |
ISBN 9781509927852 (EPub) | ISBN 9781509927845 (pbk. : alk. paper)

Subjects: LCSH: Dyson, John, Lord, 1943- | Lawyers—Great Britain—Biography. |
Judges—Great Britain—Biography.

Classification: LCC KD632.D97 (ebook) | LCC KD632.D97 D97 2019 (print) |
DDC 347.41/035092 [B]—dc23

LC record available at https://lccn.loc.gov/2019021087

ISBN: PB: 978-1-50992-784-5
        ePDF: 978-1-50992-786-9
        ePub: 978-1-50992-785-2

Typeset by Compuscript Ltd, Shannon
Printed and bound in Great Britain by CPI Group (UK) Ltd, Croydon CR0 4YY

MIX
Paper from
responsible sources
FSC® C013604

To find out more about our authors and books visit www.hartpublishing.co.uk. Here you will find
extracts, author information, details of forthcoming events and the option to sign up for our newsletters.

To my family

Acknowledgements

THE ACORN FROM which this Memoir grew was the valedictory speech that I made on my retirement as Master of the Rolls in 2016 in which I referred to my Jewish roots. That speech inspired me to write the Autobiographical Background to my book *Justice: Continuity and Change* which was published by Hart Publishing in 2018. Various people who heard the speech and have read that essay suggested that I should go further and give a full account of my life. I am grateful to all of them for their encouragement. I have hugely enjoyed writing about my journey.

I am particularly grateful to several members of my family for their assistance. My wife, Jacqueline, has read every word enthusiastically at least twice. She has made many wise suggestions all of which, I believe, have improved the book. My love for her and appreciation of her support in my life is a motif that runs right through the book from our chance meeting which I describe in chapter five to the end.

My children Michelle and Steven have made valuable comments on the family history chapters. My brother Robert has been especially helpful on chapters one to three where the Journey starts. And my brother-in-law David Levy has made astute observations which have helped me to focus on the kind of memoir I wanted write.

Finally, I wish to thank Sinead Moloney, the Publisher and General Editor at Hart Publishing for her encouragement and wisdom. She and her team have produced a book of which I am very proud.

Contents

Acknowledgements vii

1. My Mother's Family 1

2. My Father's Family 14

3. A Leeds Childhood 22

4. Oxford 51

5. New Beginnings: London 64

6. Engagement and Marriage 70

7. Practice at the Bar 75

8. The High Court 89

9. The Court of Appeal 113

10. The Supreme Court 129

11. Master of the Rolls 141

12. Master of the Rolls: Memorable Cases 186

13. On Being a Judge 196

14. No Longer a Judge 206

15. A Jew in England 221

16. My Family Life 228

17. Epilogue 237

Index 241

1

My Mother's Family

MY MOTHER WAS born on 4 June 1915 in Sofia, Bulgaria. Her mother, Malvine, was born on 9 May 1892 in Sofia. Malvine's parents, Karl and Hermine Goldstein, seem to have been well off. At some stage (probably in the early 1900s) they moved from Vienna to Sofia. Karl was a leather merchant and was proud of his business connections with the Bulgarian royal family. They moved back to Vienna in the 1930s where they lived in a flat in the smart Prater district. My mother used to visit them during her school holidays. Hermine lived in Vienna until she fled back to her birthplace Zemlin in Serbia, Yugoslavia to escape from the Nazis during the Second World War. In 1942, she was murdered by Nazi sympathisers in Stara Gradiska, a concentration camp in Croatia, Yugoslavia. Her father, Issak Guttmann, was born near Bratislava, which was then in Czechoslovakia, and went at some stage to Vienna and then to Budapest. He owned a salt mine in Pestszentloerinc, which is now a suburb of Budapest and died in 1905 in Budapest.

My grandmother Malvine had a comfortable middle-class life in Sofia. She told me that in her view *La Belle Epoque* (the period between 1871 and 1914) was the best time in the whole of history to have been alive. I have little doubt that in many ways this was the case for those who had money. She had little interest in the working classes or understanding of their situation. The upheavals generated by the various European revolutions of the late eighteenth and the nineteenth centuries seem to have had little or no impact on her life and that of her family. She never had to work. Her role in life was to be the matriarch of her own family, cultivate friendships and generally to lead an active social life with members of the upper strata of Bulgarian society. She held musical soirees in their flat. Balls, concerts and operas were the order of the day. This made the appalling experiences that she was to suffer during the Second World War all the more devastating and difficult for her to bear.

She met Jenö Kremsier at a dinner party in Sofia in about 1910. He was born in Budapest, Hungary on 11 March 1879. He was therefore about 13 years older than her. His father, Mihaly Kremsier, was born in Pest in January 1847. I know little about Jenö's background. According to my mother (who adored him), he had led a far from sheltered life and he continued with his wandering habits long after he married Malvine. I understand that a disparity between the standards of sexual behaviour that were acceptable for middle-class men and women was quite common at that time.

She was with her parents at the dinner party. Young women always had to be chaperoned in those days. Access to the opposite sex outside marriage in middle-class circles must have been quite tricky. Malvine claimed that Jenö played 'footsie' under the dinner table and wasted no time in asking her father for her hand.

Jenö was employed by the Bank of Hungary. By 1910, he was working as a branch manager in Sofia. In due course, he became a director of the bank. Following their marriage on 30 March 1912 in Sofia, Malvine and Jenö lived the life of well to do people, very much in the style of her parents. My mother told me that he would tease Malvine saying that she came from a sophisticated family, whereas he was a '*bauer*' or peasant. But he was a highly intelligent man as I have recently discovered from reading the fascinating letters that he wrote from Budapest to my mother during the Second World War when she was already living in England. Malvine was a social snob who judged people by their wealth and their appearance. She was also an intellectual snob. She pretended to read serious literature and to enjoy doing so. The reality was otherwise. Jenö had no such pretentions.

They had three children: Erno a boy who was born in 1913, Gisella (my mother) and Margit who was born in 1919. The girls received a good education at the German speaking school in Sofia. German was spoken by the upper middle class, just as French was the language of the aristocracy in nineteenth-century Russia. My mother stayed at school until the age of eighteen. She was a diligent student. She had a good rounded education which included the study of Latin. Much later in life, she was still able to recite the opening lines of Cicero's *In Catilinam* '*quo usque tandem abutere, Catilina, patientia nostra?*' She learnt to play the piano to a good standard. She was still able to play Chopin waltzes and mazurkas when I was growing up. She was also excellent at embroidery, tapestry and knitting and did the sort of things that refined, young, comfortably off women did in central Europe in those days. Her output of tapestry and knitting was prodigious even in her later years. I still use a piano stool whose seat is covered with her tapestry work and our daughter Michelle has dining chairs whose seats are covered with yet more of her tapestry work.

My uncle Erno was a tearaway who was too much for his parents to handle. When he was quite young, he was sent to a boarding school. He was a colourful character and quite wild throughout his life. I was told that he had an affair with a spy in Luxembourg during the Second World War. He spent most of his adult life trying to avoid paying tax. That is why he lived for a long time in Andorra.

But to return to my mother's early life, she did not see her father until she was three years old. This was because he fought for the Austro-Hungarian forces against the Russians in the First World War. At some stage, he was captured by the Russians. According to my mother, he escaped in a hay wagon and narrowly avoided being bayonetted by Russian soldiers. In one of the letters that he wrote to my parents during the Second World War, he refers to his 'Siberian experiences'. Eventually, he reached Odessa where he was hidden by a man called Warschawski.

He returned to civilian life in Sofia in 1918 and carried on working as a director of the bank. It seems that he did not work hard. He spent much time in cafés reading newspapers that were fixed to wooden poles and playing chess. Life went on much as before the war except that there were now three children in the family. Malvine and Jenö were not 'hands on' parents. The children were largely brought up by the governess and the cook. My mother spoke very warmly about them. They had little education and were not at all sophisticated; but they showed an affection for and interest in the children which they did not receive from their parents. When the children were small, they would be prepared for bed by the governess and presented to their parents for a kiss and a brief 'good night'. This was apparently typical of such households at the time.

One family activity about which my mother spoke was hiking on the Vitosha mountain which is in the outskirts of Sofia. They would go there with the governess and eat barbecued lamb kebabs and burgers. My mother always loved walking in the mountains, as do I.

As I have said, she had a good education. She frequently spoke to me enthusiastically about the writings of Heine and, in particular, Stefan Zweig. Zweig was all the rage in the 1930s in central Europe and in other parts of the world. When I was growing up, he was virtually unknown in this country. In recent years, there has developed something of a cult for his work here too. The bitter-sweet quality of his work appealed very much to the passionate and romantic side of my mother's character. I have greatly enjoyed his works too. His 'The World of Yesterday' is a wonderfully evocative account of what it was like to be alive in central Europe between 1881 and 1942.

Both Malvine and Jenö were Jewish. I know very little about their Jewish lives. They were not at all religious. They did not observe the dietary laws or the religious rites and traditions. But I believe that they were extremely conscious of their Jewish identity. It was very difficult for Jews in the 1930s not to be conscious of their Jewish identity in the face of the currents of anti-Semitism that were swirling around strongly not only in Germany, but in many other European countries too. So far as I am aware, there was no inter-marriage within the family except by the rebellious Erno, whose first wife was Jewish but his second and third wives were not.

The political life in Bulgaria between the two world wars was quite turbulent. I have no idea whether my mother was interested in politics. She never talked to me about the political situation in Bulgaria. But she did describe an incident that she witnessed when she was walking in the street in Sofia. A man who was walking in front of her dropped dead, having been shot by someone she described as a Serbian nationalist who was walking behind her. This experience marked her for life. She was by nature of a nervous disposition and always suspicious of and anxious about the police, soldiers and officials of any kind. When I was growing up, each time we passed through customs control after a holiday, she would become very tense, as if fearing that something unpleasant would happen to her.

At some stage in the early 1930s, Jenö decided to retire and take his family back to his birthplace, Budapest. I don't know the reason for the move. It may have been partly because Budapest was a more cultured and sophisticated city. A further factor was probably that anti-Semitism was on the rise in Sofia, although life was not easy for Jews in Hungary either. By 1936, the family was living at Kossuth Lajos Ter 4 in Budapest V.

On 9 May 1936, my mother, who was now almost 21 years of age, married Imre Majer. He was a bank official who had been born in Novi Sad, Serbia. The marriage was a disaster and after two or three weeks, she left him and returned to Budapest. It seems that there had been problems over the ownership of her dowry. Imre's father had designs on the cash and wanted to use it to purchase a forest for his timber business. She resisted and Imre was caught in the cross-fire between his wife and his parents. He tried to save the marriage, but she would have none of it. I am sure that there was more to it than that, but she never told me. They were not divorced until April 1939, when he gave her a 'gett' (Jewish divorce document). Being divorced in those days was a matter of shame in the kind of social milieu in which my mother's family moved. When she met my father in 1939, her brother told her not to mention her first husband. But she ignored this advice. She did not, however, feel able to tell me about it until I was 16 years old. The news came as a great shock to me. Worse still, she told me not to tell my younger brother Robert who was then 14 years old. I complied with her instruction, but he found out by other means and did not tell me that he had found out the dark secret. I mention all of this because it is indicative of the huge change in attitudes to divorce that has taken place during my lifetime.

When I was growing up, she frequently talked to me about her life in Budapest. In her memory, Budapest in the 1930s was a beautiful city where it was wonderful to be young and it was possible to savour all that life could offer. The family continued to enjoy the comfortable life that they had enjoyed in Sofia. My mother and her younger sister went to dances, even then always accompanied by Malvine. They still did not work. If she was aware of the darkening political situation in Europe, she never spoke to me about it. She did not mention Admiral Horthy, who served as Regent of Hungary from 1920 until 1944. He led an extremely conservative government, which in the late 1930s formed an alliance with Nazi Germany against the Soviet Union. Under his regime, the Hungarian Jews were persecuted with increasing vehemence. Quotas were introduced restricting the numbers of Jews who could enter the universities and the professions. She must have been aware of what was going on, but she said nothing about this to me. I suspect that she had expunged it from her memory.

I did not question the picture that she painted of life in Budapest. I had no knowledge of the history of Hungary in the 1930s other than what my mother had told me. It was not until much later that I got a more balanced understanding of the situation. When I was at Wadham College, Oxford in the 1960s, Sir Maurice Bowra, who was the Warden of the college, would invite small groups of students to dinner on Sunday evenings. Most of the talking was invariably be done by him. On the whole, the students listened reverentially. He had a great many interesting things to say. In an endeavour to contribute something fascinating and a little exotic to the conversation, I mentioned at one of the dinners that my mother had lived in Budapest during the 1930s. I said that I understood it had been a wonderful city at that time. The Warden asked me how I could say this in view of the terrible things that had been done by the Horthy regime. I had no answer to his question, not least because I had not even heard of Horthy. I was embarrassed and felt that I had been misled by my mother's nostalgia and her selective memory.

In 1938, she was encouraged by her father to go to Paris to learn about the fashion industry. She went to classes and learnt about different aspects of fashion, including millinery and how to make women's clothes. Her study of women's fashion was to prove most useful to her in later life. She told me that she loved her time in Paris. I am sure that her happy experience of life in Paris was the reason she encouraged me to go to Paris after I left school and before I went to Oxford. She was quite sentimental and my time in Paris enabled her to relive her own life there.

In January 1939 when she was still living in Paris, she decided to go on a skiing holiday to Chamonix. Her father insisted that she could only go if Erno and Margit went too. He was a strict and controlling father who was fearful of what might befall his daughters.

Chamonix was then a far less bustling place than it is now. But it was already established as a winter sports resort. It had hosted the first Winter Olympic Games in 1924 and by 1939, some cable cars had already been installed. But there was nothing like the profusion of skiing installations that there are now. Also in Chamonix were two young men who had travelled from Leeds, England to do some skiing. They were my father Richard Dytch (later Dyson) and his friend Harold Deutsch (later Denton). They were by no means affluent, but my father (and possibly Harold too) stayed at one of the smartest hotels in Chamonix. My mother, always very careful with money as her father had taught her to be, stayed in the garret of a small pension.

My parents were together for at most one week before he returned to Leeds and she to Paris. She spoke some English which I think she had learnt at school. She was fluent in German and Bulgarian and strong in French. During those few days, they spoke in English. It seems that they were both struck by a *coup de foudre*. After the disaster of the first marriage, one would have thought that my mother might have been more cautious this time. But she was a passionate and impetuous woman. She was determined to marry my father.

Between January and the end of May, they exchanged letters almost every day. They soon decided to marry. The correspondence shows that it was my mother who made the running. He said that he could not come to Budapest for the wedding until July. My mother kept pressing him to come sooner. It is also clear from her letters that she was becoming increasingly concerned about the political situation in Hungary. Her parents seriously considered emigrating to Santiago in Chile. Apparently a number of her friends had already emigrated there. She mentioned none of this to me during our many conversations. But she did say that her father was keen that she should marry my father and move to England because she would be safe there. It was not however merely a question of safety. The reputation of the United Kingdom as a fine and reliable country carried a great deal of weight in Europe in those days.

Jenö was also keen that Margit should marry Harold, although Margit said that she did not love him. Jenö felt sure that she would come to love him in time. It would be a great relief to Jenö that his two daughters would be living in the safety of England and be able to give each other support. Margit and Harold married in May 1939. Sadly, their marriage proved to be loveless and unhappy, but it staggered on until Harold died in 1987.

Meanwhile, in March my mother had come to Leeds with Jenö to visit my father's family. They stayed at the Great Northern Hotel next to Leeds Central Railway Station. The hotel was converted into flats many years ago. Each morning, Jenö retired to the Writing Room in the hotel to catch up with his correspondence. He and Malvine were great letter writers. Years later when we visited Malvine's apartment in Vevey, Switzerland, my brother Robert and I would soak off the stamps from letters that she had received from all over the world. She kept writing in her idiosyncratic spidery handwriting, which was very difficult to decipher, until she died in 1983.

The Leeds visit went reasonably well, which was quite an achievement in view of the huge cultural, educational and economic gap between the two families. The differences will become apparent when I describe my father's family in the next chapter. In addition to these differences, there was the fact that my father, who was the youngest and favourite child of the family, was marrying a divorcee and a foreigner. It seems that Jenö liked my father's mother Freda, who was warm and lovable. She will have spoken to him in Yiddish. I think his English was limited. Sadly, she died of cancer in 1940.

My father arrived in Budapest towards the end of May. The civil marriage ceremony took place on 27 May. It seems that none of my father's family went to the wedding. This was probably on account of the cost and difficulty of arranging travel. The religious ceremony took place in a synagogue in Budapest on 1 June. My mother did not wear a white wedding dress and only a few people attended. A white dress with its connotations of purity would have been thought to be inappropriate. The divorce clearly cast a considerable shadow.

My parents went on their honeymoon to Switzerland. They visited the World Exhibition in Bern. From there they travelled to Luzern, the Rigi, Vitznau and

Engelberg among other places. This sealed their love affair with the mountains of Switzerland, a love of which I and Robert have inherited.

Malvine and Jenö decided to move from their large flat in Ut Poszonyi 40 overlooking the Danube and the Margit Island to a smaller flat in a nearby square at Budapest 5, 25 St Istvan Ter where they still retained their maid.

Jenö corresponded frequently with my mother and Margit before his death from kidney failure on April 1943. The letters that we have show him as a warm, caring father, and a man who, even from more than a thousand miles away, tried hard to manage his children and their spouses and tell them what to do. He was an astute businessman. He was interested in the stock market and concerned that his family, now settled in England, should make wise investments. All the letters and instructions came from Jenö and, it seems, very few from Malvine. She would often add a few bland flowery good wishes at the end of Jenö's letters. However, as I was later to discover, she too was interested in the stock market and had a shrewd business sense. Despite his attempts to reassure my parents that they had no grounds for concern and that all was well, he could not conceal the rising sense of anxiety and alarm that was being generated by the situation in Europe.

On 26 July 1939, he wrote from Budapest:

> My secret hope is that in the new year we will at last have quietness and peace, which will allow us to sort out our affairs by investing our money wisely. We can look to settle in a modest house somewhere in France. We would have to have a small flat here in Budapest, where we could spend a few months each year.

He went on to say why he was convinced that there would be no war 'at least not this year'.

On 22 August 1939, he wrote from the spa town of Karlsbad (in Czechoslovakia) in response to my parents' 'anxious telegram':

> Your telegram caused us to be alarmed, but your concern moved us deeply ... We know that underneath we are boiling and burning, but on the surface we are cool. Here everything is calm, and life goes on as normal. Without excitement – we are not thinking about War, but instead thinking that there is taking place a peaceful reorganisation of lost territories ... Should there be a disaster, in spite of all this, we are Hungarians and our place is in Budapest.

On 15 June 1940, he wrote to my mother from Budapest that the post was now 'getting more difficult'. He continued:

> Our friends from Paris have gone all over the world, Bela to Bordeaux, Kuyum to Biarritz, Leo Rintel to New York, Eibschutz to Monte Carlo; many have gone to concentration camps, joined the forces or have died. Nice Choice!!

The last letter that we have from Jenö before his death is dated 28 November 1941. It includes the following:

> Your telegrams always give us courage and hope to live happily through the crises, but otherwise one ought surely to have doubts. When one sees and hears about all the

general and personal tragedies, one must thank the good Lord that not everything is going badly. As things stand, I have no fears about the fate of our family and feel that we will come through the War fit and well.

I hope that you have strength and hope to live through it all, especially you, my little Gisula [my mother], with your sensitive nerves and your not very great courage – or have you toughened up in the meantime?

Great strength is needed to keep the close and wider family together. By that I mean man and his wife, then children to parents and brothers and sisters. Everything is so easy if people are reasonable, have their heart in the right place and act without selfishness.

Don't worry about us, because at the moment we are a long way away from danger, and even if we were, we would be in much less danger than you. Because of this concern, we always eagerly await your telegrams, because we fear that the normal operation of the post will soon stop.

I sign off now with many kisses from your loving father.

Although her marriage to my father was my mother's second marriage, her parents were keen to provide her with a dowry which is what comfortable middle class parents did in those days. My mother refused her parents' offers of money. She considered that the money that she had received from her parents on her first marriage had been the cause of its catastrophic failure. In 1941, Jenö optimistically arranged for a consignment of furniture and other domestic items to be transported from Budapest to Leeds. The consignment reached Bordeaux in about November or December 1941. It never reached England.

When I went to Paris in 1961 before going to Oxford, I stayed with the family of Pierre Hardy (whose previous name was Oscar Arditti). He had been a school friend of my mother in Sofia. He and his brother had been deported to Auschwitz during the war. I can still recall that, like everyone who was incarcerated in that terrible camp, they had numbers tattooed on their forearms. They both survived and went to Paris after the war where they built up an extremely successful retail business in the centre of the city. Their experience of the war led them to change the family name from Arditti to Hardy, to decide not to have their son circumcised and to have him and their daughter brought up as Catholics. They hoped that these drastic measures would provide them with a degree of protection against persecution.

By 1961, my mother had accumulated a large number of documents relating to the missing consignment of furniture. She had been hoping that she might be entitled to receive compensation from the French Government. I gave the file of documents to the Hardys' lawyer. He advised that the prospects of compensation were remote and my parents wisely decided not to pursue the matter.

Contact between my mother and her parents became impossible. My mother became pregnant with me in the autumn of 1942. One of her great regrets was that Jenö died without knowing that he was to become a grandfather: I would have been his first grandchild. My mother wanted to call me Eugene (Jenö). For once, my father refused to agree with her. The resultant compromise was John. For a long time, my mother did not know that her father had died. Nor did she know what had happened to her mother.

It must have been very difficult for Malvine after Jenö died. She had never worked. None of her siblings had remained in Hungary. Otto, who was born on 4 November 1893, had been living with his German wife Edith in Berlin since before the war. He was described in some family papers as a merchant. Attempts to secure their safe passage to London were unsuccessful. They were both murdered by gassing in Auschwitz in 1943. Edith was gassed on arrival. Otto was gassed four months later after he had been working in a coal mine in the Auschwitz 3 complex. Irene, who was born in 1895, had married a businessman called Julius Balogh in Vienna. He ran a transport company using barges and motor boats which plied up and down the Danube. After the Germans invaded Austria in the *Anschluss* in 1938, the Baloghs moved from Vienna to London. At some stage, they moved to Bishops Stortford, Hertfordshire.

Emil was born in Sofia in 1896. He was passionate about classical music and married Elerica, a Rumanian pianist who, on marriage, promptly gave up the piano, to Emil's great distress. In 1938, they came to England and lived at 37 Compayne Gardens, London NW6. Emil lived there until he died in 1992. During the Second World War, he worked in Caversham, Berkshire, doing some kind of intelligence work. This included preparing propaganda leaflets which were dropped over Germany. From there, he went to work in 'strategic services' at the US Embassy in London. After the war, he attended the Nuremberg War Crimes trials and was involved with military intelligence and questioning Nazis. At some point after his return to London, he worked for the Bulgarian service at the BBC World Service. I recall driving him to Leeds in 1982 to attend a party organised by my parents for Malvine's ninetieth birthday (which she attended). He was a fascinating man who told us about his life in Sofia before the First World War. It was a long journey and we thought that he might need to stop for a rest and to use a toilet at a service station. But his bladder was in excellent order and he was happy to do the whole journey without a break. Malvine's family was tough and determined.

The youngest sibling was Rosa who married Isaac Freedman, a Yugoslav businessman. I don't know where they were living in 1943, but I am sure that it was not in Hungary. I met Rosa and Isaac once in the 1950s in Switzerland. They had two daughters, Lydi and Hanni, both of whom settled in Israel. After the death of Isaac, Rosa lived for a time in Israel. In the 1960s, she met a Mr Meyer who came from Munster, Germany. They married and she lived in Munster for the rest of her life. She died in 1974.

Although Malvine had some cousins and friends in Budapest, she must have been very lonely. Her husband was dead. All her children had left Hungary and none of her siblings was in Hungary either. Nor did she have the comfort of the routine of a job and work colleagues. The stress that she had to endure must have intensified when it started to become clear that the Germans had been systematically murdering the Jews of Europe. Although the anti-Jewish laws that Horthy had introduced in Hungary caused great hardship, most of the Hungarian Jews lived in relative safety until 1944. In March 1944, German troops invaded Hungary. Accompanying the German forces was a *Sonderkommando* unit headed by Adolf Eichmann whose task was to implement the 'Final Solution' in Hungary. Between 15 May and 9 July 1944, about 430,000 Hungarian Jews were deported mainly to Auschwitz. They represented almost the entire Jewish population that had been living outside Budapest.

Eichmann's plan was to complete the job by deporting the approximately 300,000 remaining Hungarian Jews, most of whom were living in Budapest. Throughout the spring of 1944, Reszo Kasztner, Joel Brand and other members of the Relief and Rescue Committee started negotiating with Eichmann in an attempt to save Jewish lives. Eichmann offered to exchange 'Blood for Goods' whereby a number of Jews would be spared in return for large amounts of goods, including trucks. In June, Kasztner persuaded Eichmann to let some 1,700 Jews leave the country by train. He and other Jewish leaders drew up a list of Jews to be released, in exchange for the equivalent of $US 2,000 per person. The idea was that those selected for release were to be a kind of Noah's Ark of the Hungarian Jewish community. They included children, many orthodox Jews and people from diverse social backgrounds. There were also 30 members of Kasztner's family as well as some 300 wealthy Jews (one of whom was Malvine) who were, in effect, to pay the ransom demanded by Eichmann as his price for the release. The plan was that they would be sent by train via Spain to Lisbon in Portugal from where they would be transported to Palestine. The train left Budapest in the early hours of 1 July containing 1,684 Jews. The journey was extremely slow. They went via Vienna and Linz into Germany as permission was refused to cross France. I assume this was because the Allies had by now landed and there was fierce fighting in Normandy. The result was that they could no longer go to Portugal or Spain. On 8 July, they changed trains near Hanover.

The final destination was Bergen-Belsen, which, although at the time not an extermination centre, was an appalling concentration camp. The 1,684 Jews were placed in what was called 'the Hungarian camp'. This was a separate part of Bergen-Belsen for the *Ungarnlager* or a place for the Hungarian 'exchange Jews'.

Starvation and illness accounted for a huge number of deaths in the camp generally. Towards the end, before the camp was liberated in January 1945, many of the inmates died of typhus (including Anne Frank) and some of those who survived were murdered by the SS. Although the Hungarians were treated less harshly than the other inmates in the camp, nevertheless life was terrible for them. Within a few weeks of their arrival, approximately 300 of them were allowed to leave by train for Switzerland. They arrived in Basel from where they were moved to Caux, high above Montreux on the Lake of Geneva. They were placed in a hotel which had been requisitioned by the Swiss authorities and converted into a displaced persons' home. Malvine was not among them. She stayed in the camp at Bergen-Belsen with the remaining Hungarians. Many of these succumbed to illness and suffered from hunger, lice, as well as the cold and damp. They did not know what was going to happen to them. At the end of November they were told that they too would be sent to Switzerland. They left the camp by train on 3 December 1944. A few days later they arrived at Bregenz in Austria from where they entered Switzerland. They were sent to join the others in Caux. Two hotels had been requisitioned by the Swiss authorities. The Regina Hotel became the home for the orthodox Jews and the Palace Hotel the home for the others, who included Malvine.

The Palace Hotel was constructed in slightly more than two years and completed in 1902. It sits on a huge terrace 700 metres in length, commanding a wonderful view over the lake and the mountains. It comprised enormous public rooms and more than 200 bedrooms. In its heyday, it had been a magnet for the wealthy. But tourism had come to a halt in the Second World War. The refugees slept on bunk beds, between four and eight persons per room. We visited the building in July 2018. It is now used as a catering school for ten months each year and occupied by a Peace Foundation for two months each summer. The building has lost all the glamour that so appealed to wealthy guests like the Maharajah of Baruda, who was a frequent visitor. At the time of our visit on that glorious summer's day in 2018, I found it impossible to imagine what it must have been like for Malvine and the other refugees to live there.

Malvine had spent about five months in Bergen-Belsen. She was released shortly before the dreadful outbreak of typhus that was to kill huge numbers of sick and emaciated inmates. So it was that Malvine escaped from the horrors of Bergen-Belsen and survived. Like many survivors of the camps, she found it very difficult to talk about her experience. The only thing I recall her saying was how terrible it had been to be forced to clean the latrines. My brother tells me that she also told us that she had witnessed a fight between two inmates, one of whom had stolen a piece of bread that the other had hidden under his pillow. She must have witnessed the most shocking and horrendous suffering and cruelty which she could not bring herself to describe. This would have been unbearable for anyone. It must have been particularly unbearable for her because, until the war, she seems to have sailed through life free from hardship of any kind.

My mother knew nothing about any of this at the time. I regret that I do not know how or precisely when my mother came to learn of her father's death and her mother's survival.

In the post-war period and while I was growing up, it was rare for people to talk about the Holocaust and for survivors to talk about their experiences. I have the sense that people wanted to look to the future and get on with their lives. I have no recollection of any discussion about it at home, although members of my mother's family had been victims. It was only later that the momentum of writing and talking about the subject began to build up.

Sometime in 1945, my mother learnt that Malvine had survived and was living in Switzerland. She came to Leeds to stay with us. I have no recollection of her visit, but I know that it was not a success. There were rows and many tears were shed. The idea that she might settle in Leeds and be close to her two daughters was rapidly abandoned. Apparently, on one occasion when Malvine was crying for some reason, I picked a daffodil and gave it to her saying: 'don't cry grandma, have a yellow flower'. I only know of this incident because she recounted it to me countless times in later years. It was on account of the yellow flower that I became her favourite grandchild. But the yellow flower was not sufficient to persuade her to stay in Leeds. So she returned to Switzerland.

In 1948, she married an elderly Swiss widower who originally came from Schaffhausen in northern Switzerland. His name was Lajos Hausner. She took his surname. So she was known as Madame Hausner. He seemed to my parents to be a gentle person. He was an observant Jew. Malvine was not particularly gentle and she had no interest in orthodox Judaism so they were a rather unlikely couple. I imagine that he was rather smitten by her colourful background and strong personality. She could be quite coquettish too. The attraction of the relationship for her must have been his devotion to her and the fact that he gave her companionship and stability. It must also have helped that he owned a building at Place de l'Ancien Port in Vevey as well as other property. He did not last very long. He died in early 1952 and left the Vevey building to her in his will. It is perhaps not surprising that his son by his first marriage was unhappy about this.

Malvine lived until 1983 when she was 91 years of age. I have a vivid recollection of her. During the 1950s and early 1960s, my parents, Robert and I would go abroad on holiday by car. Motoring holidays from England to Europe were not so common in those days. My mother was drawn to Europe for obvious reasons and my father was happy to go along. So we would take the cross-Channel ferry which sailed on the Dover–Boulogne route in those days. Cars were hoisted by crane one by one on to and off the boat. This process could take two hours.

Most summers, we stayed for a few nights in Malvine's apartment in her building in Vevey. The flat overlooked the Lake of Geneva and across to the mountains of Savoie in France. Robert and I spent many hours sitting on the balcony rather bored staring out at the view and waiting for the occasional lovely old steamer to go by, honking its horn and making a wonderful haunting sound. There was little for us or for our father to do. But it was important for our mother to have time with Malvine. They spoke in German except when they didn't want us to understand when they spoke in Bulgarian.

Vevey is a pretty little town, but there never was much to do there, except talk, eat and walk up and down the *quai* of which Malvine was very proud, not least because it boasted a statue of Charlie Chaplin who had lived in a house on the mountainside above the lake.

The flat was in a large building which comprises two interconnecting buildings. The front building is a fine nineteenth-century structure on whose façade there are beautiful friezes which were sculpted by Gustave Courbet. The building at the back is older and constructed in a more traditional Swiss style. The flat was rather old-fashioned. It included a living room which was too smart for daily use, but where the occasional visitor whom Malvine wished to impress could be entertained.

When we visited her, she frequently complained about her agent who, she said, was incompetent. And then there were the endless discussions about whether she should sell the building that she owned in Berlin. This had been bought some time before the Second World War. Every year, she would ask my parents whether she should sell it. Although she was probably interested in their views, she knew her own mind: she would sell it when she thought the time was right. She was shrewd and intelligent. Eventually she did sell it. No doubt it is now worth vastly more than the price for which she sold it.

She was a social snob. She was also an avid reader of journals such as *Paris Match* and others which reported gossipy 'news' about our royal family which was not covered by our press. Sadly, she did not live long enough for me to able to tell her about my knighthood and my audience with Her Majesty the Queen in 1993. That would have impressed her far more than any of my other achievements.

After I married in 1970, I continued to visit her well into the 1980s, but now with my own family. She made quite an impression on our children when they were quite young. When he was a small boy, our son Steven described her as 'furry-face'. This was a good but cruel description: her face was covered with a haze of hair.

She was a strong-willed, tough and colourful person. Without that toughness, she could not have survived her terrible experiences in 1944. Nor could she have coped with living on her own in Switzerland for almost 40 years after the war. The burghers of Vevey were not particularly welcoming of a Bulgarian/Hungarian Jew. She made friends, but most of them were emigrés from different countries. Some of these lived in Geneva. And she was sustained by constant correspondence with friends from her early life who had emigrated to many different countries.

She continued to live on her own in her apartment until towards the end of her life when she moved into the Hotel de Famille in Vevey. This was an old-fashioned hotel which specialised in housing elderly long-term residents who were still able to lead a more or less independent life. She died in 1983. Although I did not see her very often, I still see her clearly in my mind's eye. And still hear her voice. She was a memorable person who probably had more influence on my life than I realise. I am sure that my life and my character have been strongly influenced in ways that I would find difficult to articulate by the complex European background of my mother's family.

2

My Father's Family

M
Y FATHER WAS born on 18 April 1909 in Leeds. His father, Louis Dytch, was born on 23 December 1875 in Shad Kovno (today known as Seda), which was then in part of Russia, but is now in Lithuania. He had been a tailor since the age of 14. His last recorded residence in Russia before he came to England was in Libau, on the Baltic coast in what is now Latvia. My father's mother, Freda Damelin, was born in 6 March 1877 in Zagare, Russia which is in the north of what is now Lithuania and close to the present border with Latvia. At some point during the 1890s, Louis would from time to time see Freda pass by the tailor's shop where he was working. He contacted a *schadchen* (a Jewish marriage broker) who arranged a marriage. They married in Zagare in about 1896 and shortly thereafter came to England.

Members of the two families emigrated to a number of countries apart from England. These included the United States, Canada and South Africa (although some of those who went to South Africa left following the introduction of apartheid). Although I have not researched the matter, my impression is that on the whole they flourished. This is not intended to be a family history, but it is worth recording that American members of the Damelin family have traced that family back to 1680.

So when my grandparents arrived in Hull, Yorkshire, he was 20 and she 18 years of age. Like so many Jews who came to this country, their ultimate dream may well have been to go to the United States via Liverpool. They had left Russia in order to avoid his being conscripted to serve in the Russian army for up to 30 years. They spoke Yiddish but no English. They had received little secular education.

They planned initially to settle in Leeds where there was a significant Jewish population and where Freda's sister was already living. But when they arrived in Hull, a Mr Morris persuaded Louis to run a tailor's shop for him in the Shambles in York. So instead of going to Leeds, they moved to York and lived above the shop. At some point, they learnt that York was the subject of a *Cherem* (a curse) on account of the massacre of Jews in Cliffords Tower in 1190. According to the *Cherem*, no Jew could eat or spend the night inside the city walls. On learning this, my grandparents quickly left the city and went to Leeds. This was in 1896 or 1897.

Their first home was in a very small rented 'back to back' terraced house at 49 Gower Street with an outside lavatory which was shared with the others who lived in the terrace. The house was in an area called The Leylands. This was an unsalubrious part of the city near Sheepscar/Mabgate Beck and close to the city centre. It was damp and liable to flooding. Sometime after 1901, the family moved to another back to back house at nearby 41 Cloth Street. In about 1907, they moved to 29 Kenealy Street, which was a street-lined through terraced house. This was better accommodation since it was up the hill from the beck and out of The Leylands. This is where my father was born. He was the youngest of the five children who survived into adulthood. There were two more moves to terraced houses in Oatland Avenue and Samuel Street before, in 1924, they moved to 14 Wellclose Mount, which was even further up the hill towards the university and further away from the damp and squalor of The Leylands. For the first time, the family had a small front garden and a rear yard.

Finally, after six homes, each of which was slightly better than the one before, they moved in about 1938 to a pleasant semi-detached house at 29 St Martin's Road. This was in Chapeltown, part way between the city centre and the leafy suburbs to the north of the city to which most of the Jews were eventually to migrate. I recall visiting Louis from time to time on Sunday mornings. At that time, he was living there with Rosie (Raisky) who was his eldest daughter together with one of his granddaughters. Rosie was already a widow and never remarried. To me, Louis seemed a very grumpy old man. Whenever we visited him, he was sitting in an armchair and said very little. So far as I am aware, apart from one visit to the United States in 1947, he never travelled outside England. Nor did he ever acquire British citizenship. He was stateless. In 1947, he went to the United States for six weeks to visit some of the members of his family who had emigrated there. He was able to travel on a certificate of identity that had been issued by the Home Office. Many members of the family in the United States have become very successful. Louis died at the age of 77 on 25 December 1952.

Freda had died on 12 August 1940. Everyone spoke warmly of her. She seems to have impressed the far more worldly and cultured Jenö when they met in 1939. She was very kind and welcoming of my mother. She was devoted to her family and particularly favoured my father, who was the Benjamin of the family. Louis was a tailor throughout his working life, and eventually ran his own business. In the 1911 census, he was described as an 'assistant tailor manager'. During the First World War, he worked part-time in Carlton Barracks repairing army uniforms. In 1919, he was working for Fox Parkinson Tidwell Limited as manager of a large sweat shop in which rows of machinists worked in appallingly cramped conditions.

When he started his own business, he rented premises at 84 Grafton Street. My brother found an advertisement that Louis placed in the *Yorkshire Evening Post* on 19 November 1926 which reads:

> L. Dytch. Reliable Bespoke Tailor. 84 Grafton Street is open to CMT [Cut, Make and Trim] or make suits, overcoats etc; lowest prices. Satisfaction guaranteed.

Freda and Louis had six children, all born in Leeds. Large families were very common at that time. Rosie was born in 1899; Simpson or Sim for short (Simsky) was born in 1902; Oscar was born in 1903; Annie (Rivki) was born in 1905; and Issie (Richard, my father) was born in 1909. There was also Elke who died in infancy before 1911. The route by which the name 'Richard' was arrived at is interesting. Freda and Louis wanted to name him 'Gabriel' and his Hebrew name was 'Gavriel'. For some reason, the Registrar thought that his name was 'Israel' and this was the name recorded on his birth certificate. He was called 'Ickey' at school and by his friends. 'Ickey', which was shorthand for 'Israel', then morphed into 'Dickie' which in turn became 'Richard'. One of the forenames of one of my grandchildren (Justin) is Gabriel.

At the time of the 1911 census, all of the surviving children were described as being school children except for Rosie (who must have left school by the time she was 12) and my father, who was only two. The minimum school leaving age at the time was 12.

Our family papers include a declaration issued by the Leeds City Police on 23 September 1918 in respect of Freda. Her nationality at birth was described as 'Russian Jewess'; and her declaration that the particulars stated in the declaration were true was evidenced by her thumb print. This suggests that she was either illiterate or, more likely, that she only knew how to write her name in Yiddish, a language which is written in Hebrew characters. Another police document described her 'business' as 'housekeeper'. So far as I am aware, she did not work for anyone: in modern parlance she was a 'housewife'. The papers include various official documents relating to Louis. These show that he was able to write and sign his name, although in 1898 he had signed with a cross ('X') on Rosie's birth certificate. His nationality at birth was described as 'Russian Jew'. In a certificate of identity dated 28 January 1947, his 'nationality of origin' was described as 'Russian' and his occupation as 'tailor'.

My father went to Leeds Central High School, which was the first local authority secondary school opened by the Leeds School Board. He stayed there until he was 16 and passed 'Matriculation' or 'Matric' as it was called. This was the predecessor of 'O levels' which in turn were the predecessor of 'GCSEs'. He obtained his Matric. According to his diary for August 1925, he was the only member of his class to do so. But he must have had quite a good education. He was good at arithmetic and he was keen on English literature. He particularly loved Shakespeare. His diaries show that he read serious books. He understood the importance of a good education, and he was later to insist that his two sons should have one. On 17 July 1953, when I was almost 10, he gave me *David Copperfield* for successfully playing J. S. Bach's Minuet in G at the Leeds Grammar School Junior School Music Festival. I am still the proud possessor of the book which he inscribed. His ideas of what literature I could cope with at that age may have been unrealistically ambitious, but the gift of this book gives a good insight into his view of the importance of good literature and his hopes for his children.

But to return to the 1920s when my father was going to school, the fact that there were seven people living in far from spacious accommodation made it difficult for him to study at home. He did much of his studying at the City Reference Library or 'the Ref' as he referred to it in his diaries. His diaries for 1925 are fascinating. They show that, although he was an active and fully committed member of the Jewish community, who went to the synagogue, belonged to the Jewish Institute ('the Club') and was a keen Zionist, he was also very interested in the outside world. Apart from reading widely, he went almost every week to the cinema. He went to the theatre and attended lectures on diverse subjects ranging from the League of Nations to trade unions and medieval architecture. The diaries record that he attended a debate at the Club on 'Should girls smoke?' and that Yorkshire beat Surrey at cricket by 10 wickets. He seems to have had a much wider view of the world than his parents and his siblings. This is not at all surprising in the case of his parents. Nor is it so surprising in the case of his siblings who all left school at about the age of 12 and lived at home until they married.

Rosie was the first to marry. In December 1925, she married a man called Joe Stankler. In his diary for May of that year, my father recorded: 'Rosie's chap's parents came to talk business. £200 and wedding suite (sic). Seemed quite satisfied.' So dowries were the order of the day whether for a well-off family like my mother's or a far poorer family like my father's. The wedding was celebrated at the Victory Hotel, Briggate in the centre of the city. The couple had their honeymoon in Blackpool.

So my father had a better education than all of his siblings. It was unusual for children in the Jewish community to go to university at that time, although a few did. Some of the young of my father's generation went into the professions of law and accountancy. In those days, they were not obliged to obtain a university degree and most of them went into professional practices as articled clerks (now called 'trainees'). Those who went into the medical profession were obliged to go to medical school. But the majority of my father's generation who grew up in the Jewish community of Leeds went into the retail business.

All of my father's siblings went into retailing in Leeds. Freda wanted my father to become a chartered accountant. Louis would have preferred him to start earning a living as soon as he left school. Freda prevailed. So he obtained articles for five years with the firm of Norman D Vine, for which the family paid £150 which was a significant sum at that time. They had to negotiate to pay this in instalments over the entire five-year period. We have my father's diaries for the whole of 1927. They give a fascinating insight into his life when he was in articles. He described his studying in detail, including the various law examinations that he had to pass. He referred to his studying as 'swotting'. He was an active and keen Zionist. He was elected the Honorary Auditor of the Leeds Jewish Zionist Association. He was always short of money, yet he was able to go frequently to the cinema, theatre, cafés and play snooker and whist. During 1927, he was also able to go to Scarborough for a few days where he stayed in 'digs'. And he had a holiday for a few days in Southport. The impression I have is that he enjoyed life and did not work too hard and that he spent all the money that he earned.

He passed Part 1 of the accountancy examinations, but failed one of the subjects in Part 2. He could have retaken the paper, but his principal demanded a further substantial sum for the continuation of his articles. This was in about 1933. My father thought this was unreasonable and refused to pay. That is why he never qualified as a chartered accountant. But he was able to practise as a non-chartered accountant and did so in partnership with a Mr Sayers under the name of 'Dytch, Sayers & Co' from 81 Albion Street in the centre of Leeds. Eventually, he sold his interest to his partner for £200.

Meanwhile, his sister Annie had started a small business selling knitwear. In November 1933, she and my father formed a company called Gown and Mantle Limited with a share capital of £200. Initially, he was not involved in the running of the business. But at some stage, my father and his brother Sim and Sim's wife Helen all joined the business. They opened more shops and started selling cheap ladies' fashion. By 1939, they were renting three shops in Commercial Street, which was in the centre of the shopping district of the city.

Before I come to the point when my parents married, I should say a little about my father's love of foreign travel. He derived an income from his practice as an accountant and then from the women's fashion business. The capital sum he received from the sale of his share in the accountancy practice will have helped him to be able to afford to undertake some quite expensive travelling abroad.

In the summer of 1936, he went to Canada and the United States with his friend Bernard Lyons. Bernard Lyons was the son of S. H. Lyons who was a wealthy Leeds businessman. He founded Alexandre Limited, a successful manufacturing and retail clothing business which was later acquired by United Drapery Stores, a substantial public company. My father told me that S. H. Lyons had invited my grandfather Louis to join him early on in his business life. Louis refused the offer, preferring to stick to the safe harbour of the life of a tailor.

On 25 July 1936, Bernard and my father sailed from Southampton to Quebec on the Empress of Britain. My father kept a detailed diary of the visit which lasted a whole month. It is very well written. From Quebec they went to Montreal and then on to Toronto where they met Bernard's mother. There they visited large modern factories and department stores. Bernard at least was interested in learning about business techniques which might be useful for his family's company in England. They then went via Niagara Falls (which my father found stunning) into the United States. They visited Buffalo, Pittsburgh and Washington DC. My father described some of the iconic public buildings including the Supreme Court. He wrote:

> From the Capitol I walked across the Square to the new famous ten million dollar Supreme Court building. This huge monument to American justice is built entirely of white marble both inside and out and it is the most lavish building I have ever seen.

He would not have believed that 81 years later, one of his sons would be standing alongside the Chief Justice of the United States, making a speech in the great court room of the very building that had so impressed him.

From Washington he travelled to Philadelphia and Atlantic City before going on to New York. He was bowled over by New York, not least because he had never seen skyscrapers before. While he was there, he visited New Jersey where he met one of his uncles. From New York he went to Boston where he met an aunt and saw Harvard. Then back to New York for museums, shows and films.

One of the things that is striking about the diary up to this point is the lack of any reference to Jews or Jewish things. In view of the intense Jewishness of his family and the community in which he grew up, this is remarkable. My father seems to have been far more open to outside influences than other members of his family. But he did go on to visit Brooklyn with his uncle during his second stay in New York. He described the 'ghetto' and the crowded tenement blocks in which Jewish immigrants were living.

A few days later, on 26 August he returned to England on the Queen Mary. Her maiden voyage had been on 27 May 1936. My father was hugely impressed by this beautiful vessel.

I doubt whether many members of the Jewish community of Leeds went skiing in the Alps in the 1930s. But my father and his friend Harold Denton went to Murren in the Bernese Oberland on a skiing holiday in the winter of 1937/38 and then again to Chamonix in January 1939 as I have already described in chapter one. To judge by what I saw of his skiing in the 1950s, he was not a great skier. But then, the boots and skis of the 1930s did not make for easy skiing.

The arrival of my mother in Leeds had a dramatic effect on my father's family. Annie left the business to run her own clothing business called Mayfair Modes. My parents became the owners of Gown and Mantle Limited and ran their women's fashion business under the name 'Chanal' from 22–23 Commercial Street. And Sim and Helen ran their women's fashion business under the name 'Lafayette' a little further down Commercial Street. From the outset, Chanal, Lafayette and Mayfair Modes were in direct competition with each other to attract women's fashion custom. The potential for explosive disharmony was only too evident, although, under the influence of my mother, Chanal went upmarket and started to attract a wealthier clientele than shopped at Lafayette. But when I was growing up, the rivalry between Chanal and Lafayette in particular persisted. Its most obvious manifestation was in the attempts made by each to persuade wholesale suppliers in London not to supply the other. So relations between my parents and Sim and Helen were strained and patchy at best. Sometimes, an incident would occur which caused passions to boil over so that they even stopped speaking to each other, sometimes for long periods of time.

At the outset, my parents struggled to make a success of Chanal. They found it difficult to pay their debts and business life was rather hand to mouth. It is interesting that from an early stage my mother took an active part in the business. This must have been hard for her, not least because she had never worked before. No doubt what she had learnt in Paris was very useful. Gradually, the business started to prosper, largely on account of my mother's skill in advising women what clothes to buy. She had a real flare for this and slowly built up a large, loyal clientele who trusted her taste and judgement.

Her arrival caused something of a stir in the family, and to some extent, in the community too. My father was extremely handsome and was much fancied by girls in the community. He had great charm and was popular. The fact that he had married someone from Hungary did not go down too well in the family or the community. My mother was a strikingly beautiful red-haired woman. She was also quite outspoken and could be tactless. For example, she had been used to living in a smart apartment in Budapest and to central heating. She commented with surprise on the fact that in Leeds people lived in houses which had dirty coal fires and no central heating.

As for the family, she was warmly welcomed by Freda. Her relationship with the rest of the family was at best wary and respectful, although she tried hard to make it work. The fact that business links with Annie, Sim and Helen were severed so soon after my mother came on the scene indicates that they all knew they would never get on sufficiently well with each other. My mother wanted to move upmarket.

The saga of the change of the family name illustrates the problem only too clearly. My mother did not like the name 'Dytch', which I understand to have been a corruption of 'Deutsch'. She thought it was ugly. She convinced my father to change it. He was willing to agree partly because he tended to do what she wanted, but he was also influenced to some extent by his memory of being teased at school over his name. He never forgot how one of his teachers poked fun at him in front of the class, asking mockingly how the name was spelt and how it should be pronounced: for example, was it 'Ditch'? He did not want his own children to experience such humiliation. My parents chose the name 'Dyson' because it was unquestionably English and bore a reasonable resemblance to 'Dytch'. In fact, it is a common Yorkshire name. Throughout my life, I have been asked whether I am related to one Dyson or another; and more recently, whether I am related to Sir James Dyson. I have always had to explain why my Yorkshire roots do not run deep.

When my father informed his family that he intended to change his name, they were outraged. This was seen as yet another example of my father surrendering to the foreign interloper. What could be closer to the identity of the family than its name? But in time, Sim too changed his name from Dytch to Dyson as did Oscar's son Michael (but not Oscar himself).

Britain declared war on Germany on 3 September 1939, no more than three months after my parents married. My father served in the Auxiliary Fire Service during the Second World War. He was understandably reluctant to volunteer to serve abroad in the armed forces and leave his newly wedded wife in a strange land and with a somewhat less than welcoming family to provide support and comfort. My impression is that with the death of Freda in 1940, my mother lost her one true friend in my father's family. Louis lived on for another 12 years, but I never heard my mother say anything to suggest that there was real warmth in the relationship between the two of them. Unlike Malvine, he had no impact on my life at all.

3

A Leeds Childhood

I WAS BORN at about midnight on 31 July 1943 in a huge thunderstorm. My father was convinced that this was a portent of something momentous. I had a strikingly large mop of black hair which resulted in my having for many years only a modest forehead. I was the progeny of the union of a most unlikely pair. My mother was a well-educated, cultured woman who came from a well-to-do, upper middle-class Middle European family that was reasonably well integrated into the wider community. My father was a less well-educated man who came from a poor, unsophisticated, Russian and intensely Jewish family that was not at all integrated into the wider community.

By the time I was born, my parents had moved to a house in Broomhill Drive in the Moortown area of Leeds. This was the area on the Harrogate side of the city to which many Jews had moved from Chapeltown. They moved again in 1945 to 4 Belvedere Road before my brother Robert was born. This was further north and closer to Alwoodley, which for many Jews was the most desirable part of the city in which to live. This house was to be my home until I moved to London in 1968. It was not particularly large, but it had four bedrooms (one of which was tiny). It had only one inside lavatory. It had a nice garden. Like most of their friends, my parents were not at all interested in gardening. Surprisingly, my brother and I were and have maintained that interest throughout our lives. I recall that we used to retrieve wallflower plants which had already flowered from a nearby rubbish dump and try to recycle them by planting them in our garden. Predictably, this was a hopeless exercise.

My parents' business fortunes improved rapidly after the war. They were able to afford to have a 'mothers' help' to look after the two of us. I have only the most limited recollection of life before I went to school in September 1948 at the age of five. We did not have a television until shortly before the Coronation of Queen Elizabeth II on 2 June 1953. I recall that our mother's help, Elsie, had the radio on a great deal of the time. She listened regularly to the thriller series *Dick Barton, Special Agent* which was broadcast on the BBC Light Programme (predecessor of Radio 2). I was too young to understand what it was all about, but do recall the theme music and much excited chasing about the house when the programme was on.

I recall going down the road to the parade of shops which was a few minutes' walk away on Sandhill Parade. We could not buy certain goods without handing over stamps from a ration book. A loaf of white bread cost 5d (approximately two pence) plus a stamp. There were small grocer, butcher and greengrocer shops on the parade. Shops like these have long since fallen victim to the irresistible march of the supermarket.

The school to which our parents chose to send both of us was Ingledew College. This was an old-fashioned 'prep school' most of whose pupils stayed on until the age of 13. If they passed the 'common entrance' examinations, they went on to a 'public school', usually of the boarding variety. There was a boys' school and a girls' school in separate parts of the building and there was remarkably little contact between the two. The school was no more than five minutes' walk away from our home, which must have been one of its attractions for my parents. The school uniform was red and green and included a green cap with a red star. We wore the uniform even outside school hours and on social occasions. I have seen photographs of us wearing our school uniforms on the beach at Scarborough! This was symptomatic of the formality of those days. If we possessed any informal clothing, we rarely wore it.

I do not know why my parents chose this school in preference to the small private school run by a Miss Rider a few doors away from our house in Belvedere Road. I only had one encounter with Miss Rider which was when I was seven years old. I started throwing snowballs for fun at the children from her school as they were passing our house on their way home. Miss Rider saw me doing this and, in effect, arrested me. She marched me back to her school and locked me in one of the schoolrooms for about 15 minutes. To use the language that judges used when I started to sit as a judge in the 1990s, I was given a 'short sharp shock'. It was a very frightening experience as it was intended to be. She then released me from custody and allowed me to go home. I never threw snowballs at the pupils of any school again. I doubt whether my parents made any complaint. It would not have occurred to them to do so. Anyway, any complaint would presumably have been made to Miss Rider herself and she would undoubtedly have rejected it on the grounds that my incarceration was necessary to punish me and teach me a lesson. Parents were generally far more accepting and respectful of what teachers did in those days. In today's world, what Miss Rider did would probably have been regarded as a criminal offence and certainly a breach of the European Convention on Human Rights.

The Ingledew College school building was a stone-built house which had probably been built for a successful businessman in the late nineteenth century. It seemed huge to me at the time. I later discovered that it was not especially large. There was what seemed to me to be an enormous room on the ground floor where the school assembly took place and where we listened to *Music and Movement*. This was a BBC programme which was broadcast each morning for young children. We had to float about to the accompaniment of wafting music, taking on various guises, such as clouds or trees by raising our arms towards the ceiling. It was a gentle way to start the day which called for no input from the teachers.

The school was very traditional. It was modelled on institutions which educated children to become good citizens of the British Empire. The Empire had only just begun to disintegrate following the end of the Second World War. The granting of independence to India in 1947 was a hugely important step along the way. The map of Africa still showed unbroken pink (denoting at least some form of connection with the United Kingdom) from Egypt to South Africa.

The syllabus was traditional and Victorian in flavour. For example, we learnt Latin from the age of five or six. The teaching of Latin comprised the mindless chanting of declensions and conjugations in unison. We studied French as well as other mainstream subjects. I have little recollection of the detail of the teaching. But I well recall how violent some of the teachers were. They deployed different techniques. One would punish miscreants with a whack of the slipper. Another would throw pieces of chalk at pupils who were misbehaving (the chalk was intended to be used by the teacher for writing on a blackboard). Yet another teacher would hurl board dusters which were designed for the erasure of chalk script from the blackboard. The schoolroom was quite a dangerous place. Parents must have known what was going on, but I suppose that they regarded this kind of behaviour as a normal and acceptable way for the teachers to keep control. They will have thought that the teachers were the experts and that they knew best.

Sports were very important. I remember the annual Sports Day when, in addition to the usual mix of running and other athletics, there were peculiar races such as the sack race, which involved staggering along in sacking that was drawn up to one's chest and which made running impossible; and the egg and spoon race, which involved running whilst holding an egg in a spoon: if the egg fell off, one was disqualified.

In the autumn, we used to indulge in 'conker fights'. We would drill a hole through a conker and thread a piece of string through the hole. The conker was now fit for a contest with another similarly prepared conker. The fight was won or lost when one of the conkers was destroyed in the fight. Some pupils hardened their conkers by baking them in an oven. I am not sure whether this was permissible according to the conker conventions. Another popular activity was playing with glass marbles. This harmlessly involved rolling a marble along the ground with the aim of hitting or merely touching one's opponent's marble. One day, a slightly older boy than myself called Nigel Rodley was watching me play marbles in the school yard. He accused me of cheating and told me to stop. I can't now recall the details of the transgression. Nigel was to become Sir Nigel Rodley and a dear friend in later life. He had a most distinguished life, becoming inter alia a professor of Human Rights Law at the University of Essex and a member and later chairman of the United Nations Human Rights Committee. His sense of fairness and outrage at injustice was already evident at an early age.

I was happy at the school because I did well academically and did not get into trouble too often. Indeed, I was regarded as one of its star pupils. The school hoped that I would stay on until the age of 13 and then go to a boarding school. I think this idea appealed to my father who would have liked his sons to spread their wings and fit comfortably into wider society. Consistently with this, he wanted me to learn boxing so that I could stand up for myself. But my mother had very firm contrary views on both issues. As usual, she prevailed and I did not go to boarding school and did not learn how to box. I would have been hopeless at boxing. I have never been able to watch boxing contests and have always found all forms of violence upsetting.

In retrospect, I do not think that Ingledew was a particularly good school. Its academic standards were not high and it was very old-fashioned: its ethos and approach to education were firmly modelled on Victorian ideas and values. But my assessment of the school may be unfair. It was not shared by one of its most illustrious alumni, Lord (Michael) Mustill of Pateley Bridge. Michael became one of the United Kingdom's outstanding judges of the late twentieth century. He was the son of a family with strong Yorkshire roots and was at Ingledew from 1936 to 1940. He then went to other schools before going on to board at Oundle School at the age of 13. In his old age, he clearly felt affection for the place which he described to me as a school for the sons of Yorkshire gentlefolk.

The traditional flavour of the school is perhaps well captured in the sentiments expressed in the five-verse school song, whose first two verses were:

(1)
Ingledew's sons are not many,
Ingledew's sons are not old,
But Ingledew's sons are valiant men,
As Time will soon unfold.
One, two, one, two,
March the straight road at Ingledew.

(2)
Ingledew's men are fighters;
They scrap and they box and spar,
But they're ready to fight for the weaker side,
As the boldest always are.
One, two, one, two,
Fight the straight fight at Ingledew.

So it was that in September 1951 I went to the Junior School of Leeds Grammar School (LGS). The Junior School was a private fee-paying school. The Senior School (or Main School as it was called) was at that time a Direct Grant Grammar School, which took some fee-paying pupils and some whose education was paid for out of public funds. LGS was founded in 1552. It had a fine reputation like similar northern grammar schools such as Manchester Grammar School and

Bradford Grammar School. It was usual for a few LGS boys to go to Oxbridge each year. Like most secondary schools in those days, it was a single-sex school. There was a sister school, Leeds Girls' High School, which was approximately one mile away in Headingley. In the 1950s, apart from coming together for the limited purpose of putting on school plays, the two schools were hermetically sealed from each other.

The Junior School was housed in a large nineteenth-century house in Clarendon Road. It was about half an hour's walk from the commercial centre of the city. Pupils spent two years there. The first year was divided into three classes, J1, J2 and J3. J3 was for those who appeared to be the ablest and J1 for the least able. The second year was divided in order of ability into J4, J5 and J6. It must have been rather a shock to my parents that their star pupil son only managed to scrape into J1.

The Main School occupied a large site about half a mile up Clarendon Road away from the city and towards Woodhouse Moor. The school building was a typical grandiose Victorian gothic edifice which had been opened in 1858. Like most Victorian buildings in the 1950s, it had been blackened by deposits of soot over many years. On the right hand side of the entrance to the Main School was a Victorian gothic chapel; and on the left hand side a Victorian gothic porter's lodge. There was also a sports field and a sports pavilion. The main sports facilities were several miles to the north-west at a site in Lawnswood. The school also had a gymnasium and swimming pool. All in all, it was very well equipped and the facilities were modern by the standards of the 1950s. Many years later, the Main School site was sold to the University of Leeds whose Law School building was constructed where the school swimming pool had been. I was later to give a lecture to the law students more or less on the site where I had tried with only modest success to perfect my diving skills.

I recall my first day at the Junior School in September 1951. The journey from our house to the school involved two buses and a walk. The first bus journey took about 15 minutes and was from the main road at the top of Belvedere Road to the Central Bus Station in town. The second took about 10 minutes and was from the bus station to a stop opposite the Main School. The final leg of the journey was a 10-minute walk down Clarendon Road. My father accompanied me on the first day. Thereafter, I went to school and came home on my own. There were no school buses or coaches in those days. It was only towards the end of my school career that my parents drove me and Robert to school on their way to the shop in the morning. By this time, there were also school buses for the return journey. It was not unusual in those days for young children to undertake journeys of this kind on their own. Parents were less anxious for their children than they were later to become. I think this was mainly because there were relatively few cars on the roads.

On my first day, I was shown into my classroom. The form teacher of J1 was Miss (Hilda) Jones. She was a kindly woman who had grey hair that was squashed into a tight bun. Miss Christie, who was the form teacher of J2, was rather less kindly. Her favoured punishment for misbehaviour was a fierce tug at the pupil's hair. Both teachers seemed incredibly old.

I did reasonably well academically, because at the end of my first year I was placed in J5. If I had done really well, I would have been placed in J6. I worked diligently. Miss Jones was astute enough to recognise in me a certain earnest anxiety which to some extent has dogged me all my life. In the report at the end of my first term in J1, she wrote 'I hope he has a carefree holiday'.

I have a fairly limited recollection of life in the Junior School. Every day, we would be marched in 'crocodile' formation (ie two by two) up to the Main School for lunch and then back again. We wore navy blue and yellow school uniforms and navy blue caps with yellow stripes. Hence the nickname for boys at LGS of 'banana skins'. We were always sent out to play during the mid-morning break. Life in the playground was very physical. This led to many minor injuries. Both of my legs were usually covered in healing scabs. Another regular and compulsory feature of life was the school assembly. LGS was a Church of England school and prayers were regularly conducted before any assembly announcements were made. There were a number of Jewish boys in the Junior School, but there were no separate prayers for them. So the entire school was present for prayers. I remember being embarrassed that I did not know any of the prayers, whereas they seemed to be familiar to almost everyone else. And I did not know the hymns that they sang either. I tried to pick up some of the hymns and prayers by listening intently. The most important prayer seemed to be the Lord's Prayer. When it came to 'forgive those that trespass against us …', I was defeated by the word 'trespass'. I had never heard the word before and did not know what it meant. In a vain attempt to reproduce it at the appropriate point in the prayer, I muttered 'pss, pss' and hoped that nobody would notice. I was acutely self-conscious about it.

As in all schools, sports were very important and success on the sports field was greatly prized. There were two houses in the Junior School, Nicholson and Smeaton. I was in Nicholson. My ability did not match my keen spirit, but I tried.

Cricket has always been an important part of my life. We played at Ingledew College where I found that my under-arm 'grass cutter' bowling was more accurate and more effective than my rather wayward attempts at bowling over-arm. Robert and I used to play French cricket on the lawn of our back garden. We would frequently hit the ball into neighbouring gardens and crawl through gaps in the hedge to retrieve it. One neighbour used to get very cross and confiscate the ball. His wife was of a more understanding disposition and would throw the ball back if she found it.

At some point we also started to play in the short driveway of the front garden. We spent hours playing what passed for a version of conventional cricket (but with each team comprising one player). The wicket was drawn in chalk on the wooden garage door. I assumed the role of my hero Len Hutton and Robert the role of his hero Willie Watson. Len Hutton played for Yorkshire and captained

England. Willie Watson also played cricket for Yorkshire and England. We also used to play cricket with a few friends on the local recreation ground ('the Rec') which was about 10 minutes' walk away from home.

By the time I left the Junior School, I was becoming passionately interested in cricket. In 1953, my father took Robert and me to one of the Yorkshire v Lancashire or 'Roses' matches at Headingley. It is difficult now to imagine the excitement that used to be generated by the Roses matches in those days. The ground was always full to capacity. There was a buzz in the air. The outcome of these games really mattered to the populations of Yorkshire and Lancashire as well as to me and my brother. Thereafter, we used to go to Headingley from time to time. I followed the fortunes of Yorkshire cricket obsessively through-out our school lives and for some time thereafter. In those pre-internet days when television was limited to a single station, which corresponded with what is now BBC1, the main source of information was the radio and news-papers. It was occasionally possible to hear live cricket commentary on the radio. John Arlott was the most famous cricket commentator at that time. He had a wonderful turn of phrase and spoke with a distinctive Hampshire burr. Every day, we would study closely the newspaper reports of the previous day's matches. During the England tour of Australia in 1954/55, I recall listening to the crackly sound of live commentaries at 06.00 (our time). We were hugely excited by the bowling feats of Frank (Typhoon) Tyson who was the fast-est bowler of his day. These helped England to a rare and convincing victory in the series. This contributed to a sense of happiness and well-being in both of us.

During the 1950s and 1960s, I used to look forward to the start of the cricket season with great eagerness. I never bought *Wisden's Cricketers' Almanack* because it was too expensive (it has been my great pleasure in recent years to buy it for our cricket-obsessed grandson Oliver). Instead, I bought the more compact and cheaper *Playfair Cricket Annual*, which included the batting and bowling averages of all the county players. I studied these intently and learnt many of them by heart. During the 1950s, Yorkshire usually came second in the County Championship table to an outstanding Surrey side. In the 1960s, Yorkshire came top for several seasons. Following the fortunes of the Yorkshire and England cricket teams absorbed much of my time and emotional energy.

Although we played rugby union at school, my main football interest was in soccer. I never followed the fortunes of the Leeds Rugby League Club (now the Leeds Rhinos) and have never been particularly interested in rugby union even at international level. I was probably about 10 years old when Robert and I started to watch Leeds United play soccer at Elland Road. My father took us on Saturdays for a short time. Then we went with some of his friends. They had seats and we would stand in the six-penny schoolboys' area behind one of the goals. In those pre-Premier League days, the game was far less commercial than it has since become. Leeds United were not very good in the 1950s. They made some progress following the arrival of John Charles who was known for some reason as 'the gentle giant'. But it was not until Don Revie became manager in the 1960s that the club started to prosper. I have to confess that I was a fickle supporter. There was a direct correlation between the enthusiasm of my support and the team's success. Over the years, I lost interest. But I did play a good deal of soccer with friends on the Rec and also at weekends on the Soldiers' Field in Roundhay Park. As with all my other sporting endeavours, my ability did not match my enthusiasm.

In addition to playing cricket and football, I used to spend hours playing various games in the garden at home. From as far as back as I can remember, like most children of that time, Robert and I were encouraged, if not ordered, by our parents to go outside and play unless it was raining. We played with a few friends who lived nearby. In the early years, we played hide and seek and a chase game called 'tig'. There were plenty of trees and bushes which were suitable for hiding. We also had a passion for making dens. These were simple structures which were designed to have the appearance of modest rustic houses. Sometimes we would make use of the branches of a tree to construct an upper floor. These dens were unstable and tended not to endure for very long. Over the years, we constructed dens in various parts of the garden and one den would be replaced by another. The construction of dens, and spending many hours in them, formed an important part of our lives in the early 1950s.

I suspect that our love affair with dens was in part inspired by the books of Enid Blyton which Robert and I loved. In particular *The Famous Five* series and the series of *Adventure Books*. Many of the stories in these books were set in caves and similar outdoor places which were suitable for hiding from and spying on men who were up to no good. I devoured these books from the age of about seven to 11. It was only much later that I began to discover that serious-minded people condemned them because they reflected the values of a narrow middle class which was out of touch with modern life and that they were badly written with a limited vocabulary. When I reread one of the books many years later, I saw at once that these criticisms were justified. But the storylines were gripping and the books appealed to children of that era and sold in millions. They were of little interest to my children or grandchildren. Other books that I read in the early 1950s were the *Just William* series by Richmal Crompton and the *Billy Bunter* series by Frank Richards. I loved William because he was always getting into trouble for his mischievous pranks and doing things that I was not brave enough to do. I knew that none of these books was regarded as improving literature, but I thoroughly enjoyed reading them. I knew that the Arthur Ransome series of books starting with *Swallows and Amazons* were thought to be 'good literature', but for some reason, I never managed to get very far with any of them. A particular favourite was *Our Island Story* by H. E. Marshall. This was a child's history of England from the Romans until the death of Queen Victoria which was first published in 1905. I reread it many times in the way that children do. Although I knew the storyline well, it continued to excite my imagination.

Almost all of my friends throughout my childhood were Jewish. Many of them were the children of my parents' friends. This was reflective of the closeness and inward-looking nature of the Leeds Jewish community and its reluctance to engage with the wider community. But I did play with some non-Jewish boys who lived nearby and formed some friendships with non-Jewish boys at school. I recall one boy with whom I used to play and who did not go to my school asking me 'why did you kill Jesus?' This question came as a shock to me and I did not know how to answer it. I have often been asked whether I have encountered anti-Semitism during my life. I am not sure that my young friend's question was evidence that his parents or his school were anti-Semitic. But it made a big impression on me, since I recall it well to this day. Apart from this incident, I have only encountered anti-Semitism directly once in my life. The occasion was when I was about 16 and was having a Classics lesson at LGS. One of the Jewish boys in the class was making some complaint to the teacher. He kept pressing his complaint. The teacher, Eddie Scott, was a very quietly spoken, impeccably dressed, seemingly gentle individual. His patience was being taxed to breaking point. Suddenly he snapped and, raising his voice, boomed 'you people are all the same'. I was deeply shocked. The storm then subsided as quickly as it had erupted and the teacher resumed his usual calm, superficially gentle demeanour.

But that is to leap ahead. Other things that we did at home included spending hours playing games such as *Monopoly, Totopoly, Cluedo* and *Wembley*. Some of these games have survived in a slicker and more modern form. Others have disappeared. In retrospect, these games seem to have been simple and unsophisticated. A world away from the games that my grandchildren play, all of which seem to involve a screen of some kind.

At weekends, we frequently went by car into the lovely nearby countryside. We visited such places as Bolton Abbey and other places in Wharfedale; Scarborough, Filey, Bridlington and Ravenscar on the East Coast, where we would dip into the freezing waters of the North Sea; and Blackpool, Southport and St Anne's on the West Coast, where we would dip into the rather less freezing waters of the Irish Sea. More than 50 years after leaving Leeds and moving to London, I still miss the beauty of the Dales and the North of England. For all their loveliness, the Chiltern Hills are no match for them. It was these visits to the country as well as early holidays in Switzerland that inspired in me a lifelong love of walking.

I was introduced to classical music early in my life. I started having piano lessons with a Miss Sadie Marks quite early on. She was something of a dragon and did not inspire any love of music in me. The result was that I did not practice as I should have done. I recall one week when I had done no work on a piece and decided to hide the music under the carpet. She demanded to know where the music was and I pretended to search for it. She became suspicious and ordered me to swear on some religious text that I did not know where it was. This was all too much for me and I rolled back the carpet to reveal the missing music.

I was not conscious of having any religious scruples at the time. But I do recall being told by at least one of the Catholic Swiss mothers' helps who came to stay with us that, if you misbehave, you are likely to face eternal damnation in hell. This made a big impression on me. It is possible that I was moved by the fear of this terrifying prospect when I was asked to swear on the religious text that I did not know where the music was. In any event, it was not long after this incident that I gave up having piano lessons. I started again when I was 10 with Christine Brown who had been a pupil of Fanny Waterman. She was a good teacher and I enjoyed my lessons with her. When I was 12, I took part in a competition at the Harrogate Music Festival. I played one of J. S. Bach's Little Preludes from the Anna Magdalena Notebook. I was runner-up to one of the Waterman pupils. When I was just 13, I started having lessons with Fanny myself. I will describe these later.

I had no understanding of politics or the world situation in my early years at LGS. I have a vague recollection of the two elections that were held in 1951. I recall very clearly hearing of the death of King George VI on 6 February 1952. I relayed the news of the death to another boy who was travelling with me on the bus going home. He witheringly told that this was 'ancient history'. I have never forgotten this putdown. I also recall learning of the death of Joseph Stalin on 5 March 1953. I understood very little about the Soviet Union, but I knew that he was a bad and dangerous man. His malign influence and the threat that he represented to mankind had frightened me. His death came as a great relief. I felt that we were entering a more peaceful and happy era.

On 2 June 1953, the Coronation of Queen Elizabeth II took place in Westminster Abbey. We watched it on black and white television (this was well before the introduction of colour television). Everyone I knew was happy and enthralled. At school we had the bonus of being given glass coronation mugs and a day off. The entire Junior School went on a hike from Otley to Ilkley. I remember having a picnic on the bracken covered moors above Wharfedale. The sense of happiness engendered by the Coronation was enhanced by the news, which was also announced on 2 June 1953, that Hillary and Tenzing had been the first to climb Mount Everest. These seemed to be good times to be alive.

At Whitsuntide, the four of us used to go to Stratford on Avon to see Shakespeare plays. Both my parents were keen on Shakespeare. We also went from time to time to Bournemouth. When I was about 10, we stopped at Oxford en route for Bournemouth. Our parents wanted to show us the city of 'dreaming spires'. I recall a visit to Magdalen College, where our son Steven was to go many years later. In the window of one of the undergraduates' rooms that we approached from the outside was a note which read 'if you are close enough to read this, you are too close'. I was so impressed with what I thought was the cleverness of this note that I have never forgotten it. My young unsophisticated mind needed no further evidence that all Oxford undergraduates were brilliant and stunningly original. I cannot, however, pretend that this was the life-changing experience that put me straight on the course that would inevitably lead me to Oxford University. It is unlikely that I had even thought about going to university at that time. If I had done so, Oxford would have been beyond my imagination.

My career at the Junior School came to an end in July 1953. I had done sufficiently well academically to be placed in the highest of the three first-year classes in the Main School. There were eight houses in the Main School all named after famous Leeds men. We had been asked in the Junior School whether we had any relatives in the Main School. The school liked the idea of placing members of the same family in the same house. I had a cousin in the Main School. I told the teacher this. When I was asked what house he was in, instead of saying that I did not know, I blurted out the first house name that came into my head. This was Sheafield. In fact, my cousin Melvyn was in Ermystead. The result was that I joined Sheafield and my brother and several generations of Dysons who have since gone to the school also joined Sheafield.

In the summer of 1953, as in the previous two summers, we went on a family holiday by car to Europe. In those days, the principal cross-Channel ferry route was between Dover and Boulogne. English cars on the roads of the Continent were something of a rarity. In 1951, we had driven down to St Jean de Luz in the south-west corner of France. In 1952, we had gone to a place called Cavalaire on the Cote d'Azur. There were no autoroutes in those days. I can remember driving through towns and villages and seeing the buildings that were pock-marked from Second World War gunfire. France was far from prosperous. We were under strict instructions from our parents not to drink tap water. It was many years before I had the courage to drink French tap water.

In 1953, we drove to Vevey to spend a few days with Malvine in her apartment en route for a beach holiday in Italy. It was exceptionally hot and one night I had quite a bad attack of asthma. This was a frightening experience. It caused my parents to have a change of plan and decide that we should go to the mountains instead of the Mediterranean Sea. Esther Melchioretto ('Esti') had been one of our former mothers' helps. She was Swiss and recommended that we go to Klosters in Graubunden. At that time, this was a small mountain resort. It had not achieved the fame that Prince Charles and other members of our royal family and others were subsequently to bring to it. We had a wonderful holiday walking in the mountains and returned there the following summer. I think this holiday marked the beginning of my love affair with the Swiss Alps.

In 1955, we went by car to Portschach in Carinthia, the southernmost province of Austria. This was an unusual thing for a British family to do in those days. Perhaps even more unusual or extraordinary so soon after the end of the Second World War was to drive through Germany. I recall our spending a night in a rather dark and dingy hotel in Munich. Wherever we went, I could not help wondering what the people we encountered had done during the war.

The fact that we were having such holidays so soon after the war shows how strong a force the pull of Europe was in our family. In this respect, as in so many others, my mother's influence was dominant. It extended to the food that we ate and the music that we heard. I also picked up many German and Viennese aphorisms and words from her such as '*der Apfel fallt nicht weit vom Baum*'. ('like father, like son'); '*Hals und Beinbruch*' ('break a leg – good luck'); '*zwei linke Hande*' ('clumsy'); '*Krampus*' ('killjoy'); and '*Sitzfleisch*' ('ability to sit still and concentrate'). I could give many other examples. Although I never studied German or spent much time in Germany, I have always felt a strange affinity with the German language.

I started in the Main School in September 1953. Our form master (they were called masters rather than teachers) was a bluff geography teacher called Rex Farebrother. Like most of the masters in the school, he relied on corporal punishment to keep us in order. They deployed quite a range of weapons. The favoured one was a rectangular piece of wood which was used to 'whack' the boy's bottom up to a maximum of six times. Naturally, the severity of the sentence bore some relation to the gravity of the offence. But many of the offences were minor infractions of the school's code of law and order. Running in the corridor or talking in class could qualify for corporal punishment.

Mr Farebrother warned us about our Latin master, Dr (Fred) Wilson, sometimes known as 'the Doc'. He told us that Dr Wilson's bark was worse than his bite. The evidence suggested otherwise. Dr Wilson had his own special weapon, which was a piece of wood in the shape of a thin pole. He called the pole 'Eustasia'. When he introduced us to her (he told us that the pole was a female), he explained that the name had a Greek origin. '*Eu*' meant 'well' or 'good' and '*stasia*' was derived from '*histemi*' which meant 'I stand'. In other words, the intended effect of being struck on the bottom by Eustasia was that the victim would be unable to sit down for a while. Dr Wilson used Eustasia freely, even to punish a boy for making excessive mistakes in translation from English into Latin or vice versa. Beatings were carried out in front of the entire class. Even more sinister was the fact that, if a boy found that Dr Wilson had made a mistake, the boy was required to turn the tables and apply Eustasia to his bottom. In hindsight, I am in no doubt that he made deliberate mistakes in order to achieve this result. I doubt whether any of us appreciated the significance of his behaviour at the time. Much later in my school career when I was in the Classical sixth form, he was kind enough to give me and other scholarship boys some extra tuition after school hours. He often chose erotic poetry for me to translate. I particularly recall passages in the works of Horace which described things that I did not really understand. He was keen to explain. So far as I was aware, apart from corporal punishment which was universal, Dr Wilson was the only master who behaved in this distinctively inappropriate way.

But I later came to understand that he was an excellent classical scholar. He had studied Classics at Balliol College, Oxford before the Second World War and had been taught by the great Russell Meiggs. He had been on archaeological digs at the ancient Roman port of Ostia and in Cyrene in North Africa. The rumour was that he had caught malaria during the Second World War and had become an alcoholic. I don't know the source of this rumour. I am sure that it did not emanate from anything that Dr Wilson told us. I can now see that he was a sad and lonely man. I am sure that at the time I knew nothing about and had no interest in his personal life or that of any of the other masters. They did not talk about their families or themselves or their passions and interests unless, improbably, these were directly relevant to the subject that they were teaching. So far as we were concerned, masters were there to teach us, no more and no less. I learnt subsequently that the school was the main focus of Dr Wilson's life. He used to take groups of boys to visit Roman York. One of his favoured destinations was the basement of a pub which was not open to the general public and which contained the remains of Roman baths. He was good at communicating his enthusiasm for the ancient Romans, their literature and building skills.

I do not think that he was a good teacher. But very few of the teachers were inspiring. Most of them made little attempt to engage in a dialogue with their pupils. Most of them failed to excite us and open our eyes to the excitement and beauty of knowledge. They were quite efficient at imparting information in a didactic fashion. We were not encouraged to examine what we were being taught critically or engage in conversation with the teachers or indeed each other about it. In my experience, this continued to be the case even in the sixth form. There were exceptions. One of these was Tom ('Froggy') Beckett who was one of our Classics masters. He was a lovely man who inspired real affection in the boys. He exuded enthusiasm for Latin and Greek poetry. He persuaded some of us to enter a Latin reading competition. The text was a piece of poetry from Virgil's *Aeneid*. His love of the poetry was infectious and we were inspired to work hard and to read the passage with great passion. To the delight of us all and especially Froggy, we won the competition.

I made solid progress during my first three years in the Main School. Each year, I was in the highest class, but it was already becoming clear that I was not destined to be an outstanding scientist. I was reasonably proficient at Mathematics and Chemistry. But I had real difficulty with Physics. I could just about cope with elementary magnetism and indeed was mesmerised by the behaviour of iron filings when they danced to magnetic forces. But I found electricity and light difficult to comprehend. The cause of Physics was not helped by the fact that our teacher, Larry Moore, was unable to explain things to pupils who did not have a natural talent for Physics. He also had no idea how to control a classroom of 12-year-olds. One of our pranks was to place pieces of smouldering string beneath the inkpots in our wooden desks and occasionally lift the inkpots to enable the smell of burning string to drift around the classroom. The teacher would go to the window and comment how odd it was that the gardeners always seemed to be burning rubbish. Another prank was to construct marble runs on our desk tops. These were ingenious works of construction comprising pairs of books placed on top of each other, with channels between them. The channels served as gulleys for marbles, which we placed at the highest point of the construction, to run from the top of the piles at various angles down to the desk surface and then noisily along the desk surface into a school cap. I have no recollection of anyone being punished for these escapades. It was no wonder that few of the boys were any good at Physics.

During these early years in the Main School, and indeed throughout my school career, I played rugby and cricket with more enthusiasm than skill. I enjoyed both sports. During the spring term, we had to do cross-country running. I was a reasonable short-distance runner, but I was hopeless at long-distance running and hated it. There were no opt-outs except, I assume, on medical grounds, so I had to do it. The key to popularity in the school was sporting prowess. Boys who excelled at sports were treated as heroes. Those who were good academically were regarded as 'swots' and not admired. Likewise, those like me who were keen on music and chess (as I was later to become) were of little interest to the school community. For the most part, excellence in intellectual activities was treated with indifference. Exceptionally, at the end of my second year when I was approaching my twelfth birthday in 1955, I and one other boy were awarded a school 'foundation' scholarship. Bizarrely, to mark this event some or all of the boys of the school were given a half-day holiday. This went down well and did much good for my street credibility. I do not understand why my success in the scholarship examination led to others being deprived of half a day's education.

In 1956 at the end of my third year, when I had not even reached the age of 13, I had to make a crucial choice. I had to decide whether to go into 4CM (Classics and Modern) or 4SM (Science and Mathematics). For me the choice was easy, although in retrospect I think it was appalling that we were required to make such a critical decision at so early an age. It was inevitable that I would go into 4CM. I stopped having Physics and Chemistry lessons. The only science subject that I was now to study was Biology. I did, of course, continue with Mathematics. Since I had already had to choose between German and ancient Greek the previous year and I had chosen Greek, it looked as if I was already heading towards the Classical Sixth form and an education in Classics. I was still studying English, History and French, so that it was possible that I would go down the 'Modern' rather than the 'Classics' route. But there were two reasons why that possibility was somewhat remote. First, there was a tradition that clever boys who were not pursuing an education in science studied Latin, Greek and Ancient History. This was the course favoured by the best schools in Victorian England. It was the route that led from the best schools to the best universities and then to the professions and the civil service.

The second reason was that I showed no talent for the study of English. I was proficient at analysis and comprehensions. But my writing style was not well regarded my English masters. When I was criticised for writing a piece on the grounds that it was too short and unimaginative, I produced work that was criticised for being too long and out of control. My English master when I was in 4CM was also my form master. He was R. C. S ('Apple Face') Shepard.

When my parents met him at the parents' evening, he told them that he was concerned about my performance in English. On hearing my mother's strong foreign accent, he said that it was not surprising that I was not doing well at English because it was a disadvantage to have a foreign parent. My mother was extremely upset. I have always thought that what he said was both insensitively hurtful and plainly stupid and wrong. One of the books that we were studying with him was Joseph Conrad's *The Nigger of the Narcissus*. Conrad, who was one of the masters of modern English literature, did not have contact with the English language until he joined the British marine when he was about 20 years old. The irony of this fact must have been lost on Apple Face. By now, I had graduated from reading Enid Blyton, Richmal Crompton and Frank Richards. I had discovered the novels of Alexandre Dumas fils, such as *The Three Musketeers* and *The Count of Montecristo* which I found far less heavy going than Conrad. When Apple Face discovered that I was reading these books, he dismissively said that I should not be reading foreign books in English translation. Such appetite as I was to acquire for reading literature owed nothing to his teaching skills.

On 7 July 1956, I had my Bar-Mitzvah. For a number of years, I had been learning Hebrew and preparing for my Bar-Mitzvah with a teacher called Mr Knopf. I found him totally uninspiring. I rarely did the preparation for my weekly lesson which took place at home after school hours. Sometimes, he and I travelled on the same bus. I would race home pretending that I needed time to wash. The real reason was that I needed the few minutes before he arrived to do some last minute learning. Not at all impressive on my part. I staggered through the lessons. Ours was not a religious or observant household. In this respect, as in so many others, my mother prevailed over my father. He had come from a reasonably observant family which, for example, did not shellfish or pork. She knew nothing of Jewish rites and customs, still less did she observe them. She had been accustomed throughout her life to eating pork (what she called '*schweinerei*') and shellfish. My father gradually lost his inhibition about eating such things, even at home. They rarely went to the synagogue on Saturdays, although they usually went for Rosh Hashanah (the New Year) and Yom Kippur (the Day of Atonement). So I did not come to my Bar-Mitzvah from a family background of Jewish learning or familiarity with the religious rites and customs. But I had then, and have never lost, a profound sense of being a Jew and the importance of what is often called Jewish culture, that is, an awareness of belonging to a minority which has retained its separate identity for some 3,000 years.

I had to sing in Hebrew *Maftir* (a portion of the Torah) and *Haftorah* (a passage from one of the books of the prophets) as well as some blessings. Although somewhat nerve-racking, this was not an unduly arduous undertaking for a reasonably intelligent boy of almost 13 who had had more than enough time to prepare himself. I regret to say that I did not perform especially well and needed to be corrected or prompted *sotto voce* from time to time by the

Rabbi who was sitting behind me. I suspect that these glitches were not noticed by many in the congregation, and certainly not by my mother who knew no Hebrew whatsoever. She was wearing a smart new outfit and sitting high up in the balcony to which the women were consigned during the service. There she revelled in the congratulations that were showered on her by people who could not distinguish a good performance from a bad one. After the service, we went to lunch at the nearby Moortown Corner House where Bar-Mitzvah celebrations were often held in those days. Many members of both my father's and mother's families attended. These included Malvine who had come from Vevey and my great uncle Emil who had come from London. Emil disgraced himself by eating too much and being sick in the presence of the guests. He was a very modest man who usually ate little. On this occasion, the delicious and plentiful food was too much for his tiny stomach. He gave a repeat performance in 1986 at the Bar-Mitzvah of our son Steven when, once again, Emil gorged himself on the food and was sick. Like any Bar-Mitzvah boy, I received many gifts. I recall receiving several fountain pens and alarm clocks, gifts which were typical of the 1950s, but which would be of little interest today.

In the summer of 1956, Robert and I went for a month to a Swiss summer school in Zugerberg, above the Lake of Zug in central Switzerland. The previous year, my cousins had gone to a similar establishment somewhere else in Switzerland and had returned claiming to have had a wonderful time. This gave rise to my own desire to spread my wings too. My parents knew that, if anything went wrong, Esti, who lived in Zurich, was not too far away. The first two weeks or so were great fun. Lots of sport, hikes, making dens in the forests, indulging briefly in illicit smoking and, less enjoyably, having some French lessons. But four weeks was too long and by the end we were longing to go home. It was our first taste of life away from home.

In the winter of 1956, all four of us went on a skiing holiday to Wengen in the Bernese Oberland. The skiing equipment was probably closer to that used by my parents in the late 1930s than to that used today. I enjoyed it very much. In due course, I became a competent skier, but I was never outstanding. We went to Arosa in eastern Switzerland the following winter, and again to Arosa the winter after that, although on this third occasion Robert and I stayed in a winter school which was far more fun than a hotel.

1957 was my *annus mirabilis* on the sports field. During this year, I reached my full height and was taller and stronger than some of my contemporaries. This gave me a considerable, but fairly short-lived, advantage over them in competitive sports, although not in cross-country running at which I did not excel even in 1957. Success in Athletics was assessed by 'standards'. These were the yardsticks set by the school for measuring achievement in running short and medium distances, jumping and throwing various objects such as javelins and cricket balls. I practised very hard to improve my performance. I recall in particular spending many hours at home practising the high jump. I was very proud of the fact that I achieved no fewer than seven standards that year. I was never to match this feat again.

It was at about this time that I also started to try to improve my performance on the cricket field. I practised my batting with great application and seriousness in the school cricket nets. I was greatly encouraged by the kindly Biology master, who was called 'Beefy' Hoggett. I was no great batsman, but under Beefy's instruction, I learnt to improve my forward defensive shot. The trouble with that is that it rarely produces any runs. However, I was considered to be good enough to have some training at Johnny Lawrence's famous cricket academy in Rothwell. I think it was in the summer of 1958 that I was selected to play as a batsman for the School Colts XI (under 15s). I was incredibly nervous and excited. My parents bought me some smart new white kit. The match was against Drax Grammar School. We batted first. I was number five. One of the Drax opening bowlers fired very fast balls at us with a prodigious swing. We lost our first three wickets very cheaply. Far sooner than I had hoped, I was on my way out to face this bowler. I had never encountered bowling of this ferocity or quality. The first four balls that I faced swung so far and so fast that I failed to make contact with any of them. The fifth ball crashed into my stumps. What a humiliating debut. It was made all the worse by the fact that one of our batsmen, George Papworth scored 81 runs. I have relived this day many times in my imagination, with me scoring a century and taking a number of wickets. I am not proud to admit that, instead of working hard to improve my game, I abandoned my aspiration to play cricket for the school. But I continued to play cricket and rugby reasonably well at House level.

1957–58 was my 'O' level year. I took examinations in eight subjects. I passed well in most of them. In view of Apple Face's earlier attitude, it was particularly satisfying that I did well in English language and composition. None of us did particularly well in English literature. Perhaps we were not well taught. But I thoroughly enjoyed studying *Macbeth, Kipps* by H. G. Wells and a selection of eighteenth- and nineteenth-century English poetry. The school wanted me to go into the Classical sixth form. I don't recall much discussion about what I should do. In those days, pupils and their parents were more deferential to teachers than they are now. There was still a widely held view that the study of Latin and Greek was the most rigorous and therefore the best form of education for bright pupils who did not wish to study Mathematics and Science.

By now, I had discovered chess. I joined the chess club at school and started playing regularly. I enjoyed the game, but never studied it seriously to the point of reading books about the various openings and gambits. I started playing for the school against other Yorkshire schools. I never rose to higher than Board 3, that is, the third best player. Chess was of limited appeal in a traditional school such as LGS. Most pupils and masters were not interested in it. This was long before the days of well-known superstars like the American grand master Bobby Fischer who, in the glare of international publicity and to great public acclaim in the West, defeated Boris Spassky of the Soviet Union in 1972.

Nor in my case did the fact that I played the piano make up for my shortcomings on the sports field. As I have said, at the age of 13, I had started having weekly lessons from the already well-known Fanny Waterman. Some of her pupils had already become quite famous. These included Allan Schiller, Michael Roll, her niece Wendy Waterman and Kathleen Jones. Even before I started having lessons, they had played piano concertos in London under the baton of famous conductors such as Sir Malcolm Sargent and Sir John Barbirolli. To me, these brilliant young pianists were demi-gods. To play cricket with Allan in the garden of Fanny's house (as I did) was the stuff of dreams.

My weekly lessons were on Sunday mornings between 11.00 and 12.00. Fanny always insisted that one of her pupil's parents sat in on the lesson so that they could supervise the intense practising that she demanded and expected would take place between one lesson and the next. Allan, accompanied by his mother, had his lesson between 10.00 and 11.00. Michael, accompanied by his mother, had his lesson between 12.00 and 13.00. Michael was 10 years old when I started having lessons with Fanny. In 1963, when he was 17, he won the first Leeds International Piano Competition, the famous competition that was founded by Fanny. It was rather disconcerting for me when, a few minutes before the end of my lesson each Sunday, Michael and his Viennese mother, Greta, came into the room and listened to the last few minutes of my playing. Greta was an excitable, colourful character. So far as I could see, her main role in life was to nurture her son's prodigious talent. She even went so far as to insist that he did not shake the hands of anyone unless he was wearing gloves. In this way, she minimised the risk of his succumbing to some disease. This neurotic tending to her young child reminded me of what I had read about Yehudi Menuhin's upbringing. Such talent needed to be encouraged with a combination of tender love and fierce control. It was remarkable that Michael grew up to be a delightfully normal boy who liked football.

The lessons were testing affairs. Fanny was an exacting teacher. I don't recall her ever raising her voice, but she was tough. Although very small, she could be intimidating if she was displeased with one's playing. She would always say that the real challenge for a pianist was to get what is essentially a percussive instrument to sing. I still possess the scores of the pieces that she taught me. The pages are covered with heavy pencil markings in her hand including many instructions such as 'sing', 'tops' (bring out the top note), 'too flimsy' and 'pedal properly'. She did not believe in requiring her pupils to enter the examinations for Grades (Grade 1 to 8) set by the Associated Board of the Royal School of Music. I can't now remember why. Nor did I study musical theory. Scales and arpeggios were important to her and she was superb at teaching pianistic technique. No matter how easy or difficult the piece that the pupil studied with her, she expected him or her to perform it to what she called 'concert standard'. The result of this exacting approach was that I was only studying a small number of pieces at any one time. I was quickly able to play them from memory, which was good for the quality of the performance, because I could concentrate on producing a good sound rather than finding the notes. But it was less good for promoting excellent sight-reading. I continued having lessons with her until shortly before

I took my 'A' levels in 1960. The last piece I learnt was Liszt's third *Liebestraum*. This is a difficult piece to play to the high professional standard that Fanny was looking for. I was still practising every day, but I was not able to satisfy her. I found this rather frustrating. So I stopped having lessons. I think my mother was quite relieved that she no longer had to accompany me on Sunday mornings. I owe Fanny (now Dame Fanny) a great debt, because she fostered in me a lifelong great love of classical music and in particular of the piano and its repertoire. I owe my mother a great debt too. She helped me considerably. She also persuaded me to continue having lessons when, at the age of about 14, I wanted to stop. She said that, if I stopped then, I would regret it in later life. I carried on until I was almost 17 and as a result have played the piano with great pleasure all my life.

In the years before I started to have lessons with Fanny, she used to showcase her pupils at an annual concert in the war-damaged Leeds City Museum. Our parents used to take us to these concerts and I recall my sense of wonder that young pianists could play to such a high standard. But by 1956, these concerts had ceased. Perhaps this was because the Museum had been rehoused. But I suspect that the more likely reason was that by now her best pupils were established and, more importantly, her own reputation as an outstanding teacher was also well established.

So it was that the only events at which I performed during my time as one of Fanny's pupils were at school. Each year, there was a House music competition. And for several years at least, there was a summer concert at the school. The standard of music at school was not particularly high. My success in the house music competitions was not an indication that I had great talent. But I did play at these competitions pieces such as Schubert's Impromptu in A flat Op 90 No 4 and some Chopin Nocturnes. On two occasions, I also played fairly easy piano concertos with the school orchestra. One was the little concerto in C major by Haydn; the other was a rather attractive concerto by the seventeenth-century English composer, John Stanley. I had never played with an orchestra before nor have I done so since. In view of the limited part that music played in the life of the school, it was not surprising that the orchestra was not of the highest quality. But I can still recall how thrilling it was to play the piano with an orchestra.

After that diversion into music, I need to return to 1958 and my entry into the sixth form. The Classical sixth form comprised only five pupils. We studied Latin, ancient Greek and ancient (ie Roman and Greek) history. Our classroom was tiny as befitted such a small class. It was high up in the main school building and rather isolated from the rest of the school. It had a commanding view over the city of Leeds. In the middle distance was the glowering black Armley prison. Our form master had a small desk on which we used to play a miniature game of table tennis at lunchtime using books as table tennis bats.

I was quite proficient at translating English prose and verse into Latin and Greek prose and verse. *Pace* Apple Face, one can be taught to write reasonably good English prose. I always thought it rather odd that we were required to write Greek and Latin verse. Fortunately, we were not required to translate Latin and Greek verse into English verse. I enjoyed the rigour of the analytical skills that were required in order to produce the clear and accurate translations that were asked of us. The fact that there was no scope for fudge here appealed to me. I would have to deploy similar analytical skills later in life when I became a lawyer.

We were introduced to some of the great Greek and Roman literature. I recall in particular being enthused by the ardent love poems of Catullus. We were well taught by the trio of Classics masters all of whom were Oxbridge-educated. I have already described The Doc and Froggy Beckett. Eddie Scott (whose anti-Semitic explosion I mentioned earlier) was dapper and neat in dress and everything he did. The precision required of a good Classics scholar suited his temperament well. The teaching of Roman and Greek history was less impressive. We did not even quite cover the syllabus. For some reason, much of this teaching was assigned to a fourth teacher, A. F. (Chips) Chippendale. He was a delightful man who seemed to be something of a part-timer when it came to teaching Ancient History. He was one of the art teachers and, as if that were not enough, was in charge of the school workshop as well. For a time, I used to go to the workshop at lunchtime and attempt to do some woodwork. I recall trying to make a boat out of a small rectangular piece of wood. I tried in vain to produce a symmetrically shaped prow. The result of my continual shaving with a plane was that I managed to produce a tiny asymmetrical piece of wood.

The syllabus mainly comprised Greek, Latin and Ancient History. This over-specialisation at an early age was typical of the English educational system at the time. There were two modest gestures towards something broader. The first was an 'O' level course in which I was taught some of the basic laws of Economics. The only thing I can remember about this course was being taught the reasons why paying women less than men for doing the same job was said to be economically justified. The second was an 'A' level course in General Studies. The only thing I can now remember about this was 'studying' the causes of the First World War. We were taught in all seriousness that the first and most impor-tant cause was the defeat of Roman forces by a German tribe in the Teutoburg forest in 9AD and the consequent failure of the Romans to inspire the German people with the benefits of Roman civilisation. According to this ridiculous theory, the result of their being deprived of the civilising influence of the Romans was that the Germans were an aggressive people who were bent on imperialism and destruction.

At some stage during my time in the sixth form, I was made a school prefect. Prefects were appointed by the headmaster, I assume on the recommendation of other masters. The views of the pupils were of no relevance. I must have been told what the duties of a prefect were, but I do not recall receiving any training for the role. One of the duties was to assist in the keeping of order in the school. It is extraordinary that prefects had penal powers. There was a quasi-court called the 'Prefects' Executive' which comprised the entire corpus of the prefects and which met every Friday after school hours. If a boy was unfortunate enough to be seen by a prefect during school hours behaving badly or breaking an important 'rule', the prefect might 'put' him on Prefects' Executive. The boy and the reporting prefect would appear before the assembled prefects on the following Friday at a kind of Kangaroo Court. After the conclusion of what passed for a hearing, the prefects decided what punishment to mete out to the miscreant. This could be a number of whacks to the bottom with a wooden stick. The punishment was administered by the prefect of the week. There was no right of appeal to a master. But even if there had been, the school culture was such that it would have been pointless to exercise it. I am now embarrassed that I participated in this process and wish that I had had the courage to refuse to do so. But it was so much a part of the accepted way of school life that nobody thought to question it. I once had to execute a punishment. I did it fairly gently. Others were less inhibited and delivered savage blows to the unfortunate boy.

A more attractive and worthy side of school life was its encouragement of debating. I was a member of the Debating Society. I was not a natural public speaker, but I enjoyed debating. I particularly enjoyed taking part in 'balloon' debates in which each debater represented the cause of a famous person and had to argue why this person should not be thrown out of the imaginary balloon in which there was only room for one. I did not realise at the time that I was probably sharpening my tools for a future career as a barrister. I recall the visit to the school by Mr Justice Ashworth, a high court judge who was sitting at the Leeds Assize Court (now the Crown Court). I cannot recall a word of what he said. But I do recall being inspired and excited by him. I now know that he was not one of our greatest judges, but to an impressionable young man, he seemed remarkable.

Unlike me, my brother Robert was a good sportsman. Apart from my single disastrous game of cricket for the Colts against Drax Grammar School, I never represented the school in any sport. Robert played in the First Rugby XV and represented the school at athletics and in his last year was Deputy Head Boy. I played a full part in various activities at House level. I was appointed Deputy Head of Sheafield. I competed for the House at various sports. I also recall working hard with a group of enthusiastic boys to produce a choral performance of *O Isis und Osiris* from *The Magic Flute* for a House Music Competition. I had no experience as a conductor and some of the boys could not sing in tune. But we all worked very hard. The fact that we won says something about the standard of music in the school in those days.

In the summer of 1960, I took 'A' levels in Greek, Latin and Ancient History and 'S' (scholarship) levels in Greek and Latin. Apart from a modest performance in Ancient History, I did well in these examinations and was awarded what was called a 'state scholarship'. This meant that I would receive public funding for university education.

The third year in the sixth form was for the boys who had done badly at their 'A' levels and needed to have another go as well as for those who were trying to gain admission to Oxbridge. By this time, it had been decided by the school, I assume with the agreement of my parents, that I should try for Oxford. I do not know why the choice was Oxford rather than Cambridge. Perhaps I had some say in the decision, since I had always supported Oxford in the annual boat race against Cambridge. Perhaps I was also still in awe of Oxford after that visit to Magdalen College when I was about 10. I had decided that I would read Law if I was successful. My father was the driving force behind this decision. Most members of the Jewish community of his generation had gone into business. He wanted his sons to acquire a professional qualification and all the security that it was thought this would bring.

The school believed rightly that Wadham College Oxford had a good reputation for Law. So in September 1960, I started to prepare for the scholarship examinations that I would have to sit in Oxford in December. I confess that I had never heard of Wadham at the time. I worked hard that term and was given extra tuition out of school hours by the masters. I was very grateful to them for this. They were very keen that I should succeed. I recall all three of them giving me a mock interview and asking me to explain the meaning of the words 'Classics' and 'classical'. I had not had to apply my mind to questions like this before. I found the exercise stimulating and useful. Of the five members of the class, three were preparing for Oxford scholarship examinations. In those days, the colleges were divided into three groups for the scholarship examinations. The first group held its examinations in December 1960 and the second and third groups held theirs in January and March 1961 respectively. If you did not succeed in the first examination, you could have another go in the second or third examination.

Wadham was in the first group. All the candidates had to spend four days in college, writing papers and attending interviews. It was a gruelling and stressful business. The weather was freezing. The papers were difficult and challenging. I remember having dinner in the ill-lit Hall under the baleful gaze of the portraits of distinguished alumni. I gained the impression from talking to other candidates that, as I had expected, many if not most of them were self-confident, brilliant and far cleverer than me. My interview with the Wadham Classics and Law Fellows was friendly and not especially tough. The Warden (Sir Maurice Bowra) asked me why I wanted to read Law: if I intended to become a lawyer, why not read Classics? There would be plenty of time to pick up the Law. I did not have a ready answer to this question.

I also had interviews at Pembroke and Keble Colleges. They were also in the first group and they interviewed me to see whether I was of interest to them in case I was rejected by Wadham. The interview at Pembroke was dispiriting.

The Law Fellow asked me what I thought of the jury system and whether I supported the death penalty (which was not abolished until 1965). I had not thought about either of these issues, although I should have done. They were fair questions to ask of a person who had aspirations to become a lawyer. I cannot remember how I responded but I imagine that my answers did not impress my interlocutor. I thought that the interview at Keble went well. After four difficult days, I was convinced that neither Wadham nor Pembroke was interested in me. Keble was a possibility. But overall, I thought it most unlikely that I would be offered a place, still less a scholarship at any of the colleges. But I was determined not to give up. On my return home, I decided that, after a short break, I would continue slogging away and would have another go in the March group of examinations.

One of the sweetest moments of my life occurred when a letter arrived by post from Wadham offering me a scholarship to read Law. It arrived on the very day on which I had decided that I would start working again. Mindful of what the Warden had said, I decided quite soon that I would study Classics.

I wanted to leave school without delay. I liked the idea of doing some voluntary work overseas: there was a VSO programme. My parents were not keen. The headmaster put pressure on me to stay at school until Easter. One of the reasons he gave was that he wanted me to play in an important chess competition in which the school had hopes of success. There must have been other reasons too, but I can't remember what they were. So I agreed to stay on for a term. I abandoned my life in the Classical sixth form and joined the 'A' level French set for the term. I enjoyed reading some serious French literature. But in retrospect, I should have left school at Christmas and escaped from the protective cocoon of my family. I was no longer a fully committed member of the school and I felt that I was marking time. It was time to move on.

Overall, I was very happy at LGS. I received a solid rather than an inspiring education there. The school had not shaken off the rigid stays of the Victorian era. It is easy enough to be critical of some of the things that were done there, such as corporal punishment. But there was nothing unusual about that in those days. The ethos of the school is well captured by the school song which was always sung in Latin:

> *Voce clara gaudeant Leodenses cuncti*
> *Strenui per omnia, numquam non conjuncti*
> *Sive labor nos vocat, fortes laboremus;*
> *Sive ludus placuit, impigri certemus;*
> *Floreat per saecula, schola Leodensis;*
> *Salus sit fidelibus, malae res infensis.*

Roughly translated, this means: 'Let all the Grammar School boys rejoice in a loud voice; strong in everything and always united; if we are called to work, let us work boldly; if we take to sport, let us contest with integrity; let the school prosper throughout the generations; let it be a haven to the loyal and let bad things befall its enemies'. These sentiments are somewhat reminiscent of those expressed rather less solemnly in the Ingledew school song. The flavour of the school's confident self-image was also captured by the school motto: '*nullius non mater disciplinae*' ('the mother of every discipline').

I left school at Easter 1961. Although I spent considerable periods of time at home thereafter until I finally left Leeds to go to London in 1968, leaving school was an important milestone on my journey towards an independent life. I had enjoyed a happy childhood. My parents were loving and cared deeply about their two sons. I can see now that they were over-protective of us. My mother was the dominant influence on me. Her strong personality left little space for my father. She spoke endlessly to me about her own earlier life. He spoke little about his.

The success of the smart dress shop that they ran until the lease expired in 1970 was almost entirely attributable to her flair and hard work. Once he transferred the book-keeping to a secretary, there was little for him to do. They opened a second shop at 48 King Street in the centre of Manchester. My father used to go across the Pennines once a week to keep an eye on it. Sadly, it did not prosper, partly because the person they had chosen to manage the shop embezzled large sums of their money. He felt badly let down but also, I think, knew that he had been naïve and felt that he had been responsible for the failure.

My mother had a real love of clothes and an innate ability to choose well. Her regular customers bought whatever she advised them to buy. Twice a year, she and my father went to the wholesalers in London to buy clothes for the following season. She took the lead in making the decisions. Understandably, she found the experience stressful and worried that they might be left with an unacceptably large amount of unsold stock at the end of the season. Once a year, she organised and hosted a fashion show at the Queen's Hotel in the centre of Leeds. She acted as commère (female compère) as the models (called mannequins) displayed some of the outfits. She never ceased to be nervous on these occasions.

It is not surprising that by Saturday evenings, she was tired and was looking forward to Sunday which was her only day of leisure. This makes it all the more remarkable that every Sunday morning for four years, she accompanied me to my piano lesson with Fanny Waterman. In those days, Sundays were oases of calm. Most of the shops were closed and there was very little traffic on the roads. Leeds was not a vibrant city in the 1950s. It was proud of its heritage of fine Victorian buildings. Foremost among them was the famous Town Hall which was opened in 1858. Like so many other buildings in the city, it was black with soot from the particles of coal dust that were in the air that we breathed. In the 1950s and 1960s, a great deal of rebuilding took place. The city had suffered little damage during the Second World War but the City Council planners encouraged the wholesale demolition of many old dwellings to make way for the high rise council housing of which they were very proud at the time. They believed that this would solve the problem of the acute housing shortage. Many of the demolished buildings were terraced houses such as those in which my father's family had lived in the early part of the twentieth century. Some elegant older buildings also fell victim to the bulldozer. There was a great deal of commercial development in the city too. It was exciting to see these large structures going up all over the centre of the city in the 1950s and 1960s. Some of them have since been demolished. In hindsight, most would agree that they were poorly designed, unimaginative and unattractive. The post-war buildings that have survived have few friends. Fortunately, the famous arcades and quite a few of the other wonderful buildings of the eighteenth, nineteenth and early twentieth centuries have survived.

Heavy engineering and the textile industry dominated the commercial life of Leeds. It would not be until later in the twentieth century that financial and legal services came to the fore. By the middle of the twentieth century, there were many firms of solicitors in the city. Many of the larger firms were long-established. Both their partners and their employees were for the most part Christian white males. The majority of the increasing numbers of Jews who had gone into the legal profession were not welcome in these firms. The Jews responded by forming their own firms, just as they had responded to their exclusion from golf clubs by establishing their own Moor Allerton Golf Club. There was little social intermingling between the Jews and the wider community and far less intermarriage than there is today. The Jewish population of Leeds had been about 25,000 at its peak in the 1920s and remained at that level during the next few decades. By the 1960s, it had declined to about 18,000. Today it is approximately 10,000. Over the years, the Jews came to play a more prominent part in all aspects of the life of the city. I am sure that one of the reasons for this was the fact that over time most of the young members of the Jewish community went to university. When I was growing up, it had already become accepted that most boys would go to university. But many girls did not because their protective parents feared that a terrible fate would befall them if they did. Gradually, this all changed. A consequence was that there was inevitable socialising between young Jews and other members of the wider community. And intermarriage increased.

But these changes occurred gradually after the 1950s. When I was growing up, there was a certain mutual wariness between the Jews and the wider population. To some extent, this was reflected in the LGS. So far as I am aware, there was no official quota restricting the number of Jewish boys who could attend the school. But it was noticeable that the Jews never exceeded about 10 per cent of the school population. I do not know how this percentage was achieved. The other striking feature of the population of the school and the city in the 1950s was the lack of black and Asian people. I do not recall there being a single black or Asian boy or indeed, with one exception, a boy from any foreign country at the school. The exception was a boy from Finland. Both the school and the city were essentially white and of Yorkshire birth. This fostered an almost jingoistic passion for all things Yorkshire.

All of my parents' friends were Jewish. Their main social activity was bridge. Bridge games could be excitable affairs in which voices were raised and complaints made about the quality of the bidding and the playing of hands. This may have put me off learning to play the game. Most of my friends were Jewish too. I went to parties but, owing to my shyness, I was slow to discover girls. Robert and I were very close and happy in each other's company. Neither of us felt the need to have a hectic social life.

There was a great deal of classical music in our lives. We listened to 78s records (78 revolutions of the gramophone turntable per minute). This meant that a typical symphony occupied two or three records which had to be changed by hand. The arrival of 33s (33 revolutions per minute) was a cause of great excitement. I used to go to the Central Lending Library most Friday evenings after school to borrow records as well as books. We often went to excellent concerts in the Town Hall on Saturday evenings. Robert and I sat in the rises behind the orchestra. Our parents sat more comfortably in the main body of the hall. For a short period I collected the autographs of the famous artists who performed there. For many years, we also went to the Harrogate Festival at the beginning of July to hear Sir John Barbirolli conduct the Halle orchestra. The orchestra would perform every night for a whole week. Friday nights were Beethoven nights. Saturdays were devoted to Viennese music. Barbirolli would positively dance on the podium to the rhythm of Strauss waltzes. Another feature of our musical lives was the annual visit to the Leeds Grand Theatre of the D'Oyle Carte Opera Company. This company toured the country performing the Gilbert and Sullivan Savoy operas from the 1870s until 1982. We loved the words and music. So there was much music in my life as I was growing up.

But there was no choral music. I do not know whether this was because it was associated with the church and therefore of no interest to Jews. At school, we never went to services in the chapel. The Jewish boys were segregated from the rest of the school at early morning prayers. When I became the most senior Jewish prefect, I had responsibility for managing Jewish prayers. I did not have the skill or desire to lead these prayers. That task was entrusted to someone who was more knowledgeable than me. But I did have the responsibility for maintaining a degree of decorum and keeping the noise levels down. This was difficult and occasionally, to my great embarrassment and anger, the noise was so great that one of the masters came in to complain.

Robert was more enterprising than I was and joined the school choir. The first work he sang was Haydn's *Nelson Mass*. He did this despite objections from my parents. They were unhappy that their son should be singing church music and doing so in a church. He was bold enough to withstand the pressure to which they subjected him not to sing. It is easy to criticise them for being narrow-minded and even bigoted. But they were merely reflecting the Jewish social mores and insecurity of the time. This insecurity engendered in a few Jews a desire to lose their identity and assimilate with the wider community. But the majority wanted to preserve their identity and protect it from influences that might undermine it. My parents would have been far from alone in thinking that singing a mass in a church was just such an influence. But to their great credit, they came to the performance of the Haydn in St Michael's Church, Headingley and so enjoyed it that they bought a recording of the work.

I was not a voracious reader, but I read quite widely. I enjoyed reading classic English and European novels. I particularly enjoyed reading the great Russian novels. But I also enjoyed the rather cloying and overblown works of Lawrence Durrell (such as his Alexandrian Quartet) and the novels of D. H. Lawrence: books that I now find almost unreadable. Lawrence's *Lady Chatterley's Lover* was published in its unexpurgated form in 1960 while I was still at school. News spread as to where to find the salacious passages which had previously been expurgated. Like many other boys, I went to W. H. Smith's bookshop and furtively turned up the well-thumbed page. It seemed an exciting thing to do, although by today's standards, the text is fairly bland. The publication of the unexpurgated edition of the book and the enactment of the Obscene Publications Act 1959 were evidence of a distinct departure from the stifling formality of the 1950s.

Ours was not a religious household. As I grew up, visits to the synagogue became a rarity. The one religious event that I recall with pleasure was *Seder* night at *Pesach* (or Passover). Most families celebrated two *Seder* nights. I don't recall our ever having *Seder* nights at our house. I suspect that my mother would not have known what to do. Anyway, she did not have much time for religious rituals. For some reason, we went for a number of years for the first night to the home of an Irish couple and their son. This was the only time we used to see them. We sometimes celebrated the second night at the home of uncle Sim and auntie Helen. But that came to a crashing end when one of the many rows that periodically broke out between them and my parents boiled over and led to a serious breakdown in relations. After that relations cooled for a number of years.

As I have already said, my mother suggested that on leaving school I might like to go to Paris to improve my French. I could stay with her old school friend Pierre Hardy who lived with his wife and two children in the sixteenth arrondissement. They had generously said that I could stay with them while I attended a three months' course at the *Institut Britannique* in the Rue de la Sorbonne. This was an institution where Anglo-phones studied French and Franco-phones studied English. I was to discover that there was little intermingling between the French and British students.

Within a short time of my enrolling on the course, I became friendly with a group of young English men all of whom, like me, were going to Oxford University in October. One of them had been at University College School,

London (UCS), a school which our grandson Oliver now attends. The rest had been to well-known boarding schools. One of them had won the organ scholarship to Magdalen College, the college that we had visited when I was 10 and to which our son Steven was to go in 1991. The organ scholar had an ability to improvise on the piano and play simple pieces in the style of different famous composers. I thought this was an astonishing skill. The whole group seemed very sophisticated. The UCS boy told me about a debate at his school on the motion 'the plug end is the better end of the bath'. I had no idea what one would say for or against such a motion. But I thought it was quite brilliant and far more exciting and imaginative than the subjects of any of the debates at LGS. We were a happy band of carefree young men who spent a great deal of time with each other, inevitably speaking English. This did not help us with our French. Fortunately, I had the advantage that I spoke a good deal of French with the Hardys.

I recall little of the French lessons. But there was a fierce teacher who was a passionate supporter of President General de Gaulle. The political situation in France was quite fraught at the time. De Gaulle was a Second World War hero. In 1958, he founded the 5th Republic and became its president. An independence war had been raging in Algeria for some time. The settlers (the *pieds noirs*) and many in the armed forces were opposed to the grant of independence. In April 1961, they staged an attempted *coup d'état*. I recall that there was a large military presence in the streets and De Gaulle made his famous televised speech in which he pleaded with the people: '*Francaises, Francais: aidez-moi*'. The situation was very tense and the Hardys felt responsible for my safety. So I went home for a few days. After a short time, calm was restored. Following a referendum, Algeria was given its independence.

`The fierce teacher hated *Franglais*. She regarded the importation of English words into the French language as a national insult. She also took us to task if we did not speak with the precision and elegance to be expected of a master of classical French. For example, if one apologised by saying '*je m'excuse*', she would respond pedantically: '*peut-etre vous oui, mais moi non*'.

The Hardys were extremely kind to me. They lived in great comfort in an apartment in Avenue Adrien Hebrard in the sixteenth arrondissement. Pierre's brother and his family lived in an apartment one floor above. The two brothers had established a large successful clothes store in the Chausée d'Antin. They also jointly owned a large house in the country to the west of Paris in La Queue les Yvelines to which they retreated most weekends. Pierre and his wife had two children, Claudine, a pregnant married daughter aged 19 and an extremely annoying 13-year-old son called Gerard. To me, Claudine seemed a very mature and worldly young woman. Her husband, who was about 30, even more so. I enjoyed sharing their family life. All conversation was in French so I made real progress. By the time I left in June, I was able to speak reasonably fluently. Sadly, over the years I have lost a good deal of this skill through desuetude. But I can still speak with a flatteringly good accent.

When I was not having lessons or being with the Hardys, I spent much time exploring Paris both on my own and with my English friends. I did not make any French friends and had limited contact with girls. There was one French girl whom I met at the *Institut* and arranged to meet again, but she failed to turn up. There was a nice English girl at the *Institut* who was going to St Anne's College, Oxford in the autumn. We met a few times. I can't pretend that I had a successful time with the opposite sex in Paris.

But my eyes were opened to many other wonderful things. I spent a great deal of time in the Louvre and the Jeu de Paume, which then housed the superb art that is now displayed in Musee d'Orsay. I loved the famous collection of Impressionist and Post-Impressionist paintings. I also discovered the sculpture of Rodin. I had never seen any of this art before and I was overwhelmed by it. Like many people who are excited by a wonderful new experience, I felt that I had made a great discovery and wanted to share it with anyone who was prepared to listen to me talking about it.

I went to many concerts. The most memorable of these was a concert in the Paris Opera (now the home of the Opera Garnier). Artur Rubinstein, who was then aged 73 and seemed incredibly old to me, played three piano concertos. This was quite a feat for a pianist of any age. He was one of the greatest pianists of the twentieth century. I remember him as a small man who exuded amazing energy and vitality. I was particularly excited by his performance because I had the impression that this was likely to be one of his last public concerts. I was seriously mistaken. He carried on playing in public until he was 89. He gave his last concert in the Wigmore Hall, London in May 1976.

I also went to recitals in the famous Salle Pleyel. I recall spending a whole day there attending a piano competition. The competitors had to play Chopin's first piano sonata. I loved listening to the different performances. I have always been fascinated by the range of possible different interpretations of music. One of the great attributes of an outstanding musician is to be able to give a performance of a familiar piece which is so arresting that the audience listens to it with great concentration and a sense of excitement as if they had never heard it before.

On the lighter side, I enjoyed going out to bistros and to satirical performances in night clubs. Satirical sketches had been part of the theatrical scene in Paris for some time, long before they were introduced in England in the late 1950s. I recall one show performed by 'Les Quatre Barbues'. It consisted of a number of brilliantly witty sketches to music from Rossini's *Barber of Seville*. I had never seen anything so bold and innovative before. In 1963, I was to see *Beyond the Fringe* in London which ushered in a fashion for something similar in the United Kingdom.

I enjoyed my three months in Paris. It was a gentle introduction to life away from the shelter of my home. It marked the beginning of my independent life.

4

Oxford

I WAS ONE of about half a dozen boys from LGS to go up to Oxbridge in October 1961. With the exception of two cousins who had studied dentistry at Leeds University, so far as I am aware I was the first member of my family to go to any university. So my departure from home to go south was quite an event for the family. I packed my belongings into the large trunk which my father had used when he sailed to Canada in 1936. It was sturdy, but not in good condition. I had attempted to make it look smart by painting it black. It was transported to Oxford by road by British Road Services. My train journey took about six hours. On the whole, parents did not drive their children to universities in those days. Road travel was very slow in the pre-motorway era: the first section of the M1 was not opened until 1959.

On my arrival at Wadham, I was allocated a room on the top floor of staircase 12 at the back of the second quadrangle. The room was tiny and overlooked Holywell Street, which at that time was a busy road. The bed was narrow and its mattress, which was shaped like a steep-sided valley, bore the imprint of generations of undergraduates. There was a washbasin outside the room. I was fortunate that the bath and lavatories were at ground floor level and that I did not have to go outside the building to use them. That was a pleasure in store for me later in the year.

Like all new undergraduates, I arrived before the start of the Michaelmas term in order to go to the Freshers' Fair. This gave me the opportunity to see what activities the university had to offer and to join societies and clubs. It was all rather bewildering.

I joined the college rowing club although I had never rowed before. Rowing seemed to me to epitomise the traditions and ethos of the English public school. Despite the fact that in some ways LGS was modelled on these traditions and sought to reflect them, it is hardly surprising in view of my background that I felt that they were alien to me. So it is perhaps rather odd that I was attracted by the idea of rowing at Oxford. I was soon to discover that it involved a huge amount of hard training. I must have been given some elementary tuition in the art of rowing. Wadham was not known to be one of the leading rowing colleges and there was little competition to join the club. No doubt that is why I was welcomed as a new oarsman.

Every afternoon except on Sundays, the crews went down to the river Isis (the name of the Thames where it flows through Oxford). Like most colleges at that time, we stored the boats and equipment in an attractive but rather rickety wooden barge which was moored to the river bank. We practised hard and were regularly shouted at encouragingly by the coach and the cox. We were expected to row whatever the weather conditions. I was considered to be good enough to row in the first eight at bow, that is, in the position furthest away from the cox. During the second term, we trained for two races. One was called Torpids, which is a curious 'bumping' race in which college crews take part. Boats start the race at a specified distance behind each other. The object is to bump the boat in front and thereby overtake it in the table. The other race for which we trained was an altogether more exhausting affair. It was called the Reading Head Regatta which took place after the end of the Hilary Term in March. Dozens of crews raced over a course of about three miles on the River Thames at Reading. Our crew did badly. We lacked the skill and, despite all that training, the stamina to do well. By now, I felt that I had had enough of rowing. The idea of rowing six days a week was no longer appealing. Summer was approaching. My rowing career came to an end.

For the rest of my time at Oxford, my involvement with rivers was confined to punting on the River Cherwell during the Trinity (summer) terms. I spent many happy hours punting up and down the river, mooring the punt against the bank, sometimes in the company of a girl and sometimes not.

But I need to return to the beginning. Throughout my Oxford career, I was taught in accordance with the traditional Oxford tutorial system. This involved one or two tutorials per week at which the undergraduate read his weekly essay aloud to the tutor. The tutor would then comment on it and a discussion would ensue. There were about eight Classics undergraduates in my year. So each week, the tutor had to listen to eight essays on the same subject. It must have been quite a challenge for the tutor to maintain his concentration. This was an extravagant and costly system which, in retrospect, I can see was difficult to justify.

My tutor was a gentle and kindly man called Tom Stinton. He was a brilliant classicist who published essays and reviews mainly on Greek tragedy. He was painfully shy and found communication quite difficult. Sometimes I found the silences between his sentences difficult to bear. For the first five terms, I studied Classical Moderations (Mods). This was a taxing course which had remained unchanged since the nineteenth century. It involved Greek and Latin language and literature. The language entailed unseen translation of English prose into Greek and Latin prose and English verse into Greek iambics and Latin hexameters. The literature involved the study of all the works of Homer and Virgil as well as a number of other 'set books' including Euripides' *Hippolytus* and several books of Lucretius' *De Rerum Natura*.

We also had to study one 'special subject'. I chose ancient Greek sculpture which I greatly enjoyed. I spent many hours in the Ashmolean museum as well as in the British Museum. I am thrilled by the Elgin marbles to this day. I found the flowering of Greek sculpture in the fifth century BC extraordinary. There must have been something in the air in Athens at that time that led to such a remark-able explosion of activity in art and literature.

I also enjoyed immersing myself in the literature, although I had and still have doubts about the usefulness of studying the contributions made by differ-ent scholars to establishing the definitive texts (the study of textual criticism). Even if such meticulous examination of the texts of this great literature was a worthwhile pursuit for some academics, I saw little point in asking undergradu-ates to mimic their work. But we did not spend all our time considering the merits of different suggested texts and it was a real privilege to study this great literature. I became particularly interested in *Hippolytus* and wrote an essay comparing Euripides' treatment of the story with that of Seneca in *Phaedra* and Racine in *Phedre*.

I was good at translating prose from and into the two languages. I enjoyed the combination of having to be precise and at the same time trying to write elegantly and attractively. Verse was rather different. I had little difficulty in translating Greek and Latin verse into English prose. But I struggled with translating English verse into Greek and Latin verse. Sometimes, understand-ing what the English verse meant was itself a problem. But the real difficulty was producing passable Greek and Latin verse. Tom Stinton was not impressed with the quality of my work. Eventually, he suggested that I stop trying to produce verse for my weekly tutorials, but that I take the examinations and try my luck.

The examinations took place towards the end of the Hilary term of 1962. We had to sit 14 three-hour papers, every morning and afternoon over a seven-day period. I obtained alpha marks in 10 of the papers (seven were needed for a First). Astonishingly, these included alphas for my translation of English verse into Greek and Latin verse. This was particularly sweet after the humiliation of being told to stop trying. I attribute my success to the fact that, as a result of my extensive and detailed reading of Greek tragedies and the poetry of Virgil, I had learnt many phrases and acquired a rich vocabulary. By these means, I had achieved a respectable technical skill. I cannot claim that I was inspired by the Muse.

Hilary term in the second year is famously a high point of an undergrad-uate's Oxford life. There are no examinations on the horizon; just weeks of punting, playing tennis, parties and having fun. The First had also been good for my self-confidence.

Like so many undergraduates, I made friends in haste and then had the tricky task of disentangling myself from some of them as tactfully as I could. At the end of the first term in my first year, I swapped rooms with a rather obnoxious individual who had been sharing with Nick Halsted. He and Nick did not get on and I was not too keen on my tiny room. So after Christmas, we effected a swap and I shared with Nick in his large room in the main quadrangle for the rest of my first year. The room comprised a large room and two small single bedrooms off it. Heating was by means of a two-bar radiator which doubled up as a toaster: there was no central heating. There were wash basins in the two bedrooms. But a visit to the bathroom and lavatory involved going down one flight of stairs and across the quadrangle. Nick was studying Law as were many of my other friends. Their tutor, Peter Carter, was notoriously tough and austere. Life under his watch did not seem much fun. I was not sorry that I had decided to read Classics and not Law.

Nick had been to Westminster and had some of that apparent self-confidence and public school polish that I did not have. Like a number of others, he smoked a pipe. This involved much tamping down of tobacco, lighting up and puffing amidst clouds of smoke. I liked the smell of Balkan Sobranie tobacco. Otherwise, so far as I could see, there was nothing to commend pipe-smoking. He was also an excellent fencer, who represented England in a World Championship and in the 1964 Olympic Games. We had a lot of fun together.

One of the problems facing male undergraduates at that time was the lack of females. The colleges were single sex and only five of them were for women. The consequence was that the few attractive female undergraduates were in huge demand. The shortfall was made good to some extent by women who were attending secretarial colleges. But overall the situation was far from satisfactory. Nick and I hit upon a stratagem to try to ameliorate the situation for ourselves. We decided to pretend that we were putting on a play. We chose Moliere's *Tartuffe* because it had a significant number of female parts. The plan was to hold auditions and sift the applicants down to two, before calling the play off. So we placed notices in the five women's colleges (but nowhere else) for the first auditions. The few women who attended the auditions that we held in our room in College threw themselves enthusiastically into the roles. But we did not find any of them attractive and subsequently placed notices in the colleges stating that the play had been called off. This ploy was as desperate as it was unworthy. But it was the kind of thing that sex-starved 18-year-old male students did in those days. The advent of mixed colleges in the 1970s obviated the need for such elaborate and hopeless ways of trying to form relationships with the opposite sex.

My father had purchased life membership of the Oxford Union for me. He hoped that I would make a name for myself in the debating chamber of this august institution. The Union debates had been famous in earlier times. For example, the notorious 'King and Country' debate in 1933 had attracted great public attention at the time. But by the 1960s, there was little nationwide interest in these debates, although the glamour of Oxford was still a sufficient draw for public figures still to be willing to take part in them alongside undergraduates. I attended some of the debates in my first few terms. On one occasion, I had planned to make a speech 'from the floor', but failed to catch the president's eye. That was the nearest I got to making a speech. This was not auspicious for a potential barrister. I was impressed by the quality of the debating and the swiftness of the repartee. It far surpassed anything that I had seen at the LGS debating society. The only debate that I can now recall was on the motion

'The creation of the State of Israel was the greatest mistake of the 20th century'. One of the speakers proposing the motion was Edward Atiyah, the attaché to the Iraqi embassy. He launched into an extraordinary attack on Israel. He worked himself into a wild frenzy of vehemence and venom. Suddenly, he collapsed. The house fell into a state of shocked silence. Eventually, the president asked whether there was a doctor in the house. After a pause, Doctor Segal, who was regarded as the leader of the Oxford Jewish community, rose from his seat in the balcony and came down to attend to Mr Atiyah. The poor man was already dead. He had suffered a heart attack. I imagine that the orthodox Jews present would have seen this as a sign of divine intervention. It was a shocking and upsetting experience.

One of my undergraduate friends was a geologist called Brian Rosen. He was the older brother of Michael Rosen, who also went to Wadham and became well known as a children's novelist and poet. During the Christmas vacation, I went to stay for a few days with the Rosens in their house in Pinner. This was my first experience of London suburbia and the tube. I was overwhelmed by the vastness of London and the sheer scale of its underground system, which seemed far bigger than the Paris metro with which I had become very familiar. Brian's father Harold was a distinguished educationist. He and his wife had been members of the Communist Party. Although by 1961 they had both left the party, they were still committed socialists. I had not encountered red hot socialism before. My encounter with Harold made quite an impact on me.

Before going to the Rosens, I had had a very different experience at the smart Kensington home of one of my Paris friends, Mike Nassim. His father was a successful medical consultant and the family reeked of sophistication and success. Like me, Mike had just completed his first term at Oxford. I was invited to a party at their house. Mike had two sisters, both of them charming and beautiful. I was smitten by the younger one. I kept in touch with her for a time and invited her to a ball at Queen's College, Oxford the following June which I probably enjoyed more than she did. To my regret, I did not see her again.

During the Easter vacation, Brian came to stay with us in Leeds. My mother was not pleased that he had come laden with fossils and rocks which he had collected on his geology field trip to the Isle of Arran and deposited in our house. These were not like the beautiful objects that were displayed in the glass cabinets which were more to her taste. Brian had organised a five-day youth hostel walking tour from Malham to Kettlewell via Ingleton. I had not stayed in a youth hostel before. In those days, there was an age limit of 25 for youth hostel-lers, nobody was allowed to arrive by car and one had to vacate the hostel after breakfast whatever the weather conditions. Brian had arranged for his girlfriend to join us and she was to be accompanied by one of her female friends. This arrangement proved to be something of a disaster. Brian's girlfriend announced on her arrival that she was now in a relationship with his best friend. Nonethe-less, she stayed with us for the entire five days. And her friend was not much fun.

She complained about the walking and gave up after about three days. Despite these mishaps and getting lost in dense fog and snow at the top of Ingleborough, I enjoyed the experience enormously.

In my second year, I was fortunate enough to be allocated a room in college in the Goddard Building. This was an undistinguished but comfortable 1950s building. I had a room to myself and it was centrally heated. Nor did I have to go outside to use the bathroom or lavatory.

The winter of 1962/63 was the coldest that I can recall. The snowman that I made at home during the Christmas vacation was still intact when I returned at Easter. Oxford, which tends to be damp and cold in the winter, was freezing. I was very fortunate to have a warm room in college.

During the Easter vacation, Mark Sharpe, who was another pipe-smoking law undergraduate, came to stay with us in Leeds. He had been to the Dragon School in Oxford and Sherborne School. Wadham had a reputation for being somewhat left-wing even in the early 1960s. But my impression was that the majority of undergraduates had not had a state education and many of them, like Nick and Mark, had been to public schools. There were a few at Wadham who were disdainful of a person like me who came from the North and had a 'trade' background. But such exhibitions of juvenile class snobbery were rare. I recall one boy who had a working class background and came from a coal-mining village in Derbyshire. He was unhappy because he felt that he did not fit in well at Wadham, and yet his family and friends at home thought that he had disowned them. I did not feel this way about myself. I was certainly not viewed with suspicion by my friends and family as having become posh, although I had started to lose my Yorkshire accent.

I had acquired a taste for youth hostelling. Mark and I went for a few days to the Lake District. We started at Ambleside and the plan was to do a circular walk taking in Patterdale, Keswick, Buttermere and returning to Ambleside. The weather was very bad. We were drenched during a whole day of rain as we walked from Keswick to Buttermere. The following morning, it was still pouring and our clothes were still wet. We decided to call it a day and curtailed the walk.

In the Hilary term of 1963, I started studying Greats. Like Mods, this was an arduous course. It comprised ancient Greek history from 776 to 404 BC and ancient Roman history from 133 BC to 68 AD. In addition to reading large numbers of academic textbooks and learned articles on the two histories, we also had to read in the original the whole of Herodotus' *Histories* and Thucydides' *Peloponnesian Wars* as well as the *Annals of Tacitus*. We were required to master the texts sufficiently well to be able to identify short passages or 'gobbets' plucked from the texts and to answer questions about them. My tutor was George Forrest. He was a brilliant, rather scruffy and altogether delightful man. His particular interest was the history of Sparta. He was a Marxist and saw history through a Marxist lens so that history was explained in terms of class. I found his exegesis persuasive and attractive. I did not question it, although

I subsequently discovered that his approach was by no means shared by most of his fellow academics. As before, I had a weekly tutorial with George on a one to one basis. I don't believe that I said anything original in my essays or had any novel ideas to contribute to our weekly discussions. It must have been a rare ancient history undergraduate who could find anything new to say to his tutor. But he did say that my work was of high quality.

The other component of the Greats course was philosophy. The philosophy seemed a strange pot pourri to me. One element of it involved the study of Plato's *Republic* and Aristotle's *Nicomachean Ethics*. As with the history, we had to read the Greek texts in the original and be able to recognise and discuss gobbets from them. We were expected not only to master the texts, but also to understand and discuss the ideas expressed in them. In addition, however, we studied moral philosophy, epistemology and logic more generally. This involved some reading of the works of later classic philosophers such as Locke, Berkeley and Hume. But this part of the course concentrated on twentieth-century philosophy and, in particular, the linguistic analysis school as expounded by Wittgenstein and many of the so-called Oxford school of philosophy, such as Ryle, Warnock and Hare. My philosophy tutor was a quiet, very clever man called Ian Crombie. He was another pipe-smoker. His reactions to my weekly essays tended to emerge slowly from behind a screen of rising tobacco smoke after much cogitation and attention to his pipe. He rarely enthused about my work. This may have been because he was not a showy person. But the more likely explanation is that what I wrote and said was rather pedestrian and at best no more than competent. The topic that I most enjoyed was moral philosophy. I was more interested in trying to understand the ethical principles that under-pin human behaviour than the meaning of existence and theories of knowledge. In view of the course that my life was to take, it is perhaps of some signifi-cance that I enjoyed the philosophy of law (or jurisprudence as it was called) and followed quite closely the Hart/Devlin debate that was preoccupying Oxford moral philosophers at the time. One book which made a huge impact on me was *Art and Illusion* by E. H. Gombrich. This was not about philosophy but was a study on the psychology of pictorial representation. It has influenced the way I have looked at paintings ever since.

Like many non-scientists, I rarely went to lectures. I relied on tutorials and getting through the reading lists that my tutors set for me. I did, however, go to occasional lectures given by the great and the good. For example, I recall going to lectures given by A. J. Ayer. More memorable and exciting for me, however, were the lectures given by Isaiah Berlin. He had given his famous inaugural lecture 'Two Concepts of Liberty' in 1958. He was already a famous national figure. I heard him lecture on the history of ideas in the nineteenth century. He talked about Vico and Herder as well as the great Russian writers such as Tolstoy and Turgenev. He spoke fluently and at great speed, the words rushing along fast and furious like a raging torrent. He was born in Russia and did not come to the United Kingdom until he was 12 years old. More evidence of how wrong Apple Face had been to blame my mother for my poor English composition when I was 14!

I thoroughly enjoyed my ancient history and worked hard at it. Apart from the moral philosophy, I found the philosophy less rewarding. I was not in sympathy with linguistic analysis and the idea that an understanding of the way we use words gives real insight into some of the fundamental concepts of philosophy. As Sir Maurice Bowra put it to me once, the linguistic analysts are forever sharpening their tools, but with a view to what? However, I believe that this constant pre-occupation with language had a valuable consequence for me when I practised law. The combination of Latin and Greek and linguistic analysis made me particularly sensitive about the use of language and almost obsessive about the need to express myself with precision.

Apart from work, I spent most of my time socialising and playing sport. In 1963, the college organised a 'commemoration' ball. These balls were grand expensive affairs which ran through the night ending with breakfast at 06.00. I bought a double ticket early in the year. Although I did not have a girlfriend at the time, I was confident that I would have one in time for the ball which was to take place in June. I met an interesting and highly intelligent girl early in the year, but was not sure that I wanted to go to a 10-hour ball with her. Time began to run out and I began to think that I would be left stranded without a partner. I was not alone in this predicament. So I invited her to the ball and she accepted. The evening was not a great success for either of us.

I was happier playing squash and tennis. I also played a great deal of 'shove ha'penny' in the bar. I tried out various other things. For example, I was once persuaded by a friend to go horse riding. The horse quickly realised that I had little idea what to do. It was very cold and the horse moved away from the stables very slowly and with great reluctance. As soon as we turned round and headed for home, the horse made a dash for it and seemed to be constantly trying to throw me off its back. I managed to hang on. I never rode a horse again. Another time, a friend invited me to join him on a dinghy on the river at Port Meadow. The strong wind caught the boom several times. It felt as if I came close to being decapitated. I never tried sailing again either.

I tried something gentler when I went on a dig with the Oxford Archaeological Society. The mission was to find the traces of a medieval vegetable garden somewhere in Oxfordshire. We were to look for the carbonised remains of the wooden fencing that marked the boundary of the garden. It was bitingly cold. We patiently removed soil under supervision, but we found nothing. I was not inspired to try that again either.

Early in my time at Oxford, I had tried something rather more promising. I joined the Wadham/LMH choir. I had never sung in a choir before. I took part in three concerts. We sang the Brahms *German Requiem*, Carl Orff's *Carmina Burana* and Beethoven's *Mass in C*. I enjoyed the singing and can't remember why I stopped. But I started singing again in a choir in 1974 and am still singing to this day. Choral singing has become an important part of my life.

The other activity at which I dabbled was acting. I had not acted at school and knew that I did not have any acting talent whatsoever. But I thought that it might be fun to take part in one of the plays that the Dramatic Society put on each summer in the college cloisters. I landed the most minor roles in Shakespeare's *Measure for Measure* and Tourneur's Jacobean *The Revenger's Tragedy*. I was a messenger in one and a soldier in the other. I can't remember which was which. I had about 10 lines in each play.

I had only the occasional use of a piano at Wadham but I played a good deal at home during the vacations. There was much good music in Oxford and I attended concerts in the beautiful Holywell Music Room which adjoins Wadham. It was built in 1748 and is said to be the oldest purpose-built music room in Europe. I became friendly with two American post-graduate students both of whom were studying music. One was a fine French horn player who performed in the Holywell. The other was extremely urbane and cultured and knew far more about music than I did. I admired his intellect. He had a piano in his room which I occasionally used to play. One evening, I was in his room. He had had too much to drink and suddenly propositioned me. I was totally shocked since I had no idea that he was gay. I did not know how to handle the situation and fled the room. I admit that, like many others of that era, I was homophobic. I was a child of my time. It should not be forgotten that it was illegal in 1963 even for consenting adults to engage in homosexual relations. I have long since ceased to be homophobic and look back on that incident with some embarrassment.

During the summer vacation of 1963, I spent four weeks in Israel. I had never been there before. In those days, there was a great deal of support for Israel in the United Kingdom. This was partly because details of the Holocaust were becoming more widely known (the trial of Adolf Eichmann took place in Jerusalem in 1961). But partly also because Israel was seen as the underdog, vastly outnumbered by the Arab countries that surrounded it and fighting for its very survival.

In those days, it was common to travel to Israel by sea. Together with a small group I travelled from Marseille to Haifa. We spent most of the four weeks on a kibbutz called Barkai. This was situated in the narrow neck of land between the Mediterranean Sea and the then border with Jordan. This was a period of relative peace between Israel and her neighbours and there was a general feeling of optimism in the country. Barkai was founded in 1949 by South African and UK Jews. It was a classic kibbutz run on communal lines. The members were idealistic socialists many of whom had been educated in universities before they emigrated to Israel. I thought they were wonderful and inspiring people. There was no industrial or high-tech activity on the kibbutz at the time.

All the work was agricultural. So these well-educated and highly motivated kibbutzniks worked in the fields as did we. They cultivated bananas and avocados as well as the usual citrus fruits for which Israel was then famous. We had to move irrigation pipes and prop up banana plants and to load bales of dried grass on to trailers. In the intense heat, this was much harder work than I had expected.

I did not have time to explore much of the rest of the country. I spent a weekend with Hanni (one of my great aunt Rosa's daughters). I was taken to a concert in the great Mann Auditorium in Tel-Aviv. I also had a little time to visit the Dead Sea and the northern part of the Negev.

On my return voyage from Haifa to Marseille, I met a 16-year-old girl from Hull called Maureen Lipman. She was vivacious and attractive and told me that she wanted to be an actor. The fact that I can still recall her saying this suggests that she said it in a way that carried some conviction. True to her word, she became a famous actor.

I had to live out of college in my third and fourth years. In the third year, I re-joined Nick and we took 'digs' in Walton Street near Worcester College. In my fourth year, I took digs on my own further north off the Woodstock Road. I was in these digs on the afternoon of 24 January 1965 when I heard the news of Winston Churchill's death. Doubtless like many others, I had a great sense that this marked the end of an era. Although the United Kingdom had long since ceased to be a great imperial power, Churchill still seemed to embody that greatness and was a vestige of it. The playing of Elgar's *Nimrod Variation* on the radio seemed entirely apt.

Like all the law undergraduates, Nick had graduated in the summer of 1964. I stayed on because Greats was a four-year course. That summer, Nick and I went on holiday together. We had both read Hilaire Belloc's *Path to Rome*, which had been published in 1915 and was a delightful description of a pilgrimage on foot in a more or less straight line from Toul in Eastern France to Rome. Our plan was to replicate this journey some 50 years later. We started walking from Toul. It was very hot. We spent the first few hours walking close to a busy road in the company of countless thundering lorries. This did not seem like the Belloc experience that we had hoped for. When the driver of a passing vehicle offered us a lift, we accepted it without hesitation. Hitch hiking was more common in those days than it is today. So within a few hours of the start, we abandoned the hopelessly unrealistic idea of walking all the way to Rome. A walking holiday had become a hitch hiking holiday.

We had no plan. We just took lifts. We travelled in this way until the money ran out about four weeks later. We sometimes slept out in the open; but more often we stayed in youth hostels and small B&Bs. Early on, we were given a lift by a charming Frenchman who invited us to join his family for their Sunday lunch. He advised us to shave off our sprouting beards if we wanted to improve our prospects of attracting lifts. We followed this good advice and then had no difficulty in finding drivers to take us on our way. We travelled mainly in lorries and cars. The most terrifying journey for me was as the pillion passenger on a motorcycle along the twisting road in Centovalli from Locarno to Domodossola. Our journey took us into Switzerland, Austria, Italy and back through France, but nowhere near Rome.

My fourth year at Wadham should have been my last. Many of my friends had left at the end of their third year. I was expected to do well in ancient history in my Finals and to achieve a First despite the philosophy. I was due to take the examinations in May 1965. I started to feel unwell and decided to go home to be looked after and to escape from the hothouse atmosphere of Oxford. At home, I relaxed and started to feel better. But shortly before I was due to return to Oxford to take the examinations, I suffered excruciating pain in the area of my appendix. I was rushed into hospital and had an emergency operation for the removal of my appendix and part of my bowel. I was suffering from Crohn's disease. I was in hospital for two weeks during the period of the examinations. I convalesced over the succeeding weeks. I was told that, if I wanted any kind of degree, I would have to return to Oxford the following summer to sit the examinations. This was a huge blow. One consequence of this reverse was that I was unable to take up the post of a Classics Instructor which Sir Maurice Bowra had fixed for me at Cornell University.

So I was faced with the prospect of convalescence and then spending time at home before returning to college in the summer of 1966 to take my Finals. I did not know what career to pursue. During my fourth year, I had considered entering the Civil Service (Administrative Grade) and had even passed the first stage of the entry examinations. I am not sure why I decided that this was not the career for me. I think I was probably well suited to it. I was also attracted to academic life and the study of ancient Greek history. George Forrest told me that he would support me if that was what I wanted to do. But he counselled me not to go down that route unless I felt that I had such a passion for the subject that I was sure that I did not want to do anything else. I did not think that I could meet this very high test. This was wise advice because ancient Greek history was exceedingly well-trodden ground and relatively few academic posts were available. I think I would have enjoyed the life of an academic, as a number of my Oxford contemporaries did. But I believe that the career path that I eventually chose was better for me than the life of an academic classicist.

Almost *faute de mieux*, I decided that I would try to obtain articles (a trainee contract) with a firm of solicitors and then take the route that would lead to my becoming a solicitor. I did not have a burning passion to become a solicitor, but it seemed quite interesting. I was rightly rejected for articles by some of the large City firms of solicitors. They had little difficulty in seeing that I did not have a real commitment to being a solicitor. The offer of a Classics teaching post at Cornell rather gave the game away. But eventually, I received offers from two firms and I accepted one of them.

I then embarked on the conversion course that I had to pass because I did not have a law degree: in fact, I did not yet have any degree. I took a correspondence course and passed examinations in some of the basic subjects. In the spring of 1966, I had the difficult task of trying to return to studying for my degree at Oxford and to get back to where I was the previous May before I became ill. I did some studying at home and then returned to Oxford for the few weeks that remained before the examinations were held. I had forgotten a great deal in the intervening year. I knew that I had lost some of my sharpness and I found the examinations something of a struggle. I was summoned for *vivas* (interviews) to test me in both Greek and Roman history. If I had done well in either of the *vivas*, I would have made it over the finishing line to a First. But I did not quite make it. This was a huge disappointment to me. I have never quite shaken it off, although it has made no practical difference to my life. Both of my tutors expressed their anguish for me. George Forrest wrote to me: 'I'm very disappointed and very sorry. Of course, it was the year off that did it, but that's no consolation.'

I learnt of my examination results in *The Times* newspaper at Munich railway station in late July. I was on a youth hostelling holiday with Robert. We arranged to meet my parents in Vienna in order to travel together to Budapest. My mother had not been back since her marriage in 1939. She wanted to show us her beautiful city and to find her father's grave. On arriving in Budapest, we took a taxi to the hotel that my parents had booked. My mother was visibly shocked by the grey and dilapidated state of the city. It had been badly damaged during the Second World War and had suffered further damage during the uprising against the communist regime and the Soviet Union in 1956. To make matters worse, the hotel said that they had no room for us. There were police and soldiers everywhere who combined to create a general air of oppression. The upshot was that my mother decided that we should leave the city immediately. She could not face it. The visit was a complete fiasco.

On returning home, I had to decide what to do. Shortly before I sat my Finals, I had decided that I wanted to be a barrister rather than a solicitor. This was an odd time to change course and to this day I remain uncertain why I did it. I believed that the Bar would be more exciting, but I did not have much evidence to support this belief. I suspect that I may also have been influenced by the knowledge that this was the profession that my father had wanted for me.

So it was that in the summer of 1966, I decided to join Middle Temple and read for the Bar. I chose Middle Temple because that was the Inn of Court to which Peter Carter used to send all the Wadham law undergraduates who wished to become barristers. I had no contacts in the Inn, but like all Middle Temple students, I was allocated to a sponsor whose role was to act as my guide and mentor. My sponsor was a delightful Divorce Registrar called Leonard Stranger-Jones.

I would not be able to be called to the Bar until I had eaten my dinners in Middle Temple Hall and passed both the conversion and practical courses. I was exempted from having to take examinations in the subjects that I had already passed in the solicitors' conversion examinations. I sat the remaining conversion course examinations in May 1967 and the practical course examinations in May 1968 and duly ate my dinners during these two years. I remember my first dinner well. I was overwhelmed by a sense that the Hall, which was completed in 1570, was an ancient place redolent with history. And as the Benchers processed in for dinner, some of them tottering along on walking sticks, I was struck by how old most of them seemed to be. It did not strike me then that all the Benchers were white and male, but they were. I would never have guessed that one day I would be a Bencher, still less that I would be the Treasurer of the Inn.

During my two years of reading for the Bar, I lived at home in Leeds. I did not study hard and I regret that I did not make better use of my time. I did, however, spend several weeks working in a solicitors' office. I was given files to sift and analyse. The work was dull and I doubt whether what I did was of much value to them or to me. I also spent many hours at the Assize courts in Leeds Town Hall watching the leading lights of the local Bar deploy their advocacy skills in grisly murder and rape cases. It was a joy to watch the best of them weave their magic with juries. The red (High Court) judges looked remote and severe. It would never have occurred to me that I might one day become a red judge myself. I was transfixed by some of the evidence. I found it difficult to believe that the person in the dock, who looked so ordinary, could have done the terrible things that were alleged against him. But the juries usually found that he had.

In the summer of 1967, I spent a month at the *Universita per Stranieri* in Perugia. The course I attended was for foreigners who wished to learn Italian language and culture. I was still sufficiently au fait with Latin to find the Italian language reasonably easy to learn and I loved, and still love, the musicality of it. Perugia is a beautiful city which has glorious art and architecture. Umbria is one of the loveliest regions of Italy. I explored a number of its hill towns with great pleasure. It helped that I met a Brazilian girl with whom I spent many happy hours.

I passed the remaining conversion course examinations and, in the following year, the practical course examinations. Like most of the candidates, I obtained a third class pass. I applied for a Middle Temple Harmsworth Scholarship. At my interview, Lord Diplock asked me, perfectly reasonably, why I had not done better in the Bar examinations. I can't recall my answer, but it must have been good enough to satisfy him and the other members of the interviewing panel, because I was awarded a major scholarship. Armed with this scholarship and a Harmsworth pupillage award, which paid the fees of 50 guineas for each of my two pupillages, at the age of almost 25, I had finally cleared all the hurdles that stood in my way before I could cross the threshold of a career at the Bar and try to start to earn a living.

5

New Beginnings: London

WITH PARENTAL ENCOURAGEMENT, I had already decided that I wanted to go to London to do my first six months' pupillage. Unlike students in more recent times, I did not do any research into chambers nor had I done a mini-pupillage anywhere. I had not worked out what kind of practice I would like to have. I suspect that I was not alone in adopting a fairly relaxed attitude to my entry into the profession. There were only about 2,000 barristers in the late in 1960s. Today there are about 15,000. In the back of my mind was the possibility that, if I did not succeed in London, I could go back to Leeds and practise at the Bar there.

Leonard Stranger-Jones introduced me as a potential pupil to Patrick Garland, who was later to become Mr Justice Garland, and who was in Leonard's former chambers at 11 King's Bench Walk in the Temple. I had a short interview with Patrick and he offered me a six months' pupillage. In those days, pupillage was regarded as a private matter between pupil and pupil master (or supervisor as they are now called). Chambers now recognise that all their members have an interest in attracting pupils of the highest quality. The pupillage fee was being phased out in the late 1960s. For many years now, chambers have been making generous awards to those whom they choose to be pupils.

Having taken so long to embark on a career, I was keen to start my pupillage as soon as possible. The obvious time to start would have been September 1968. Patrick kindly agreed that I could start at the beginning of July and then, after the August break, resume in September. One of my Paris friends allowed me to use his flat in Hammersmith in July. As a longer term arrangement, I joined two other young men in a flat at 56 Clarence Gate Gardens, Glentworth Street close to Baker Street tube station.

The chambers were a mixed bunch. The head of chambers was an old trooper called Colonel B. Stuart-Horner. I believe that in his heyday he had a busy common law/criminal practice. By the late 1960s, he was not doing much work. There were several busy juniors who comprised the chambers' powerhouse. These included Donald Keating, Patrick Garland and Mark Myers, all of whom had substantial civil practices. There were no QCs in the chambers and never had been. Derek Hyamson, who later became a Queen's Bench Master, specialised in family law, which was then called matrimonial law. There were two female members of chambers who did family law exclusively; and two male members who had mainly criminal practices. One of these was a bluff

Yorkshireman called Stanley Ibbotson. He was known in chambers as 'battling Stan' because he refused to recognise a lost cause and always kept battling on when most would have given up. The rising star in chambers was Anthony May who had been Patrick's penultimate pupil, I having been his last.

Patrick had a mixed common law practice, but following in the footsteps of Donald, who had written a book called *Building Contracts*, he was developing a specialist practice in building and engineering law.

Towards the end of my first pupillage, I was offered a second pupillage in chambers. If all went well, this would be a stepping-stone to a seat in chambers as a tenant. It was obvious that this was a Rubicon crossing moment in my life. If I accepted the offer, it was likely that I would be excluding the possibility of a career at the Leeds Bar and a life in Yorkshire. London would become my home and, in effect, I would be cutting my ties with Leeds forever. My parents unhesitatingly recommended that I should accept the offer of a second pupillage in chambers. They knew that this would be likely to result in our seeing far less of each other but they believed that a career in London was in my best interests. London was the big stage and that was where I should be.

So I accepted the offer and was allocated to Derek Hyamson for my second pupillage. Although his practice was mainly in the field of family law, he had some civil work too. One of his great cases was *Boys v Chaplin* [1971] AC 356. To this day, it remains an important private international law authority in the law of torts. By the time I was Derek's pupil, the case had reached the House of Lords (the predecessor of the Supreme Court). Derek was being led by Tudor Evans QC, who later became Mr Justice Tudor Evans. Derek persuaded his client's solicitors to instruct me as the second junior in the case. The experience of being briefed to appear in the House of Lords so early in my professional life was as thrilling as it was improbable. Sadly, we lost the appeal. Not for the first time, their lordships produced a plethora of rather confusing opinions (or judgments as we would now call them) from which it was difficult to work out precisely what they had decided and why.

One particularly memorable case that Derek had was a contested divorce petition. Contested divorces were still by no means uncommon at that time. The husband was seeking a divorce on the grounds of his wife's alleged adultery with the well-known playwright Arnold Wesker (of *Roots* and *Chicken Soup with Barley* fame). Wesker was 'cited' as co-respondent in the proceedings. Both he and the wife unsuccessfully disputed the allegation. Counsel for the husband used one of Wesker's plays in cross-examination of him. The suggestion was that Wesker had based the plot and characters of the play closely on what had happened in real life. Counsel read out various steamy passages from the text of the play and put it to Wesker: 'that was you speaking, wasn't it Mr Wesker?' It was gripping stuff. Most of the cases that I did as a barrister lacked this kind of 'human interest'.

I find it difficult to spell out exactly what I learnt from my pupil masters. But I have no doubt that I learnt a great deal simply from watching them do

the job. Both of them were careful and skilled. On a lighter note, Derek introduced me to an interesting but necessary variant of the 'last opportunity' rule:
always use the lavatory just before going into court. This excellent advice is the
only thing that I can now specifically remember from my pupillage with him.

Before the end of my second pupillage, I was offered a seat in chambers. I
had no hesitation in accepting it. All the barristers were friendly and encouraging as were the clerks. Like most if not all barristers' clerks, our clerks were of
the old school. They had started their working lives at the age of 15 or 16 carrying trolley-loads of papers around chambers and from chambers to court and
back again. Chambers were quite small in size. It was unusual for a set to exceed
15 barristers in number. So far as I could tell, the senior clerk had little or no
skill in running a large or medium size business. It would have been unthinkable for chambers to be run by a business manager or chief executive officer.
The senior clerk was responsible for the running of chambers, doing what
in today's world is referred to as members' business development (or BD) as
well as negotiating the fees in the larger cases. This was only possible because
chambers were quite small and life was relatively simple in those days. The
photocopier had only recently arrived on the scene. Telexes and faxes did not
exist; nor did the computer. All administration and, in particular, all the book-
keeping was done by hand. I still have the book for the years 1978–84 in which
my senior clerk recorded all my fees and expenses by hand. To the young of the
twenty-first century, this must seem rather like writing on vellum in ink with a
quill would have seemed to us.

The profession was riddled with restrictive practices. A QC could not be
instructed to do anything without a junior, even if the QC did all the work.
The junior always received two thirds of the QC's fee. A QC could not be
instructed to draft pleadings or write opinions regardless of what the client
wanted and was willing to pay. No chambers could have more than two QCs. A
junior who practised outside London on circuit had to move to London chambers if he or she took silk. Advertising (or 'touting for work' as it was called)
was contrary to the professional standards of the Bar. The ban on 'network-
ing' (as it is now called) has long since been swept away. Today, chambers
routinely invite solicitors and clients to all manner of events. Most of the big
chambers now hold seminars to which they invite actual or potential clients.
When I started, it was frowned upon to hold meetings between barristers and
solicitors and their clients anywhere other than in chambers. There must have
been some ostensible rationale for these practices, but it is difficult to see what
it was.

The senior clerk was paid 10 per cent of the barristers' gross fees. All the
clerks in our chambers were male. They did not encourage female members
of chambers for all the traditional bad reasons. They did not consider the
Bar to be a suitable profession for women. Foremost among the reasons given
was the fact that, just when their practices might take off, they would retire
in order to start a family. The clerks did not recommend women to solicitors

because, they claimed, many of the solicitors and their clients did not want to be represented by women. But prejudice against women was not confined to the clerks. I was told early on by a senior member of chambers that the Bar was no place for women because they became too emotionally involved in their clients' cases and they had high-pitched voices and therefore lacked the gravitas that was necessary to win cases. The few women who had the resolve to practise at the Bar knew that they were not allowed to wear trousers in court. I do not know the origin of this strange restriction. But some stuffy judges would undoubtedly have refused to allow a woman to address him if she was wearing trousers. This convention disappeared soon after I came to the Bar. Men were also required to observe strange codes of dress, such as wearing waistcoats. The sight of a huge expanse of shirt was too much for some judges to bear. It was expected that shirts would be white and that suits would be charcoal black. Some judges would not allow a barrister who was not properly dressed to appear before them.

Having done no investigation of other chambers, I was unable at the time to assess how 11 King's Bench Walk compared with other sets. I came to know that they were not in the top league, like the smart Essex Court commercial chambers or the strongest common law or chancery chambers. But they were a good solid set of chambers which had some excellent barristers. There was plenty of small work on which a beginner could cut his teeth. Most of it was in the magistrates' court and the county court. There was a firm of solicitors which bore the wonderfully Dickensian name, Hatten, Asplin, Jewers and Glenny. They had offices in various parts of Essex, including Grays. After completing the first pupillage, a pupil was allowed to undertake work on his own account even during his second pupillage. Like all the other beginners in chambers, I received my first brief early in my second pupillage from Mrs ('Johnny') Bull, who was a legal executive employed in the Grays' office. One's first case in Grays' Magistrates Court was something of a rite of passage. Mrs Bull did matrimonial work. She acted for the hapless wives of feckless husbands who, usually under the influence of drink, tended to beat up their wives, desert them or commit adultery. This led the wives to apply to the magistrates for maintenance and separation orders. Sometimes the cases were hotly contested. These could be quite stressful affairs for the budding practitioner. There was no exchange of witness statements. One had a rough idea of what one's own client was going to say, at least if they stuck to the script of their witness statement. But one had absolutely no idea what the husband and his witnesses were going to say. Cross-examination in those circumstances could be quite challenging. It was excellent training for thinking on one's feet.

Our senior clerk was Douglas Golding. He was a good clerk after the old style: tough and wily. He was particularly solicitous of the welfare of the beginners. He was certainly very supportive of me and ensured that a modest stream of small cases came my way. Like many young barristers, I supplemented my earnings with some 'devilling', that is, doing written work for a more senior member of chambers; and with some lecturing. I lectured on company law at what is now Westminster University. I was not really interested in the subject and I fear that the quality of my lectures left a good deal to be desired.

The county court work consisted of small civil litigation with an emphasis on landlord and tenant work. Most of my work was in the London county courts. I particularly remember the difficulty one had in obtaining possession orders when acting for a landlord in the Clerkenwell County Court. The two resident judges, Judge Dow and Judge Dewar, both seemed to have a pathological dislike of landlords and an unshakeable sympathy for tenants. They were astute at finding what they considered to be fatal technical deficiencies in a notice to quit. It was rather frustrating if one was representing a landlord. It was many years before a Clerkenwell case went to the Court of Appeal and a landlord's appeal was allowed with the result that the unduly technical Dewar/Dow approach was condemned.

Our chambers occupied rooms on the north side of 11 King's Bench Walk. The rooms on the south side were occupied by another set of chambers whose head in 1969 was Lionel Blundell QC. He was later replaced by Ronald Bernstein QC. They specialised in property work, particularly landlord and tenant work. Members of those chambers were to include David Neuberger, later to become Lord Neuberger of Abbotsbury, President of the Supreme Court, and Kim Lewison, later to become Lord Justice Lewison. The two sets of chambers were very close. They were administered from the same room.

Life in chambers proceeded at a gentle pace. Long before the days of the quick sandwich at one's desk, there was time for a leisurely lunch. Barristers used to go out for lunch to a restaurant in Fleet Street or a pub called The Feathers in Tudor Street; and sometimes to the Middle Temple. There was also often time even to go out for tea and a piece of toast at the Golden Egg in Fleet Street.

At the end of July 1969, the two sets of chambers had their usual end of term party. Paul de la Piquerie was a member of 11 King's Bench Walk South. He had the most noble and illustrious-sounding name in chambers. Paul had gone to the Golden Egg for tea. There he met some students, including a pretty young Bar student called Jacqueline Levy. He invited her to the party where I spoke to her briefly. I had had several girlfriends during my first year in London. None of them had swept me off my feet. I think my mother thought that at the age of almost 26, I was already 'on the shelf'. I had decided to break off with my latest girlfriend and concentrate on building up my practice at the Bar. It was quite liberating not to be looking for a girlfriend. That was my state of mind when I first set eyes on Jacqueline.

I next saw her quite by chance early in August in the Middle Temple library. She was working there in preparation for the Bar Finals that she was to take in September. I had gone into the library to look up some point. I went over to her and asked her whether she knew where *The Times* law reports were.

What an opening line! She was a student at Inner Temple and had no idea where the reports were. Nothing daunted, I then invited her to lunch that day. She was already having lunch with another man, but this did not stop her from asking me whether I would like to join the two of them. So it was that we went out to lunch *à trois*. I outstayed the other man and that was the beginning of a brief, hectic and exciting courtship.

6

Engagement and Marriage

THE NEXT JOINT chambers event was a dinner in November 1969. This time, to the slight embarrassment of both of us, Jacqueline accompanied me rather than Paul, and she came as my fiancée. How did this happen?

After the lunch in early August, I asked her whether we could meet again and suggested a Friday night. She did not know that I was Jewish. The name 'Dyson' gave her no clue that I was and the fact that I had asked her out on a Friday night suggested quite strongly that I wasn't. She turned me down because she did not go out on Friday nights. But we arranged to meet on Sunday 24 August to play tennis in a local park near her home in Mill Hill. The weather was lovely and we had a good game. She then invited me to her home for tea and supper. Her parents had gone away on holiday and her mother, Rita had left a fridge full of food. We spent some time picking plums from a tree in the garden.

She soon discovered that I was Jewish. This came about because for some reason we talked about the Swiss watch that I was wearing. This had been given to me by my grandmother, Malvine. Discussion about Malvine and the watch naturally led to my telling her about my family. Jacqueline too had a rich and varied family background, some of the details of which are even now too complex for me to absorb. She had close relatives (on her father, Bobby's side) who lived in Switzerland and France. Most of his family had lived in Alsace before the Franco-Prussian War of 1870. Following the French defeat, some of these had gone to Switzerland and others to Algeria (some of the family had already been living in Algeria since at least 1790). The Algerians went to Marseille and Paris and Bobby's parents found their way to England.

Rita's mother was born near Minsk in Belarus, then in Russia. Her father was born in the province of Vilnius, also then in Russia. They came as immigrants to London in the early 1900s.

We had so much in common and so much to talk about. Conversation flowed effortlessly. I knew almost at once that she was different from any of my previous girlfriends. Within a very short time, I was sure that she was the girl for me.

She had obtained a First in Law from Birmingham University earlier in the summer and was now reading for the Bar. She took Bar Finals in September and duly passed them. She had applied to St Anne's College, Oxford to do the Postgraduate Batchelor of Civil Law (BCL) course. By the time she was told that her application had been successful, she had met me. It now seems extraordinary that she turned down St Anne's offer for that reason. Instead, she decided to do the LLM course at University College, London (UCL). She chose three courses in taxation and one in company law. None of the other options appealed to her. She started studying for her LLM in October 1969. Since all the lectures were in the evenings, Bobby suggested that she might wish to do a pupillage in tax chambers during the day.

Bobby was a solicitor in a small old-fashioned firm improbably called E. B. V. Christian & Co. Its offices, at 141 Moorgate in the City, were dark, heavy with wood furniture and redolent of a bygone age. He was an excellent lawyer who was not in tune with the profit-driven contemporary world of the law. He used to instruct some of the barristers in the leading tax chambers in Pump Court so he approached Charles Potter whom he used to instruct and who was a leading junior barrister at the Tax Bar. Charles was happy to take Jacqueline on as his pupil, but there were a few obstacles to be surmounted first. The problem was that they had never had a female member of chambers or even a female pupil before. The prospect of admitting a woman into their midst was too much for some of them. She subsequently learned that they had three concerns. These were that they did not have lavatories for women; they would have to be careful with their language; and they would have to stand up when she came into a room. To twenty-first century eyes, all three concerns seem ludicrous. After much deliberation, the anxious doubters were persuaded to embark on the great experiment and admit their first female. Their reservations rapidly evaporated. Jacqueline was a great success and blazed a trail for other female pupils and, eventually, female members of chambers too. So by October 1969, she was studying for the LLM and doing pupillage with Charles Potter.

Meanwhile, we had continued to see each other after that first magical meeting on 24 August. Jacqueline's parents knew nothing about me until they returned home about two weeks later. It must have been rapidly apparent that things were getting serious and, from their point of view, proceeding at an alarming pace. On 29 September, I was invited to a party at the Levy home to mark Bobby's sixtieth birthday. The guests were members of the family and close friends none of whom, so far as I was aware, had met me or even heard of me. I was introduced to Edith Greene, who was Rita's best and oldest friend. I learnt afterwards that she told Rita that evening that she was sure that I was destined to be her son-in-law.

I did not know at the time that she was still seeing my immediate predecessor. Unlike me, he had blue eyes, owned a smart art gallery in Mayfair, drove a Bentley and was rich. I did not have a car and was still scratching a living at the Bar. During October, Jacqueline's French cousin Sylvia, who lived in Marseille, came to stay with the family for a few days. I learnt subsequently that Sylvia was asked for her views on the respective merits of me and the other boyfriend and that she came down in favour of me.

On 26 October, I proposed or, to be more precise, asked Jacqueline whether she would spend the rest of her life with me. She agreed without knowing precisely what I meant. I intended it to mean that I wanted to marry her.

So in addition to studying for the LLM and doing pupillage, she was now engaged to be married. Many years later, I was asked by our son-in-law Jonathan Hall what was the rush. The answer was that, like most of our generation, we were not living together and did not intend to do so until we were married.

Rita sensed what was going on. I am not at all sure that Bobby had much idea. He was a shy man who was embarrassed by any show of emotion and was not good at small talk. Rita thrust Bobby and me into the sitting room of their home. It was clear to me that she expected the two of us to have a conversation in which I was to seek his permission to marry Jacqueline. I had not practised my lines. In the fog of embarrassment that enveloped both of us, I said something along the lines that I wasn't sure that I needed his permission, but in case I did, could I please have it. He must have said yes, because I can't recall him saying no. I am sure that it was a great relief to both of us when we were joined by Rita and Jacqueline. Bobby said that he had an insurance policy the fruits of which would pay for the wedding. He hoped that we would defer it until the policy matured about two years later.

But we were in no mood to wait that long. In fact, we decided to marry on 5 July 1970. The reason why we did not marry sooner was that I had been briefed in my first High Court case which was due to be heard in June. In fact, the case settled. In hindsight, this was a ridiculous reason for postponing our wedding. It was only a case and anyway we could have postponed our honeymoon until the case was over. But a barrister's first High Court case is an important landmark in his career and I was very keen to build up a practice. It would not have occurred to us to postpone the honeymoon until sometime after our wedding.

Rita was very keen to organise a 'big' wedding. This was partly because she had not had a big wedding herself when she married Bobby on 29 March 1942. They had planned a wedding in April 1942 which was to be followed by a reception at the Savoy Hotel. The invitations had already been sent out when Bobby, who was serving in the RAF, was told that he was to be sent abroad. He was granted a short period of 'embarkation leave' which allowed him to marry before his departure. So the date of the wedding had to be brought forward and the reception in the Savoy was cancelled. After the wedding service, there was a gathering of family and friends at Rita's family home in Shirehall Lane, Hendon, London NW4. Rita's father had died, but her mother was still alive.

The period of our engagement was not without its difficulties. Jacqueline was under great stress. She was a pupil barrister during the day and studying for her LLM in the evenings. She was being pressed by Rita to apply her mind to the plans for the wedding. And I had too much time on my hands and did not give her enough space.

In March 1970, with the assistance of our parents, we were able to buy a house on mortgage. We could not have afforded to do this without their support. The house cost £11,600. It was in Wembley Park. I did not want to live in a flat or too close to the centre of London. Both of us liked the idea of having a house with a garden. The attraction of Wembley Park was its proximity to the Metropolitan Line. Thus it was that many weeks before we were due to be married, we became house owners. At weekends we tended the garden, but it did not occur to us that we should live there until after the wedding. To modern eyes, this seems bizarre. But we were observing the conventions of the day.

Meanwhile, Rita was busy with the wedding. She was a brilliant organiser and clearly enjoyed planning it. She treated my parents with warmth and sensitivity. We were both happy to let her get on with it. The majority of the guests were members of our respective families and friends of our parents, but there was a fair number of our friends, including Nick Halsted, Mark Sharpe, Steve Novy and others from my Wadham days. All four of our parents were present as were my brother Robert and Jacqueline's brother David. I have not so far mentioned David. He was 16 and had long curly hair. He was very secretive, and we suspected that he had anarchist friends and was involved in distributing seditious literature. He probably disapproved of the conventional bourgeois attitudes of his sister and new brother-in-law. In due course, he was to have a glittering career as an academic, a journalist at the BBC and later as the Director of the Reuter's Institute of Journalism.

My grandparents' generation was represented at the wedding by Malvine and her siblings, Irene and Emil. Malvine was the only survivor of our eight grandparents. But there were plenty of members of our families from our parents' generation. The oldest of these was my auntie Rosie. Bobby's sister Mimi and her husband Rene came from Marseille as did her daughter Sylvia and son Raymond. Bobby's cousin Hedy and her husband David came from Bienne in Switzerland, as did their children.

The service was held in Mill Hill Synagogue. The officiating rabbi was Rabbi Cutler. I can't recall anything about his sermon except his saying that, as lawyers, we were familiar with the 'seamy side of life'. It was not clear what he meant by this, or how he thought that it would equip us to cope with the stresses of married life. After the service, there was a splendid lunch at the Sonesta Tower hotel in Sloane Street, London SW1 (now restored to its previous name of the Carlton Tower). There was dancing for which we had prepared by attending dancing classes; and there were speeches. Rita's planning had paid off: the event was a great success.

Robert had arranged for the cleaning of the Ford Escort car which my parents had given me. We drove off to a hotel at Alfriston in Sussex for the first two nights of our honeymoon. The weather was magnificent and we enjoyed roaming on the South Downs. From there we flew to Corfu for a fortnight's holiday. I used most of an instalment of the Harmsworth scholarship to pay for it. The holiday was a mixed success. The hotel was situated on a polluted enclosed bay; Jacqueline was sick; and I spilt red wine on her lovely white dress. We had little money to spend, not least because the Government had imposed a £50 foreign travel allowance limit. We hired a small car for two days and then, in order to save money, decided to hire a motor scooter to travel around the island. Neither of us had ridden a motor scooter before. The island is mountainous and, when attempting to negotiate a 'hair-pin' bend, I only managed to get the scooter half way round the bend. We crashed into the retaining wall in front of us. We both came off the scooter and Jacqueline suffered dramatic bruising to her legs. But there were good things as well. The island was very beautiful and we enjoyed being able to relax.

A few weeks after our return, Jacqueline took her four LLM examinations. She did very well in them, and would undoubtedly have done even better if she had not had so many distractions.

She had decided that she did not want to practise at the Bar. Instead she took a job as a lawyer in the Solicitor's office of HM Inland Revenue which was housed at that time in Somerset House. The Solicitor was Eric Moses. He was the father of Sir Alan Moses and was very kind to her. She was certainly earning more than I was receiving and probably more than I was earning too. But within a very short time, she was pregnant. This came as something of a shock to us and certainly to our families as well. Jacqueline carried on working at the Revenue until shortly before Michelle was born on 25 June 1971. In September, she started teaching tax law part-time at the Bar's Council of Legal Education. She continued with that until shortly before Steven was born on 21 May 1973. She did voluntary work, principally at a local Citizens' Advice Bureau office, for the next five years.

7

Practice at the Bar

D URING THE PERIOD between the end of my first pupillage in January 1969 and early 1972, my practice developed steadily. In the first two years or so, I did mainly family law cases. These were mostly, but by no means exclusively, in the magistrates' court. I also did undefended divorces in the county court. I found that a batch of these in a morning or afternoon session was rewarding financially, but not in any other sense. One day I had been instructed by the loyal Mrs Bull to do some case in the Royal Courts of Justice in the morning and a couple of other cases in the Southend County Court in the afternoon. At lunchtime, she offered to drive me to Southend. This placed me in considerable difficulty. I was relying on the train journey to do the reading for the afternoon cases. I believed that they were quite straightforward, although I don't know how I could have been sure if I had not read the papers. Nevertheless, I did not feel able to reject her kind offer, because I could not tell her why I would have preferred to travel by train. So I had a rather anxious ride to Southend. On arrival at the court, I rushed into the robing room and skimmed over the papers. Fortunately, they revealed no problems and all was well. But I don't believe that I was ever again so cavalier in my preparation for a case or indeed anything else.

I found the disputes over custody and access to children (now called 'contact') particularly upsetting. Expressions of concern for the welfare of the child were often merely an excuse for an attack on the other parent. By about the end of 1971, I had decided that I did not wish to continue practising in this area.

I had also decided to stop doing criminal cases. Most of my criminal cases had been in the magistrates' court. It was rather dispiriting to appear for a defendant before a Bench which usually did not utter a syllable until the end of the case, when they said: 'case proved'. On one occasion, I was representing a defendant who was charged with driving with excess alcohol. He did not dispute that he was over the limit. His defence was that without his knowledge someone else must have spiked his non-alcoholic drink with alcohol. He sounded convincing to me. I had not heard of the so-called 'laced drink defence'. But the worldly-wise Justices almost certainly had and they did not believe my client. When he was convicted, I was visibly disappointed. I apologised to him for my failure to secure the acquittal that I felt he deserved. He put his arm round my shoulder and told me not to worry. He did it in such a way as to leave me in no doubt that there had been no miscarriage of justice.

I had two jury trials in the Crown Court. In one of them, the defendant was accused of stealing a gammon steak from a supermarket. The evidence against him was overwhelming. A store detective said that she had seen him take the steak from a shelf, conceal it under his raincoat and walk out without paying. When he was stopped in the street outside, the steak fell to the ground. Despite the strength of the case against him, he insisted on pleading not guilty. While he was giving evidence, he fainted. There was pandemonium in court. At the end of the trial, he was acquitted. I thought at the time that the only possible basis for his acquittal was that the jury felt sorry for him and thought that his offence did not merit his being subjected to the full majesty of a jury trial. In fact, he had elected to have a jury trial in the Crown Court rather than summary proceedings in the magistrates' court. I can't recall anything about the other jury trial. But I decided that criminal cases too were not for me.

So by about the end of 1971, I had decided that I wanted to concentrate on civil cases. I had been mainly doing landlord and tenant work, but also a range of general contract and tort cases as well. There were no QCs in chambers, but Donald Keating's book and his construction law practice were starting to have a real impact on the nature of the work that was being done by several members of chambers. The first edition of his book was published in 1955. By the time I became a pupil, Donald was heavily engaged in single-handedly writing the third edition, which was published in 1969. He had developed a heavy construction law practice and others in chambers, notably Patrick Garland and Mark Myers, were doing the same. Anthony May, who later became the President of the Queen's Bench Division, was the rising star who was rapidly making a mark in this area too.

In the 1960s and early 1970s, 22 Old Buildings, Lincoln's Inn (now Atkin Chambers) was the only other set of chambers that specialised in construction law, which was regarded as a rather dull subject. Judges and members of the smart commercial chambers were dismissive of it. They thought that construction law was all about tedious schedules of defects and disruption and delay claims and that it concerned detailed facts and little or no law. This was true to a certain extent, although some construction cases raised fascinating technical questions of fact as well as interesting and important points of law. The latter included questions of the proper construction of contracts, causation (both of which have always proved to be problematic in the law), remoteness of damage as well as the scope of the duty of care in tort. The 1970s was a period of important development in the law of negligence generally and some of the landmark decisions of the appellate courts were in construction cases.

The judges who tried these cases were not called judges at all. They bore the strange title of 'official referees'. Although the cases often involved large sums of money (well in excess of the county court jurisdiction), the official referees were not High Court Judges. They were Senior Circuit Judges.

The appointment of Donald and Patrick as QCs in April 1972 was a significant event in the history of chambers. Appointment in those days was by Her

Majesty on the recommendation of the Lord Chancellor. The Lord Chancellor in 1972 was Lord Hailsham. There was much celebration in chambers at these appointments. It was particularly welcome in the case of Donald because he had made several previous unsuccessful applications. The result of these two appointments was that there was a need for juniors in chambers to do the heavy junior work that Donald and Patrick had previously been doing. The obvious candidates to fill the gap were Anthony May and myself. Thus it was that by the mid-1970s, I was doing mostly construction work. When I joined chambers, I had no idea that this was the direction that my practice would take. I am not a practical person and had never been particularly interested in technology or technical things. My parents were hopelessly impractical and my lack of education in science did not help. So I was not equipped by nature or training to immerse myself in engineering issues and to cross-examine specialist scientists in court. But that is what I found myself doing and by application and sheer hard work, I was able to do it effectively.

During the 1970s, my practice expanded substantially. I had good quality work from top firms of solicitors and it was well paid. I was quite often led by Donald and Patrick. Few of the cases were memorable. Many of them were reported in the specialist law reports, but few were of interest to the editors of the mainstream law reports. One exception was the case of *Lamb v Camden London Borough Council* [1981] 2 All ER 408. The defendant council had negligently fractured the water pipe outside the claimant's house. The resultant damage made it necessary for her to vacate her house. One year later, the council had still not carried out the necessary repairs. Squatters moved into the house and caused considerable damage. The official referee dismissed her claim that the council was liable to compensate her for the cost of the damage. He reached this conclusion although he held that it was reasonably foreseeable that squatters would invade the house and cause damage.

I advised the client that an appeal would be unlikely to succeed. The solicitors wanted an opinion from a QC and they instructed Louis Blom-Cooper QC to advise in consultation. He advised that the official referee's decision was plainly wrong and that an appeal would undoubtedly succeed. Louis was not impressed by my feeble pessimistic view about the prospects of a successful appeal. So we appealed to the Court of Appeal. The court was presided over by the famous Lord Denning, then Master of the Rolls. Louis made strong and spirited submissions, but to no avail. Although she lost her case and had to pay both sides' costs, the client seemed content that she had had her day in court and that her QC had fought a good fight. The case is an important authority on the subject of remoteness of loss.

This was the only case in which I came across Louis professionally at the Bar. Subsequently, our paths crossed many times at Middle Temple and at his various book launches. I was delighted when he came in February 2018 to the launch of my book *Justice: Continuity and Change*. Sadly, he died in September 2018.

Although he was physically frail towards the end, he never lost his enthusiasm and zest for justice and the law.

In 1979, Anthony May had taken silk and started to attract leading work almost immediately. In 1981, Douglas the senior clerk advised me to apply for silk. I thought that I was not ready to take this step. I was 37 years of age and had only been in practice for 12 years. But he was insistent. In those days, an applicant for silk needed two judicial sponsors to support the application. I had only made the rarest of appearances before judges of the higher courts. Most of my appearances had been before official referees and arbitrators. Two excellent official referees, Judge William Stabb QC (the senior official referee) and Judge Edgar Fay QC agreed to support my application.

I was not at all surprised that I was unsuccessful. I was somewhat despondent because I did not see how I would secure the support of a senior judge. I doubted whether the Lord Chancellor would be impressed by what official referees had to say, however glowing that might be. I then had a stroke of good fortune. I was instructed to appear in a substantial appeal in the Court of Appeal. The presiding lord justice was Lord Justice Stephenson, who was a senior member of the Court of Appeal. So early in 1982, I wrote to him and asked whether he would support my application. He summoned me to his room in the Royal Courts of Justice in the Strand. This was the first time I had been behind the scenes in that awesome nineteenth-century building and I was rather nervous. He was charming and immediately put me at my ease. He had no doubt that I was 'in the top drawer' and would be delighted to support me. He was of the old school and told me that, if my application was successful, I would have to move chambers, because it was impermissible to have more than two silks in the same set of chambers. That may have been the case in his day, but at least that restrictive practice had gone by 1982. My other sponsor was William Stabb.

This time, I was successful. It was a cause for great celebration in chambers and in my family. I recall saying to Michelle who was then aged 10, and Steven who was then aged eight, that I had gone as far as I would go in my career and now it was over to them. My father came to London for the swearing in before Lord Hailsham, who was in his second term as Lord Chancellor. It seems that there was only space for one of my parents to attend the swearing in which took place in the Moses Room in the House of Lords. My father was not good at expressing his emotions, but it was clear that he was immensely proud and very happy.

The differences between being a QC and a junior barrister were gradually breaking down. It had become possible for a QC to advise and even appear in court without a junior. But these solo performances were still comparatively rare in the early 1980s. I was told to expect that I would now be treated by judges with more respect and politeness than before. I know that some judges used to treat QCs better than juniors, but I was never aware of a stepped change in the way judges behaved towards me. When I became a judge, I believe that I treated all advocates fairly and politely regardless of their seniority. If anything, I tended to be more challenging of QCs than of juniors. I always took care to be kind to very junior advocates who were likely to be particularly nervous.

I recall the very first set of papers that I received after my appointment and being thrilled by the sight of the suffix 'QC' after my name. It was a long time before I became used to it. It was good no longer to be weighed down by the endless drafting of pleadings. But in many ways, things did not change very much. As a senior junior, I had already become used to being instructed in some of the more substantial cases without a QC and sometimes to leading a more junior barrister too.

I continued to practise mainly in the field of construction law. In 1984, however, one of my loyal solicitors asked me whether I would be interested in taking on a clinical negligence case. It would be on legal aid and I would there-fore earn only a modest fee, far lower than the fee that a typical construction case attracted. Always keen to try something new, I agreed to take it on. The claim was for a boy called Stephen Collins who was suffering from severe disa-bility as a result of the alleged negligence of doctors at the time of his birth. The claim was heard by Mr Justice Beldam, who was expert in this area of the law and an excellent judge. There was a great deal of complex expert medical evidence and the case lasted about two weeks. We were successful. I found the experience enormously stimulating. Its importance for me was that it opened my eyes to the existence of a world outside construction law and gave me an appetite for more of it.

By now, Douglas had retired and had been replaced by Barry Bridgeman as the senior clerk. I told Barry that I would like to broaden my practice. His response was 'leave it to me, sir'. By now, the chambers had become known as one of the two leading specialist construction chambers. The general work was fading away as all the new members were taken on as barristers who, for the most part, would do construction work. I knew that, even if Barry wanted to find non-construction work for me, it would be difficult for him to do so. But since this other work would be less well paid than the construction work, I had doubts as to whether Barry really wanted me to do it anyway. Like most senior clerks, he was paid a percentage of the barristers' gross fees.

In 1984, chambers decided to relocate to 10 Essex Street. This is a street just outside the Temple. At that time, there were no barristers' chambers in Essex Street and hardly any outside the four Inns of Court. The accommodation at 11 King's Bench Walk was old-fashioned and we felt that in the late twentieth century we and our clients were entitled to something better. I was put in charge of organising the move. This involved not only sorting out the refurbishment that would be necessary at 10 Essex Street. It also involved negotiations with Middle Temple since the Inn had agreed in principle to take a lease of the prem-ises and grant chambers a sub-lease. I was able to negotiate favourable terms. Donald Keating, who by now was the Head of Chambers, was not at all keen on the move. He had a lovely room on the ground floor at 11 King's Bench Walk which he ludicrously claimed had the best view in Europe. He was also horrified by the cost of the whole transaction. He told me that he saved the pennies and I spent the pounds. But when, following the move, he was congratulated by leading judges and barristers on his wisdom and far-sightedness in moving out of the Temple into modern premises, his attitude changed. Everybody thought the move was a great success.

In 1986, I was instructed in an interesting construction case called *Lubenham Fidelities Ltd v South Pembrokeshire District Council* (1986) 33 BLR 39, CA. It concerned the determination of the contractor's employment on a building contract and raised some difficult questions of law. The case was heard by an official referee called Judge John Newey QC. The claimant was represented by Simon Goldblatt QC leading Edwin Glasgow. They were both members of chambers at 2 Garden Court. The judge decided the case in our favour. But of far more significance for me was the fact that, in an unguarded moment, I must have let slip to Edwin that I was becoming frustrated by my inability to break out of the stranglehold that construction cases had on me. Shortly after the conclusion of the case, he asked me whether I would be interested in becoming the Head of his chambers. Mr Justice Macpherson (later of the Stephen Lawrence Inquiry fame) had been the Head until he became a High Court Judge in 1983. Simon Goldblatt had been acting Head since then, but the chambers were still looking for someone.

At first, I did not take Edwin's approach seriously. But he later renewed it. Using all his skill as an advocate, he persuaded me that I would be able to diversify my practice if I were to move. He said that there was a great demand for leaders in his chambers and much leading work which could not be serviced in-house. Before succumbing to his blandishments, I asked a number of leading barristers from other chambers for their advice. These included the great Lord Alexander of Weedon QC who was chairman of the Bar at the time. They all encouraged me to make the move. But a due diligence exercise would have revealed a rather less encouraging situation. There was some leading work in chambers, but the solicitors had their own firm views as to where it should go. I discovered that there were some excellent juniors in chambers (including Edwin himself), but there was also a disproportionately large number of mediocre practitioners. Most foolishly of all, I did not meet the senior clerk until after I had agreed to move. I cannot believe now that I allowed this to happen. I think I was taken in by the fact that he had been a junior clerk at Brick Court Chambers and had learnt his trade at the feet of the legendary Ron Birley.

Moving chambers was a big step to take. Barristers moved chambers far less frequently than they do today. In the eyes of many, it was rather like getting divorced, but accompanied by a stigma which no longer attached to divorce. Our children were 15 and 13 years of age. I had a successful and lucrative practice as a silk and was being instructed regularly by many of the leading firms of solicitors. To move from the safe haven of 10 Essex Street into the open seas on a voyage whose outcome was uncertain was a risky thing to do. It would also involve leaving friends and colleagues many of whom I had grown up with professionally. But I was attracted by the excitement of a new challenge and knew that, if I played safe and stayed where I was, I would always have been nagged by the question of what would have happened if I had made the move. It helped greatly that I had the encouragement of Jacqueline.

Breaking the news to fellow members of chambers was stressful and difficult. I went to each colleague individually and told them what I was planning to do and why. Naturally, I started with Donald Keating, the Head of Chambers. He was an emotional man who had led me many times before I took silk. He reacted very badly and started shouting at me. He accused me of disloyalty. He said that my departure would lead to others leaving, implying that this would lead to the break-up of chambers. I was taken aback by this outburst. Most of the other members of chambers, although disappointed to see me go, were very generous, supportive and understanding and wished me well. The senior clerk was very upset. Over time however, even Donald and the senior clerk forgave me. I remained good friends with a number of the barristers in chambers. It was a cause for great joy to me and Jacqueline when in later years, chambers (by now called Keating Chambers) honoured me with dinners when I went to the Supreme Court and following my retirement as Master of the Rolls and invited me to give the 'Keating lecture' in March 2015.

So I moved chambers in September 1986. The premises at 2 Garden Court were at least as old-fashioned and cramped as 11 King's Bench Walk had been. In the first few weeks, I received no new work. My existing construction law clients seemed to have abandoned me. Since the main reason for the move was to break out into new pastures, this was not altogether surprising. I found the new clerk totally uninspiring. He seemed to spend most of his time sitting near the telephone waiting for it to ring. In short, I thought that I had committed professional suicide. Nor was my morale lifted by being told by a number of friends and colleagues how 'brave' I had been to make the move.

Things started to improve early in the New Year. I am not sure how this happened. Gradually, some of my former clients returned. More encouragingly, I started to be instructed in other fields of practice. I will only mention a few examples.

I was instructed to represent the Football Association (FA) in the Inquiry into the tragic Hillsborough disaster at which 96 spectators were killed on 15 April 1989 during the FA Cup semi-final between Liverpool and Nottingham Forest. The Inquiry was brilliantly conducted by Lord Justice (Peter) Taylor who was later to be appointed as Lord Chief Justice. The first part of the Inquiry was held in public. It considered what happened and who was responsible. The FA was allowed to participate in this part of the Inquiry because the Liverpool supporters blamed it for the disaster. The basis of this far-fetched claim was that the semi-final between these same clubs in the competition the previous year had also been held at Hillsborough, which is closer to Nottingham than to Liverpool. It was said that this manifest unfairness to Liverpool had enraged the Liverpool fans. In his interim report which was published in August 1989, Sir Peter found that the cause of the disaster was a failure of police control by the South Yorkshire Police. David Duckenfield, the police match superintendent, had ordered a gate to be opened with the result that there was a huge influx of people into the already crowded central pens on the terrace.

The second part of the Inquiry was concerned with making recommendations to reduce the risk of any such disaster ever occurring again. This was dealt with in private and by written evidence and submissions. The FA took a leading role in it. They appointed an ad hoc committee comprising the chairmen of five football clubs ranging from Liverpool FC to an amateur club. It was my task to steer this committee and persuade them to put forward an agreed set of submissions on the key issues that the Inquiry had been asked to investigate. These included whether there should be all-seater stadia and whether identity cards should be a condition of attendance at football matches. The Prime Minister, Margaret Thatcher, was keen on identity cards in the wake of several outbreaks of violence at football grounds. The committee were not at all keen on the idea of all-seater stadia. They said that the fans would refuse to use the seats and would throw them on the pitch. I persuaded them that, if they maintained an implacable opposition to all-seater stadia, they would be imposed on all clubs without exception and without delay. After much discussion, we put forward a proposal which distinguished between the position of the big clubs, whose matches were well attended, and the minnows who had no money and few supporters. We also made out a cogent case against the requirement for identity cards. In his final report that was published in January 1990, Sir Peter adopted all of the FA's submissions.

My football practice did not stop there. In 1991, I was instructed to appear on behalf of the FA to defend the proceedings brought by the Football League alleging that the decision to set up the Premier League was unlawful. The Football League sought an order quashing the decision on public law grounds. They also sought a declaration that the FA Rules did not permit the establishing of the Premier League. This was a legally difficult case. It was also very high profile. I had two excellent juniors in Nigel Pleming and Robert Hildyard, later Mr Justice Hildyard. The Football League were represented by David Oliver QC leading the young David Pannick. We persuaded Mr Justice Rose (later Lord Justice Rose) to dismiss the claim on both grounds. The reason why the FA had decided to set up the Premier League was that they believed that the Football League was not making the most of the commercial potential of football. Many projections were made of potential future income streams. None of them forecast the extraordinary financial bonanza that was to flow from television rights and other sources within a very short time. It is no exaggeration to say that our success in this litigation changed the face of football in England and Wales.

Having spent most of my practice lurking in the shadows appearing before official referees and arbitrators, I was not used to the glare of publicity. Another case in which I appeared and which caught the public eye was the dispute that Dave Clark's production company, The Right Time Production Limited, had with Rank Theatres Limited, the proprietors of the Dominion Theatre, London over the production of his rock musical, 'Time'. In this musical, a rock star, whose role was played for the first year by Cliff Richard (later Sir Cliff Richard), was defending Earth in the High Court of the Universe. Sir Lawrence Olivier featured in hologram form. Both Jacqueline and I saw the show in order to show commitment to the client: it was not necessary for me to do so in order to gain a better understanding of the issues in the case.

The case of Dave Clark's company, for which I appeared, was that the box office had been managed negligently, particularly during the period before the show opened. The allegation was that, if it had been properly run, more tickets would have been sold and the show would have run far longer than the approximately two years that it did run. The alleged loss was quantified at about £10 million. The case was heard by Mr Justice Millett. We called a large number of witnesses who wanted to buy tickets and who said that they were unable to speak to anyone in the box office when they telephoned. This was before the days of internet booking. We also called witnesses to say that the woman in charge of the box office spent a good deal of her time in sexual activity away from the box office, rather than doing her job. This was all very entertaining, but it did not seem to me that it would do much to prove our case. The real problem was that evidence of generalised incompetence did not prove that it had caused the company to suffer any loss. However, we were able to prove a causal link between negligence and loss by calling agents who said that they were calling for a greater allocation of tickets which they were confident they could have sold, but the tickets were not forthcoming. It was largely on the basis of this evidence that the judge was persuaded to award damages of £600,000 (including interest). I thought that this was a most satisfactory outcome. The defendants had denied negligence and loss. Their positive case was that the reason why the show did not do as well as Dave Clark had hoped was nothing to do with the way the box office was run. They said that, although coach loads of Cliff Richard fans kept coming (some fans saw the show 20 times), this could not disguise the fact that the show was no good. In support of this view, they relied on the expert evidence of the theatre critic of the *Daily Telegraph* whose report had been given to us before the hearing began. There was something about the report that I felt did not ring true. I had a suspicion that the critic might not have seen the show. In answer to my first question in cross-examination, he admitted that he had not seen it. I asked no further questions and sat down. This was probably the most effective cross-examination of my career.

One weekend during the trial, I had a dreadful accident at home. Frustrated at not being able to get the charcoal of the barbecue to heat up, I foolishly tried to encourage it with some petrol. There was an immediate explosion as the petrol vapour caught fire and flames shot in the direction of my left thigh and up towards my face. I was set alight and suffered 8 per cent burns. I had a terrible shock and was out of action for several weeks. Among my many well-wishers was Dave Clark himself who sent me an enormous bunch of roses.

I had other interesting non-construction cases after I had moved chambers. I will mention only one more in any detail. The claimants in *Rance v Mid-Downs Health Authority* [1991] 1 QB 587 were the parents of a severely disabled child. A scan of the mother during her pregnancy revealed that the foetus was suffering from spina bifida. The parents' case was that, if they had been told, the mother would have had an abortion and an abortion at that date would have been lawful, because the child was not capable of being born alive. By the time they discovered the true position, it was too late to have a lawful abortion. This was a sensitive and complex case raising issues of whether there had been negligence, causation and whether at the time when it was said that the abnormality should have been detected, the child would have been capable of being born alive. The claimants were both solicitors for whom it was very difficult to go into the witness box and tell the world that, if they had been told in time, they would have had an abortion of their child. They loved the child very much and were caring parents. They brought the claim because they wanted compensation in order to pay for the best possible care for him. In addition to the difficult legal and factual issues in the case, this was a case which involved personal tragedy. My construction practice had not been a good training ground for this kind of thing. We lost the case. This was particularly hard for the parents to bear in view of the publicity that the case inevitably attracted. Nor was it helped by the fact that the judge, Mr Justice Brooke, made no secret of his disapproval of them for bringing the claim. It seemed that he did not approve of 'wrongful life' claims on principle.

I had other far less emotionally draining, but nevertheless intellectually demanding, non-construction cases. Perhaps the toughest was the 'Swaps' litigation which concerned interest rate swap transactions between local authorities and banks, and claims brought by local authorities to recover sums following the decision of the House of Lords that these transactions were legally void.

In addition, my construction practice continued unabated and other members of chambers started to do construction cases. Eventually (and after I had gone on the Bench), the chambers became known as a specialist construction set. Towards the end of my career, I did a few international arbitrations in places such as Hong Kong, Pakistan and The Philippines.

In 1990, I was elected to the Bench of the Middle Temple. The Bencher of an Inn of Court is one of its senior members who is expected to play a part in the running of the organisation. I was proposed to the Bench Committee of the Middle Temple by Mr Justice (Simon) Brown, who was a Bencher and had been a member of 2 Garden Court Chambers before he was appointed to the High Court Bench. Many years later I joined Simon, who was by now Lord Brown of

Eaton-under-Heywood, in the Supreme Court. It was a great honour to become a Bencher of the Inn. Although I did some work for the Inn, I can't claim to have formed part of its powerhouse. I would not have imagined that some 27 years later, I would become its Treasurer.

When I started practice at the Bar, it did not occur to me that one day I might wish to become a judge or that I might have the qualities required of a judge. It was not a matter to which I gave any thought at that stage or indeed until many years later. I just got on with my practice. In 1983, one year after I had taken silk, I was asked whether I wished to be considered for appointment as an Assistant Recorder. Recorders are part-time judges who have all the powers of a circuit judge. At that time, they sat in the Crown Court (trying criminal cases) or in the County Court (trying civil and family cases). Assistant Recorders, which no longer exist, were temporary Recorders. They did the same kind of work as Recorders and were, effectively, on probation pending assessment of their suitability to be appointed as Recorders.

I had to attend a residential training course at Roehampton College at which we had to do practical sentencing exercises and take part in role play. This was organised by the Judicial Studies Board, which was later superseded by the Judicial College. The Judicial Studies Board was then a recent creation. The traditional view had been that judges did not need training. Their innate ability would enable them to do a good job and training was at best a waste of time and at worst an interference with judicial independence. In the last 25 years, the training of judges has improved hugely. Its importance is now widely accepted. At an early stage in the life of the Judicial Studies Board, it was recognised that all judges who presided over criminal trials with a jury needed help with the conduct of these trials. Excellent Bench Books were produced. They included specimen directions on issues that routinely needed to be addressed, particularly in the preparation of the summing up. I relied on them to a great extent.

The other training that an Assistant Recorder had to undergo before being allowed to start was a week's shadowing of a Circuit Judge. I was fortunate to shadow Judge Blofeld QC (later Mr Justice Blofeld) who was the Resident Judge at St Albans Crown Court. I sat with him on the Bench and saw how he did things. In those days, most of the judges still drank sherry at lunch. So far as I am aware, very few (if any) judges now drink alcohol during the working day. I enjoyed my few days at St Albans, but I don't think I learnt much from the experience. Watching others do a job is a poor substitute for learning by doing the job oneself.

My first case as an Assistant Recorder was about as small a case as it was possible to have in the Crown Court with a jury. It was at Inner London Crown Court in what seemed like a temporary outhouse at the back of the main court building. The charge was the theft of 20 20p pieces. It was quite an achievement for the listing officer at the Inner London Crown Court to find such a trivial case to start me off. Because it involved an allegation of dishonesty, the defendant was entitled to elect for trial by jury and did so. I remember it as clearly as my first case as an advocate in Grays Magistrates' Court in 1969.

I was quite nervous. Being put in charge of a jury for the first time is a daunting business. It was unlike anything I had experienced before; and my knowledge of the criminal process was very limited. My first test came before I had even set foot inside the courtroom. It was extremely hot and I received a request from counsel that they be permitted to dispense with their wigs. I thought it would be wise to exercise my authority by having a message sent back that I would make a decision on this weighty matter after I had gone into court. When I went into court, I did not think it was too hot for wigs, so I refused the request. The trial proceeded without any incident that I can recall.

I sat as an Assistant Recorder in various London Crown Courts trying straightforward criminal cases. I was expected to sit at least four weeks a year. In 1986, I was invited to become a Recorder. Appointments were made on the recommendation of the Lord Chancellor's Department (a predecessor of the Ministry of Justice). I know that the Department kept a card on each judge and that information was stored on the card. I have no idea how any assessment was made of my performance as an Assistant Recorder. I don't believe that the straightforward cases that I tried had generated any appeals which would have given senior judges the opportunity to see my work. It was rumoured that the court ushers and court clerks were the source of information. I don't know whether there was any truth in this suggestion. It may be that the reason why I was invited to become a Recorder was simply that there was no intelligence about me, good or bad.

So I was appointed as a Recorder in 1986. The work was not noticeably different from what I had been doing as an Assistant Recorder. I found the criminal cases that I tried interesting, although they were not intellectually challenging. Each case gave an insight into the lives of ordinary people and how they behaved. It was only later when, as a High Court Judge, I tried heavy criminal cases such as murders and rapes that I heard evidence of unspeakably horrible behaviour. There was an element of drama even in the less serious cases. The unfolding of the story through the mouths of the witnesses was often unpredictable and fascinating. The return of the jury after they had reached a verdict was always a moment of tension. When the foreman of the jury rose to announce their verdict, the silence in the court was almost tangible. Once the verdict was given, the atmosphere in court changed immediately.

So I carried on trying small criminal cases. I found this a welcome change from the heavy civil litigation that I was conducting at the Bar. After a few years, I was appointed as a Deputy High Court Judge. This was a significant milestone in my career, because it meant that I would now be asked to try some High Court civil cases. Instead of summing up criminal trials to assist juries to bring in their verdicts, I would now have to give judgments. The work I was given to do was mainly common law cases. They were usually witness actions or procedural applications. I was able to give judgment straightaway in the short and straightforward cases. In the more complicated ones, I would defer giving judgment before giving what is called a 'reserved judgment'. My appointment as a Deputy High Court Judge was an indication that I might have been considered by the relevant people in the Lord Chancellor's Department as suitable for a permanent appointment as a High Court Judge. But it was only in about 1991 or 1992, when various colleagues started saying to me that, of course, I was destined for the High Court Bench that I began to wonder whether I might be offered a full-time judicial appointment. Bill Macpherson (1983) and Simon Brown (1985) had both been members of chambers and gone to the High Court Bench as had John Laws, who was appointed in 1992. It was also significant for me that Anthony May, who had remained at Keating Chambers, had been appointed in 1991.

In the early part of 1992, I was summoned to meet Sir Thomas Legg QC, who was the Permanent Secretary at the Lord Chancellor's Department. I thought that he might be going to offer me an appointment. I had worked out what I was going to say. If he offered me a High Court appointment, I would say that I would give the offer very careful consideration; if he offered an appointment as a Circuit Judge, I would say that I was not interested at that time, but might be in the future. In fact, he offered neither. He started the interview by saying that he had noticed that I played the piano and he asked me a few questions about music. He then asked about my children. I answered his questions politely, but with a growing sense of frustration, since I knew that the purpose of the interview was not to learn about my musical tastes or my children. He was trying to put me at my ease, but his questions had precisely the opposite effect. Eventually, he got to the point. He asked me whether I had ever given any thought to how I would hope or like my career to progress. I gave him my double-barrelled prepared answers. He said that I was a little on the young side for an appointment, but he asked me whether I would let him know if I was tempted to make some major irrevocable career move before committing myself to it. He gave as an example a possible move to take up practice in Hong Kong.

So I carried on with my practice, although I found the interview and all the talk about a possible judicial appointment somewhat unsettling. Early in 1993, I came home one evening and was told by Jacqueline that the secretary of the Lord Chancellor, Lord Mackay of Clashfern, had telephoned. The Lord Chancellor wanted to see me the following day. There was much excitement and foreboding in the Dyson household. I told the secretary that I had other commitments that day, but would be able to see him shortly. We duly met and he immediately offered me an appointment as a judge in the Queen's Bench Division of the High Court. He was utterly charming. Although it was extremely rare for anyone to refuse the offer of an appointment to the High Court Bench in those days (sadly, things are very different now), I asked for a little time to reflect on the offer. He agreed to this without hesitation. But within a very short time, I received a call from Sir Tasker Watkins V-C, who was the Deputy Chief

Justice and in charge of the deployment of judges in the Queen's Bench Division. He said that, if I did not make a decision very quickly, he would have to find someone else.

I did not like being put under such pressure, but in the end, with Jacqueline's support, I decided to take the momentous step of leaving the Bar and becoming a judge.

How different this method of appointing judges was to the complex apparatus that was to emerge after the creation of the independent Judicial Appointments Commission (JAC) which started work in 2006. I shall describe the new system of appointing judges later when I mention the significant part that I was to play with the JAC in making some senior appointments.

I had hugely enjoyed being at the Bar for 24 years. I had enjoyed the excitement of it: the plotting of strategies for winning cases, whether by preparing opening and closing submissions, the cut and thrust of cross-examination of witnesses and generally trying to persuade judges by putting a case as attractively as possible. I was not a flamboyant advocate, but I believe that, in my quiet and determined way, I was an effective one.

But now a new world was about to open before me; one in which I was to make a mark far beyond anything that I might have imagined.

8

The High Court

I WAS SWORN in as a High Court Judge by the Lord Chancellor on 30 March 1993. The words of the judicial oath have never failed to thrill me: 'I will do right to all manner of people after the laws and usages of this realm, without fear or favour, affection or ill will'. The small ceremony took place in private in the House of Lords. I was accompanied by Jacqueline, our two children, my mother and Robert, my parents-in-law, Rita and Bobby and my brother-in-law, David. Nobody else was present. There were no speeches. It was an extremely low key affair and very different from the ceremonies that are now conducted in public by the Lord Chief Justice in his court and are usually attended by a large number of well-wishers and accompanied by speeches of welcome from the Lord Chief Justice and others. Lord Mackay was charming to me and all of my family, putting everyone at their ease. He was particularly good with the children. Michelle had recently graduated from Oxford and Steven was still at Oxford, studying biochemistry. Lord Mackay had an intense conversation with Steven which showed that he had a far better understanding of what Steven was studying than I did.

The knighthood that is automatically conferred on a High Court Judge did not follow until a few months later. I was on circuit in Sheffield when I was summoned to London to receive my knighthood. I should have been hugely excited by the prospect of meeting Her Majesty the Queen but strangely, I was not. I was enjoying sitting as a judge trying cases, and was frustrated that I would have to miss a day's sitting for a fleeting exposure to the glamour of Buckingham Palace. I also had to go to Moss Bros to be kitted out in the right dress, which comprised morning suit and tails. I was early for my appointment with the Queen. It was a hot summer's day, so I wandered into St James's Park where I was photographed by large numbers of foreign tourists. I must have seemed a strange quixotic figure to them. Then, slightly nervously, I made my way through the palace gates. At the entrance to the palace itself there was an official who was gesticulating furiously at me. He said that I was late. In fact, I was not late, although I had cut things unnecessarily fine. I was on my own. For some reason, I had not been allowed even to be accompanied by Jacqueline. I was ushered into a room where the Queen was waiting to greet me. She shook my hand, touched both of my shoulders with a sword and then invited me to sit alongside her on a sofa. We spoke about this and that. I think she asked me about some legal issue of the day, but my memory of the occasion is rather blurred. I had been instructed by someone that it was wrong to initiate conversation with Her Majesty. I have no idea of the reason for this rule of etiquette which, so far as I can tell, applies uniquely to conversations with Her Majesty: it does not apply to conversations with other members of the Royal Family. At all events, she was most gracious and far more beautiful than I had expected. I was totally disarmed and charmed by her. I wondered how I could have been so churlish as not to want to come from Sheffield to meet her and receive the knighthood. After about 10 minutes, she rose and pressed a bell. Almost immediately, the door opened and I left the room. I was soon restored to the real world and it was all over. Jacqueline asked me numerous questions about what Her Majesty had said; what the room looked like; and above all what she was wearing. My answers were lacking in detail and, so far as Jacqueline was concerned, deeply unsatisfactory. Everything had happened so quickly and my mind was in a state of blur. If only I could have told my grandmother, Malvine about this experience.

After the Easter vacation, I had sat for three weeks in the Court of Appeal Criminal Division (CACD). The constitution of that court usually comprises a Lord Justice of Appeal (a judge of the Court of Appeal) and two High Court Judges. It is now more common than it was when I started to include an experienced circuit judge in the trio. The CACD hears criminal appeals against conviction and sentence. They read the voluminous papers in advance and in most cases form a strong provisional view of the case before they hear any submissions from counsel. The judges are greatly assisted in their preparation for the appeals by case summaries that are prepared for the court by caseworkers. These summarise what is relevant to the issues that arise on the appeal, including the material evidence, the trial judge's rulings, the summing up and the grounds of appeal. They do not, however, express any view about what the outcome of the appeal should be. When I started sitting as a judge in the CACD, these case summaries were regarded as confidential documents and withheld from the parties. But it was not long before the parties were permitted to see them and indeed comment on their accuracy. This is an example of the welcome trend in recent years of conducting the business of the courts in a more open way than previously.

Before a criminal appeal is heard, the presiding judge of the panel or constitution that is to hear the appeal decides which of the three judges is to give the single judgment of the court. Most of the judgments are given *ex tempore*. This is necessary to maintain the pace at which the court is required to do its work. If most or all judgments were reserved, there would be unacceptable delays or it would be necessary to have a massive increase in the number of appeal courts. In a difficult case, however, the court will sometimes reserve its judgment, but this is not common.

It was usual for the same constitution of judges in the CACD to sit together for three weeks. Initially, I found the work of the CACD very hard. Quite apart from the sheer volume of papers to read, my lack of experience in criminal law counted against me. My experience of sitting as an Assistant Recorder and then a Recorder did help, but only up to a point. Moreover, I had never sat in an appeal court before. I always found that the presiding Lord Justice of Appeal was kind and encouraging. Gradually, I began to feel more at home in the CACD. Later when I was promoted to the Court of Appeal, I had to preside over constitutions which sometimes included High Court Judges who had great experience of criminal trials both as counsel and as a judge. I enjoyed sitting with them and learnt a great deal from them. They often tended to rely on gut instinct to arrive at the answer. I tended to rely on hard analysis. These two routes usually led to the same answer. Where they didn't, we found a way through, because we had to reach a single decision.

In the autumn of 1993, I was fortunate enough to sit in the CACD in a constitution presided over by the then Lord Chief Justice, Lord Taylor of Gosforth, the judge who had conducted the Hillsborough Inquiry in 1989. We had much in common. We were both Jewish. We were both born and bred in the north east of England (he coming from Newcastle) and had both attended local grammar schools. We both had a passion for music and played the piano, although he was a better pianist than me. And we both knew Fanny Waterman. He told me that he first met Fanny when he was on circuit in Leeds and was looking for someone a little different to invite to a dinner party in the judges' lodgings at Carr Manor. He invited Fanny and they became good friends. Fanny is striking, outspoken and unforgettable. For many years, she was a regular guest at dinner parties at Carr Manor.

I was excited about the prospect of sitting with Peter Taylor. I assumed that we would hear some interesting and important appeals. I was disappointed by the diet of cases that we were given. Many of them were mundane and unmemorable. I recall one appeal in which the ground of appeal against conviction was that the 'lies direction' (the *Lucas* direction) had not been given. This required the jury to be told by the judge that a lie told by a defendant might be relied on by them to support his guilt if they were satisfied that it was deliberate and related to a material issue in the case; and that there was no innocent motive for the lie. But that they should remember that people sometimes lie, for example, to bolster up a just cause, or out of shame, or because they might wish to conceal shameful behaviour. In this appeal, the *Lucas* direction had not been given. The appeal was, therefore, allowed. I remember Peter saying that he thought the law had taken a wrong turning by insisting that the failure to give a *Lucas* direction was fatal to the safety of a conviction; but that it was now too late to do anything about it. I found this surprising and rather depressing. Not for the first time did I think that some of the directions that judges are required to give to juries are bewilderingly convoluted and betray a lack of trust in the jury system.

Specimen directions set out in the Judicial Handbook included the *Lucas* direction and many others besides. Like most trial judges, I tended to follow the recommended directions to the letter, unless the circumstances of the case required them to be adapted. The result was that a summing up was overloaded with a large number of complicated directions. I recall one occasion early in my judicial career when I was summing up to a jury in Sheffield. Jacqueline had come to Sheffield because we were having a dinner party in the lodgings. She came into my court and, for the first time, heard me sum up a case to a jury. She heard me go through the long list of directions that I was required to give, telling them what they should and should not do and what they could and could not do, before I finally reached the point in the summing up where I summarised the evidence. At the end of the case, she said to me that my directions gave the impression that I was instructing or at least guiding the jury to acquit the defendant. She was surprised that the jury convicted.

Throughout my career as a criminal trial judge, I thought that it was extraordinary to expect a jury to be able to absorb and remember the detail of all the directions that I was required to give them. Most of the directions were not handed down in written form. The traditional view was that the jury should not be distracted by written material unless it was absolutely necessary. They were expected to take in and remember everything the judge said in his summing up. They could take notes if they wished, but many jurors did not do so. To modern eyes, this seems a ridiculous approach.

I sat in the CACD for three weeks every term during the more than seven years of my career as a High Court Judge. The highlight for me was sitting in 1996 with Lord Bingham of Cornhill, who had become Lord Chief Justice following the tragic illness and early death of Peter Taylor. Tom Bingham was my judicial hero: the finest lawyer and judge of his generation. Having read the papers and identified the central issue or issues in an appeal or a civil case, he directed the argument firmly and politely to the main points at an early stage of the hearing. In this way, he was able to get through the work briskly, but always with conspicuous fairness to both sides. His judgments were always impeccable, expressed with great style and clarity. Their reasoning flowed compellingly from paragraph to paragraph. It helped that he was a master of the English language. His influence on the development of our law was great. Perhaps his finest achievement was to produce a prodigious number of judgments on the meaning and effect of the Human Rights Act 1998 and on many aspects of the European Convention on Human Rights when it was incorporated into our domestic law. His colleagues did not always agree with him. But he was a towering figure who was genuinely modest and commanded great respect. He was always kind and encouraging to me. I can disclose an anecdote which provides an extraordinary illustration of his kindness and modesty. In 1996, when we were sitting together in the Divisional Court, we had a rather difficult case which had something to do with customs duties and the port of Dover. He gave the lead judgment. I agreed with his conclusion. But since I did not agree with his reasoning, with his encouragement I wrote a judgment setting out my own reasoning. Many years later, I attended a lecture that he gave about Dr Johnson in Inner Temple Hall. I wrote to compliment him on it.

In his reply, which was written in his beautiful manuscript, he said that his main recollection of our sitting together in the Divisional Court was of the Dover case of which he said: 'I have always had an uneasy feeling that your reasoning was right and mine was not'. Objectively speaking, the case was unmemorable. In the intervening 12 years, he had been Lord Chief Justice and Senior Law Lord. It was truly astonishing that he should have remembered this unremarkable case and that he had the humility and kindness to mention it to me in this letter.

When Peter Taylor had to retire as Lord Chief Justice, there were many who thought that his successor should be a judge who was steeped in criminal law. This was understandable because the Lord Chief Justice is expected to hear the most important criminal appeals and take a lead in developing the criminal law. The Lord Chancellor, who by this time was Lord Irvine of Lairg, had other ideas. He appointed Tom Bingham, who was a civil lawyer. Apart from his experience of criminal trials as a High Court Judge, he had had little experience of criminal justice. But within a short time, he had won over all those who entertained doubts about his suitability for the job. My three weeks sitting with him in the CACD were memorable, as were my three weeks sitting alone with him in the Divisional Court hearing judicial review cases and appeals from the decisions of magistrates.

I recall one appeal on which I sat with him and Mr Justice (Charles) Mantell (later Lord Justice Mantell), who was a High Court Judge with great experience of criminal cases. Sheila Bowler, an apparently respectable piano teacher, was convicted of the murder of her elderly aunt by pushing her into the River Brede in East Sussex, where she drowned. The case had attracted considerable media interest. She appealed on various technical grounds and also sought to rely on some fresh evidence which, it was argued, cast doubt on the safety of the conviction. Tom and I adopted a rigorously analytical approach to the detail of the submissions and the fresh evidence and were persuaded with some hesitation that we should allow the appeal and order a retrial. We felt that, if the jury had heard the fresh evidence, they might have acquitted the appellant. Charles disagreed strongly. He thought that, looking at the entirety of the evidence, the fresh evidence would have made no difference. Drawing on his experience and instinct, he was sure that the appellant was guilty. He made it clear to us that he thought that we were being unrealistic and excessively analytical. I felt that he was frustrated by our lack of criminal law experience. But he did not persuade the two of us to his point of view and the appeal was allowed. At the retrial, the Ms Bowler was unanimously acquitted. They could not be sure that she had murdered her aunt. But I have reflected that, if the appeal court had been differently constituted, her appeal might well have been dismissed. Litigation, whether criminal or civil, is an uncertain business.

After this diversion into the CACD, I should go back to 1993. After three weeks in the CACD, I went on circuit for the first time. I had four weeks in

Leeds followed by three weeks in Sheffield. The judges' lodgings at Carr Manor were about a mile away from Belvedere Road where I had lived most of my life in Leeds. My father had died in 1988 and by this time my mother was living nearby in a flat in Alwoodley; and Robert, who had married Jenny in 1971, was living in Shadwell, which is another suburb of Leeds. It was strange to be staying in lodgings which were so close to their homes and to where I had grown up. Carr Manor is a spacious, mainly Victorian stone-built house. It has large grounds and a tennis court. I was to stay there again in 1995 and 1996.

Judges' lodgings were managed by a person then called a 'butler' (now called a 'manager'). There was a good deal of formality about life in lodgings when I started my judicial career. The senior judge decided on the protocol to be followed. Many of them insisted on black tie being worn at dinner, even if no guests were present. A few wore black tie even if they dined alone. Some also refused to allow a fellow judge to invite his or her spouse to stay without their permission; and some refused to permit spouses who had stayed overnight to come down for breakfast. Happily, these extraordinary practices were already disappearing in the early 1990s. The younger judges found them unacceptable.

It was the invariable practice to have dinner parties to which local guests were invited. Depending on the guests, these could be very enjoyable. The visiting High Court Judges were looked after by the high sheriffs. The high sheriffs and their spouses were always invited to one of the dinner parties. And the high sheriffs always invited the judges to a dinner party at their, usually splendid, homes. These dinner parties were quite formal affairs. At the end of the dinners, whether they took place in the lodgings or at the homes of the high sheriffs, the host invited the women to retire to 'powder their noses', while the men carried on drinking port. Quite rightly, judges started to challenge this convention in the early 1990s and when I was the senior judge in lodgings, I did not apply it. But these challenges to protocol were regarded by some of the older, more conservative judges as dangerously radical; and they were also deprecated by some of the older butlers who saw no need to change a system that had worked perfectly well in the past.

During my first stay at Carr Manor, I naturally invited Fanny Waterman to one of our dinner parties. She was proud of the fact that one of her former pupils was now a High Court Judge. I also invited members of my family to a dinner in the lodgings. This must have been a momentous occasion for my mother, although I think she found it all rather bewildering. It was on occasions such as these that I felt the absence of my father very keenly.

On the second of my visits to Leeds, I shared lodgings with two other former LGS pupils, Mr Justice (Harry) Ognall and Mr Justice (Christopher) Holland. Brian Walsh QC, who was another former LGS boy, arranged a dinner in the old school building in our honour on 27 July 1995. The three of us sang the school song in Latin and more or less in tune. I doubt whether many of those present knew a single word of it. It was quite a nostalgic affair. Not long afterwards, the school moved to its present site on the outskirts of the city in Alwoodley. Brian had been the Head Boy at the school and later the President of the Cambridge Union Society. He had been leader of the North East Circuit and was a dominant figure on the circuit. I recall him prosecuting in a case that I tried on one of my circuit visits. It was strange to have one of my school heroes appearing before me as counsel. In 1996, he became the Recorder of Leeds (a senior circuit judicial appointment). Sadly, he died in 2000.

Between 1993 and 2000, I went on circuit many times. I tended to prefer to go to the larger cities rather than places like Lewes, Norwich or Exeter. Apart from Leeds (three times) and Sheffield, I went to Birmingham (three times), Manchester, Newcastle, Nottingham, Cardiff, St Albans and Winchester. Most of the trials were heavy criminal cases.

One such case that I particularly remember was at Newcastle Crown Court. The defendant was a 25-year-old woman who had been abandoned by her boyfriend for another woman. He had not treated her well and she was very upset. One day, she met the boyfriend and the new girlfriend in a wine bar. The boyfriend turned on her and told her to stop pursuing him. She rammed the wine glass that she was holding into his face causing him to suffer serious injury. She was charged with causing grievous bodily harm with intent to cause grievous bodily harm. The boyfriend and the new girlfriend gave evidence. They gave a clear account of what happened, but both came across as arrogant and unpleasant. The defendant also gave evidence. What she said was very confusing. It seemed that she was claiming that the incident was an accident which, if true, would have been a defence; or alternatively that she had been provoked which, even if true, would not have been a defence. I was sure that she was guilty of causing grievous bodily harm with intent, but hoped that the jury might feel sorry for her and convict her of the lesser offence of causing grievous bodily harm, but without the intent. She was of impeccable good character and came across as a delightful young woman who had been badly treated by her boyfriend. I did not see how I could avoid passing a custodial sentence if she was convicted of the more serious charge. And yet, a sentence of imprisonment would probably have destroyed this young woman's life and it was not necessary to deprive her of her liberty in order to protect society: she was most unlikely to commit another criminal offence. I anguished over what to do.

In the event, the jury came to my rescue and acquitted her of both offences. The defendant and her mother burst into tears, there was an uproar in court and I was spared the difficulty of deciding what sentence to pass. This was not the first time that I witnessed a perverse verdict. It was perverse because in my view the defendant did not disclose a defence. If I had been deciding the case without a jury, I could not conscientiously have written a judgment in favour of her acquittal of either offence. But the acquittal was not irrational, because it was reasonable for the jury to consider that the wider interests of justice were served by an acquittal in this case. The boyfriend had behaved badly and, although he had been injured, he had not lost the sight of either of his eyes and none of his injuries was permanent. The jury must have thought that the defendant had suffered enough in having to cope with the stress of the prosecution and have felt sorry for her. Although the verdict was perverse, I could see why they had refused to convict her.

The jury system is firmly embedded in our constitution and commands wide support in our country. Those who defend it insist that the ability of a jury to take into account wider considerations of justice and deliver a perverse verdict is one of its strengths. I understand this view, but cannot share it. One of the hallmarks of the rule of law which underpins our democratic system is that it should be certain. This is reflected in the judicial oath 'I will do right ... after the laws and usages of this realm'. The outcome of a trial should not depend on whether the tribunal is a judge and jury or a judge sitting alone. The outcome should properly reflect the facts and the law, regardless of who is responsible for deciding it.

Having said that, I recognise the strengths of the jury system. There is something very valuable in having a system whereby those charged with serious criminal offences are judged by their peers. The fact that the system commands nationwide support is of itself a strong reason for retaining it. More importantly, there were times during my career as a High Court Judge when, trying criminal cases, I was relieved that I did not have to decide the crucial facts. In most civil cases, there are documents that help the judge to decide the facts. But many criminal cases are light on documents. In these cases, the fact-finder has to decide the case on the basis of an assessment of the witnesses and a judgment as to where the truth lies. This can be a very difficult thing to do. The combined wisdom of 12 jurors may sometimes provide a safer route to the correct answer than the reflections of even the most brilliant judge.

My seven weeks in Cardiff in 1994 were particularly memorable. I shared the lodgings for part of the time with Mr Justice (Konrad) Schiemann who later became Lord Justice Schiemann and later still became the UK judge on the European Court of Justice in Luxembourg. Sir Donald Nicholls, who was then Vice-Chancellor of the Chancery Division and later became Lord Nicholls of Birkenhead, spent a week in the lodgings with me. He wore his intellectual brilliance very lightly and was delightful company. A little later, the Lord Chief Justice (Peter Taylor) spent a week in the lodgings too. Peter was very relaxed and good fun. During his week, we had a dinner party at which one of the guests was the by now retired Sir Tasker Watkins, who in addition to having been the Deputy Chief Justice, was one of the great and the good of Wales. After dinner, Peter and I played the great Schubert F minor Fantasy for four hands. This was one of the highlights of my musical, if not my judicial, career.

In Cardiff, I tried one of the most difficult criminal cases I had to try in my time as a High Court Judge. The defendant was a general practitioner called

Dr Sinha. At the end of a busy day in the surgery where he was working as a locum, he had prescribed a beta-blocker for a young female patient who was complaining of stress. Beta-blockers are contra-indicated for asthmatics. He did not ask her whether she suffered from asthma. In fact, doctors in the practice had repeatedly prescribed inhalers for her. The patient took the beta-blocker and as a result died during the night. The following morning, the coroner's office telephoned the surgery and told them what had happened. Dr Sinha was informed. He went to the computer, saw repeat entries for prescriptions of an inhaler and deleted them. But the entries remained on the hard disk. He was charged with gross negligence manslaughter and attempting to pervert the course of justice. The trial lasted three weeks. A great deal of complex expert medical evidence was placed before the jury. The defendant admitted that he had been negligent, but denied that his negligence had been gross. The jury acquitted him of manslaughter, but convicted him of the other offence. There was a technical legal argument about whether the jury had to be agreed about the nature of the proceedings that the defendant was attempting to pervert. Was it a criminal trial for manslaughter, or civil proceedings for negligence or some professional disciplinary proceedings that he might face? I directed the jury that it did not matter. As a matter of common sense, this seemed right, but as a matter of legal analysis, I was far from sure. To my relief, the defendant's appeal to the CACD on this point was dismissed, but I did not feel that the appeal court really faced up to the legal difficulty. No doubt they shared my view that to have allowed the appeal would not have been sensible. Sentencing him was not easy either. A large number of the defendant's patients were called to give evidence of his good character. They said that he was an extremely caring doctor who readily responded to calls to visit them at home in the middle of the night. They urged me not to pass a custodial sentence. Some of them could not imagine how they would manage if they could not call him. I had to harden my heart to pass a custodial sentence of six months' imprisonment. Dr Sinha was a good man who had no criminal record. He had made a bad mistake which had terrible consequences, but mistakes are easily made and I was not sentencing him for his mistake. His act of attempting to pervert the course of justice was not planned, but done in a moment of panic. And yet it seemed to me that this was a very serious offence because it is essential to be able to trust doctors to make and keep honest and accurate medical records. That is why I passed the custodial sentence, but I found it very difficult.

I would single out for mention only one other criminal case that I tried. It was in Leeds in 1995. The defendant was a man called Mohammed Ayub. He was having an affair with a rather weak woman whom he terrified and dominated. She had two daughters aged about 12 and 10 by another man. There was no suggestion that the defendant sexually molested the girls, but he dominated and bullied them. One day, he took them to a flat in the red-light district of Bradford. He had a row and lost his temper with them. He hit the older girl so hard that he killed her. He then left the younger girl alone with her dead sister's body in the flat overnight. The next day, with the assistance of one of his friends, he buried the body of the dead girl in a grave that they dug in the basement of the house where the mother was living. He later murdered the friend. He was charged with the two murders. In the course of his defence, he gratuitously alleged that the mother had been having a sexual relationship with the older girl and generally ran a hopeless, but outrageous, defence requiring his QC to put all manner of offensive and ridiculous allegations to some of the prosecution witnesses. I was sure that he did this in order to cause as much distress as possible and that he enjoyed having this effect. Witnesses were predictably very upset and broke down in the witness box. The atmosphere in court was extremely tense. I had never encountered anything like this. I found it difficult to restrain myself from remonstrating that some of the questions being put to the witnesses were irrelevant and should not be asked. The experienced QC who was acting for the defendant came to see me in my room and urged me to keep my cool, because there was a real danger that the defendant would terminate his instructions. If that were to happen, I would be faced with having to contend with the defendant acting on his own. I took heed of counsel's salutary warning, for which I was grateful.

The jury had no difficulty in convicting Ayub of both murders. In those days, the judge did not fix the 'tariff' period. This is the minimum period that the defendant has to serve in custody before he can be considered by the Parole Board for release on licence into the community. The judge recommended the tariff period, but it was the Home Secretary who determined what it should be. I was so angry at the way the defence had been conducted that I did not trust myself to make a fair and rational recommendation straightaway. There was no difficulty in deferring making this decision, since it was made by filling in a form to which the public had no access. This was yet another example of lack of openness in our justice system. How much things have improved since then. The judge now determines the tariff period and announces it in public after taking account of any victim impact statements that have been made. I duly recommended a tariff period of 30 years. My recommendation went to the Lord Chief Justice (Tom Bingham) who reduced it to 27 years, by which time the defendant would have been 70. This revised recommendation was then submitted to the Home Secretary (Michael Howard) who restored the period of 30 years.

The previous year, I had been asked by Peter Taylor whether I would be willing to do cases in what was then called 'the Crown Office List' (now the Administrative Court). The cases allocated to the Crown Office List were public law claims, usually for judicial review against public bodies such as arms of central government, local authorities and other bodies that discharged public law functions. He said, 'You know about judicial review, don't you John?' In fact, I had only done one judicial review case at the Bar (the Premier League case) and none since my appointment as a judge. But I have always found new challenges irresistible (moving chambers was another example), so I did not disabuse him.

There was far less public law work in the early 1990s than later in my judicial career. The European Convention on Human Rights had not yet been incorporated into our domestic law by the Human Rights Act 1998 and EU law was less significant than it subsequently became. Only a small number of Queen's Bench Division judges heard cases in the Crown Office List. I was flattered and thrilled to have been authorised to hear these cases. Even in those days, some of the cases raised interesting issues of fact and law. The subject-matter often had a strong political element and the cases were sometimes high-profile. It was a new experience for me to have to rule on whether the Government had acted unlawfully in reaching some of its decisions. Occasionally, the decisions were controversial and unpopular. This was a role for which my years of appearances before arbitrators and official referees had not prepared me.

Certain areas generated particularly large numbers of claims, for example, asylum and immigration claims and education. But there was a wide range of other public law work. I shall mention only two cases, both of which attracted a good deal of media attention. The first was *R v Home Secretary ex p Norney* [1995] QBD 6 Oct. Michael Howard was the Home Secretary in 1995. He had been challenged by five IRA members who had been sentenced to life imprisonment in 1976 for conspiracy to cause explosions. In each case, the prisoner's punishment period (the tariff period) had been set by the Home Secretary of the day at 20 years. The tariff periods had almost expired. Provided that the Parole Board was satisfied that the prisoners were no longer dangerous, they were entitled to be released on licence upon the expiry of their tariff periods. It was the practice of the Parole Board not to reach a decision on whether it was safe to release an individual prisoner until some six months after it had received the individual's papers. To make sure that the board could reach its decision in good time, the IRA men asked for their cases to be referred by the Home Secretary to it six months or so before their tariffs were due to expire. Mr Howard said that it had always been Home Office practice to wait until the end of the tariff before referring a case to the board and he refused to depart from this practice. This meant that every individual would have to spend another six months in custody after the end of the tariff period in custody waiting for the board to review their case.

I upheld the challenge to the refusal to refer the cases of the five IRA claimants to the board until about six months after the expiry of their tariff periods. I held that the established Home Office practice was unreasonable and produced results which were manifestly unjust. I handed down my written judgment on the morning of 28 September 1995. The Home Secretary's QC said that Mr Howard was not seeking permission to appeal (without which an appeal to the Court of Appeal would not be possible). It was unfortunate from his point of view that earlier in the same week, the European Court of Human Rights had found against the United Kingdom in *McCann v UK* [1995] 21 ECHR 97 GC. This was the case about the shooting dead of IRA terrorists by the SAS in Gibraltar.

My decision was widely reported in the national press. Most of the reporting was neutral, measured and factual. On 29 September 1995, the *Daily Express* reported the decision in a balanced manner, but reported David Shaw MP, a Tory backbencher, as having said that he was very concerned 'about the fact that judges are running against the British population in this area because most people want terrorists to have life sentences which mean life'. On 1 October, another newspaper included an article berating the European Court of Human Rights for a 'crackpot' decision (in the SAS Gibraltar shooting case), adding that 'legal weevils here at home are practising their own brand of mischief'. This was a reference to my decision. The article concluded: 'The only way terrorists should ever leave jail is in coffins. With judges like Mr Justice Dyson around, there is much to be said for the SAS. And a few ounces of lead'.

To return to the morning of 29 September, Jacqueline and I were listening to the *Today* programme on Radio 4 when we heard Michael Howard being interviewed by John Humphries. Asked whether my ruling damaged Britain's claim to the moral high ground, Mr Howard said that he did not accept that adding:

> The last time this particular judge found against me, which was on a case which would have led to the release of a large number of illegal immigrants, the Court of Appeal unanimously decided that he was wrong. So we'll see what happens if we do appeal. These things can be quite difficult to predict ...

I was stunned to hear him say this on the radio. It was true that my earlier decision had been reversed on appeal. But I thought that his reference to this earlier case during the interview could only be interpreted as an attack on my competence. It was a clear breach of the convention that ministers do not indulge in personalised disparagement of individual judges whose decisions they do not like. They are entitled to say that they are disappointed by a decision, that they disagree with it and, of course, to appeal against it if they are given permission to do so. And what Mr Howard said was all the more extraordinary in view of the fact that his QC had said the previous day in open court that the Home Secretary was not seeking permission to appeal and he never did so.

In his book *Trial of Strength* (1997), Joshua Rozenberg discussed this case and Mr Howard's reaction to it. When interviewed by Mr Rozenberg in 1997, Mr Howard denied that he had been making a personal attack on me on the *Today* programme. He saw nothing wrong in what he had said. In pointing out that I had been overruled on a previous occasion, he was simply giving an illustration of the unpredictability of judicial review. This was a clever explanation, but in my view it was totally unconvincing.

Sometime after this incident, I happened to meet Mr Howard by chance. I asked him whether he remembered the case. He said that he did. Rather charmingly, he asked me whether I had forgiven him. We laughed about it.

More seriously, however, he held the office of Home Secretary from 1993 until Labour came into power in 1997. His illiberal populist decisions gave rise to a considerable number of successful judicial review challenges. He was a QC and it was my sense that he sometimes made decisions which he must have known were vulnerable to legal attack. If he was prevented by judges from doing what would appeal to the right wing of his party and their supporters, he would not mind too much. Better that than choosing policies which would be castigated by the right-wing media as soft and liberal.

I have spent some time on this case because, so far as I can recall, it was the first time that I had been subjected to serious criticism in the public domain. I did not find it too upsetting, not least because I had no doubt that my decision was correct and I was reassured by the strong support that I received from colleagues. But it was annoying not to be able to answer back.

The second judicial review case was the claim by Kenneth Fisher against the North Derbyshire Health Authority's refusal to fund his treatment with beta-interferon, a new drug for multiple sclerosis which had been prescribed by neurologists. I upheld the claim on the grounds that the authority had failed to take account of national guidelines contained in an NHS circular and had introduced a blanket ban on the provision of beta-interferon for local sufferers of multiple sclerosis. They had therefore failed to consider whether it was appropriate to supply the drug to Mr Fisher. The decision attracted a good deal of publicity. There was a piece about it on the BBC 2 current affairs programme, *Newsnight* which, quite by chance, I watched. An 'expert' criticised the judgment in terms which made it clear to me that he had not read it in any detail. He said that he was sure that my decision would be overturned on appeal, although he did not specify what the grounds of appeal might be. Permission to appeal was never sought and there was no appeal.

Most of the civil trials on circuit settled on the day fixed for the trial. I found this frustrating. One that did not settle was a series of claims for damages for negligence against a dentist called Barry Garrett which I heard in Leeds in July 1995. The claims were brought by a number of patients who had suffered appallingly at his hands. I heard eight test cases. The allegations were that he had performed many procedures on these patients which were unnecessary and, to make matters worse, that the quality of this unnecessary work was very poor. He had been suspended from practice by the General Dental Council, but was permitted to return to practice two years later after retraining. In my view, this penalty was totally inadequate. It was true that he needed some training, but performing unnecessary treatment was not a matter of incompetence: it was a criminal act, because he had obtained the consent of the patients to the treatment by dishonestly telling them that it was necessary when it was not. He did not need training to avoid a repetition of conduct which he must have known was wrong. The public needed greater protection from him than they received.

The penalty imposed by the General Dental Council was not relevant to what I had to decide, although I had to determine whether some of the treatment that the eight claimants received had in fact been necessary. This depended to a large extent on the interpretation of X-ray images. I heard expert evidence from distinguished professors who gave their opposing views as to the correct interpretation of the patients' X-rays on the question of what they showed about the pre-treatment state of the patients' teeth and what treatment was necessary. Images, which to a layman like me appeared fuzzy, were projected on to the wall of the court room and each professor tried to explain to me why his interpretation was correct. I found it impossible to choose between their interpretations, either on the basis of my view about their comparative general competence or on the basis of my interpretation of the X-ray images. I felt that I had no alternative but to decide these issues in favour of the defendant on the grounds that the claimants had not proved their case. I thought at the time (and still think) that this case showed one of the weaknesses in our system. I would have been greatly assisted by having one or two assessors sitting with me to help me to decide technical issues which I was not equipped to determine for myself.

I tried some interesting civil cases when I was sitting in London. One that stands out was a claim by the widow of Mr Hedley against Mr Cuthbertson. Mr Hedley had engaged Mr Cuthbertson, a climbing instructor, to take him up Tour Ronde which is a mountain in the Mont Blanc range in the Alps. Mr Hedley had never climbed before. Mr Cuthbertson allowed him to lead the way, placing belays in the ice as they climbed. They set off too late and made slow progress. In order to speed up and find the shadow out of the line of falling rocks, Mr Cuthbertson took the lead and started fixing the belays with a single ice screw rather than two or even three. At some point, a belay became detached from the ice and Mr Hedley fell to his death. The case attracted a good deal of media interest. I heard expert evidence on the question of whether it was acceptable practice to fix belays with a single screw. The experts disagreed and I preferred the evidence of the claimant's expert and found that Mr Cuthbertson had been negligently responsible for the death.

I was concerned that my decision might be interpreted as encouraging claims for damages for injuries suffered in the course of any sporting activity: a contribution to what was later called the 'compensation culture'. I said in my judgment that the decision should not be regarded as opening the floodgates for claims against mountain guides whenever there was an accident. Climbing was an inherently dangerous sport and only those who failed to take reasonable steps to minimise the danger to their charges would be liable for an accident. But these cautionary words did not convince Libby Purves, the journalist who wrote a regular column for the *Times* newspaper. In an article entitled 'The heights of folly', published on 24 June 1997, she criticised my decision at least by implication. She said that judges:

> should allow a generous margin of respect for the guide or teacher's presumed professional judgment, and for the exigencies of the moment. They should err on the side

of robustness and remember that people who take up adventurous sports are in a very different position from cinemagoers or Saturday mall shoppers. Caveat emptor: if you buy a dog it might bite you. If you buy an adventure you accept a risk.

Several months later, I happened to meet Libby Purves at an event for training students for the Bar at Cumberland Lodge, Windsor Park. We talked about the case which she said she remembered well. Her article had generated a large post-bag, the readers being fairly evenly divided between those who agreed with her and those who did not. With disarming candour, she told me that, having read the judgment carefully, she now understood why I had decided the case in favour of the claimant. It was obvious that she had not read the judgment in detail before she wrote the article. I had the strong sense that she was surprised that the judge was a youthful-looking man who enjoyed hiking in the Alps, and not a decrepit frequenter of a London club who spent his life sitting in large leather armchairs sipping sherry and port.

Another fascinating civil case concerned claims by Raymond Petch against various government departments. Mr Petch was a very clever civil servant who had been employed by a number of departments. He suffered from manic depression. He brought a number of claims alleging amongst other things that he had been denied pension rights. The government departments were represented by leading and junior counsel. Mr Petch represented himself brilliantly. The claims were extremely complex and the case lasted several days. He was not in the least outshone by his professional opponents and his mastery of the documents and his ability to marshall the facts and the law was remarkable. It seemed to me that his intellectual fire was burning with a real intensity and that he was in a manic phase of his illness. But unsurprisingly he was unable to apply the cold detachment to his case that would have been expected of an independent lawyer. He issued subpoenas requiring the past and present permanent secretaries of the departments that he was suing to attend to give evidence. He even subpoenaed Sir Robin Butler (later Lord Butler of Brockway) who was Cabinet Secretary at the time. I suspect that these distinguished senior civil servants had little idea of why they had been asked to come to court. But they all dutifully attended court and answered Mr Petch's questions clearly and politely. Most of the questions did not touch the central issues in the case, but I allowed Mr Petch to ask them. He was easy to deal with. I had a strong sense that, because I treated him politely and with respect and showed every sign of understanding his arguments, he thought that he was going to win.

At the end of the hearing, I reserved my judgment. I circulated my draft judgment in due course and handed it down on a Monday morning. I had rejected all of his arguments and his claims. The contrast between the confident and upbeat man who had conducted the hearing and the dishevelled, crestfallen man who appeared at the hand down of the judgment was distressing. He seemed a broken man. Manic had given way to depressive. I was very upset to see him cut down in this way.

A few days later, I received a charming letter from Sir Patrick Nairne who was a former permanent secretary and one of the witnesses who had been subpoenaed by Mr Petch. He wrote that he had greatly admired my 'clear, succinct and cogent judgment' with respect and considerable enjoyment. He added:

> As you foresaw, Mr Petch is very distressed; but I hope that your generous words about him and his performance will encourage him to use his considerable talents and energy in some fresh field of activity. I hope that does not sound Pecksniffian!

A short time later, I read an obituary of Mr Petch in the *Guardian* newspaper. He had committed suicide by throwing himself into the River Cam in Cambridge. This came as a terrible shock to me. I read the obituary carefully. It said that he had never recovered from losing his case against the Government and that this was why he had taken his life. Although I did not see how I could reasonably be blamed for the suicide, nevertheless I found it upsetting to read the suggestion that I had caused Mr Petch's death. It was of a little comfort to see that the obituary had been written by one of Mr Petch's friends who had given evidence on his behalf at the trial.

One of the attractions of being a High Court Judge was the wide range of cases one was asked to decide. I found this endlessly fascinating. One of the strangest was an election petition by the Liberal Democrats challenging the June 1993 European Parliament election result in the Devon and East Plymouth constituency. I and Mr Justice Thayne Forbes were constituted as the election court. Mr Richard Huggett had stood as a candidate and described himself as a 'Literal Democrat'. Mr Huggett got 10,203 votes. The Conservative candidate defeated the Liberal Democrat candidate by some 700 votes. The petitioners claimed that thousands of electors mistakenly voted for Mr Huggett, believing that he was the Liberal Democrat candidate. They said that the acting returning officer should not have accepted Mr Huggett's description of himself as a 'Literal Democrat' because it was calculated to confuse. We ruled that under election rules approved by Parliament in 1968, the minimum requirements for identification were a candidate's full name and home address. The rules did not prohibit candidates 'whether out of spite or a wicked sense of fun, from describing themselves in a confusing way or indulging in spoiling tactics'. We, therefore, dismissed the petition. I was most reluctant to reach this conclusion because it seemed obvious that the Liberal Democrats had been denied victory by a combination of Mr Huggett's spoiling tactics and the failure of a disturbingly large number of voters to read their ballot paper carefully. But the statutory language was clear. All that was required of candidates was that they gave their true name and home address as Mr Huggett had done. We recommended that Parliament consider whether a system of registration of political parties should be established and whether a statutory provision should be introduced limiting the ability of candidates to use the name of a registered party. This was done by the enactment of the Registration of Political Parties Act 1998. I thought that this was a satisfactory outcome.

Far better that Parliament should tackle what was essentially a political issue than that unelected judges attempt to do so by a process of exorbitant statutory interpretation.

During the hearing, Jeremy Thorpe and his wife Marion came into court and sat at the back to listen to the legal argument. He had been leader of the Liberal Party from 1967 to 1976. Notoriously, he had been tried and acquitted at the Old Bailey on charges of conspiracy and incitement to murder Norman Scott. By the early 1990s, he was suffering from Parkinson's disease. Marion (as Marion Stein) had been a concert pianist. She had also (as Marion Harewood) collaborated with Fanny Waterman in writing a series of piano lessons books. The Thorpes hosted a party for Fanny in their Bayswater flat in about 2005 to which I was invited. A very disabled Jeremy Thorpe was wheeled in during the party. I was asked by Marion to talk to him. Conversation was very difficult because he could not speak. But I formed the clear impression that he had a full recollection of the case. He was unable to indicate what he thought of our decision.

But to revert to the 1990s, my career as a High Court Judge had, on the whole, been running smoothly. There had, of course, been successful appeals against some of my decisions: Mr Howard had referred to one on the *Today* programme in 1995. But these were comparatively rare. I was greatly enjoying the work. Senior judges were complimentary and I began to think that I might even one day be promoted to the Court of Appeal. But in March 1999, storm clouds suddenly appeared out of this apparently blue sky. A Mr O'Callaghan was waging a battle with Corals, the bookmakers, who had refused to pay out the winnings to which he said he was entitled on a bet that he had placed with them. Angered by this refusal, he opposed an application by Corals to the Bristol licensing committee for a renewal of their bookmakers' licence in respect of premises in Bristol. He failed, but he was granted permission to apply for judicial review of the committee's decision. He failed to progress his application for judicial review and, almost 14 months late, applied to me for an extension of the prescribed 14-day time limit. I refused to grant the extension of time. So far as I was concerned, this was a simple application and I expected to hear no more about it.

Meanwhile, however, the *Sunday Times* newspaper had been investigating the question of judges' commercial interests. I had been appointed a non-executive director of Dyson Properties Limited many years before I went on the Bench. This property investment company had been established in 1959 by my parents principally to provide an income for their retirement. I took no part in the running of the company, but drew an annual salary of a few thousand pounds. It had never occurred to me that it had any relevance to my position as a judge. Journalists from the *Sunday Times* interviewed a number of the company's tenants in Leeds with a view to seeing whether they could dig up any dirt. One or more of the tenants told my brother, who at this time was running the company, that he should be aware that they had been approached.

Fortunately, none of the tenants had a bad word to say to the journalists about their landlord. The first I knew about the involvement of the *Sunday Times* was when I received a peremptory demand from a journalist that I answer a series of questions about my relationship with the company, including the size of my salary. The journalist threatened that, if I did not answer the questions before expiry of the short deadline that he gave me, he would write a piece saying that I had refused to answer his questions and invite the readers to draw unfavourable inferences. I had done nothing wrong and I had nothing to be ashamed of but I did not like the intrusion and found the whole affair very unsettling. I consulted Tom Bingham (then Lord Chief Justice) as to what I should do. He was extremely supportive and advised me in extremely robust terms and colourful language to refuse to answer any of the questions. But I decided to answer the questions, uncomfortable though I felt in having to cope with what I regarded as importunate prying into my private business.

My answers to the questions were so dull that the piece that the *Sunday Times* ran, at any rate so far as it related to me, was of little interest. But it did mention that Corals was one of the company's tenants. Mr O'Callaghan (or those representing him in his battle with Corals) must have read the article. He said that, if he had known that I was a director of a company one of whose tenants was Corals, he would have objected to my hearing his application for an extension of time for his judicial review application. So he appealed against my refusal to grant him an extension of time on the grounds that my connection with the company and its connection with Corals disqualified me for apparent bias from determining his application for an extension of time. I made a statement for the Court of Appeal hearing and informed them that the premises let to Corals were in the north of England and I was not even aware that Corals was a tenant of the company. The Court of Appeal dismissed the appeal. It was heard together with four other cases which raised different issues relating to judicial impartiality. The lead case was *Locabail (UK) Limited v Bayfield Properties Limited* [2000] QB 451. I regarded Mr O'Callaghan's appeal against my decision as ridiculous, opportunistic and a waste of public money (it was funded on legal aid). But the whole saga was very stressful for me. It reminded me that judges are constantly under public scrutiny and need to be extremely careful in everything they do, both in and out of court. Under the pressure of the constant flow of work and the need to produce decisions without delay, it is easy to forget that. This was a salutary experience for me. I derived huge comfort from the support that I received from many of my fellow judges.

In 1997, I had been asked by Tom Bingham to become the first High Court Judge to become head of the official referees. Since my appointment to the High Court Bench in 1993, I had not done a single construction law case. I enjoyed the rich diet of cases that I had been asked to try. To return to the official referees was not a cause for rejoicing but I felt that I had no alternative but to do what I considered to be my duty. My appointment was formally made by Lord

Irvine of Lairg QC, who when he saw me said rather delphically, *'festina lente'* ('hurry along, but slowly'). I took this to mean that he believed that there was much wrong with the court, but that I should not try to make too many changes overnight.

The convention had previously been that the head of the official referees was the most senior man (it had never been a woman). His Honour Judge Peter Bowsher QC was expecting to take over from His Honour Judge Esyr Lewis QC. Tom's expectation was that the advent for the first time of a High Court Judge would add status to the court and that I would be able to recommend as my successor one of the other senior circuit judges of the court who, on becoming the head of the court, would become a High Court Judge. That was the plan.

My arrival came as a shock to Peter Bowsher. He was older than me. I had appeared before him quite often when I was still at the Bar. He was clearly very upset, although he knew that I had not sought the position that he coveted and expected to be his as of right. But after an initial *froideur*, he decided to help me make my appointment a success. I made a point of seeking his advice on difficult issues as well as working in a collegiate manner with the other judges too. At that time, the court was located on the top floors of St Dunstan's House in Fetter Lane. This building has since been demolished and replaced by a block of flats. I introduced some changes which were cosmetic, but which I thought were important for enhancing the standing of the court. I changed the name 'official referee' to 'judge' and the name of the court to the Technology and Construction Court (which soon became known as the TCC for short). I persuaded the Lord Chief Justice and the Lord Chancellor to agree that the judges should now be addressed as 'my Lord' (the mode of address for High Court and appellate judges and one or two other senior judges) rather than 'your Honour' (the mode of address for circuit judges). I also changed the position of the TCC cases in the daily 'cause list', so that they were listed after the High Court cases and not at the very bottom of the list after all manner of other cases. The combined effect of these cosmetic changes was to boost the morale of the judges and raise the profile of the court. The judges particularly enjoyed being called 'my Lord'.

More substantively, I had to tackle a problem of delay in the production of judgments. Some of the judges were excellent and efficient. Two, however, were extremely slow in producing their judgments. I found this an intractable problem. I gave them generous judgment-writing time. One of them accused me of putting him under such pressure that he was in danger of having a nervous breakdown. Another was chaotic as well as slow. He would sometimes agree to start a long trial before he had completed an outstanding judgment in another big case. I found it difficult to know how to deal with these problems. The nuclear option was to report them to the Lord Chief Justice, but that was a course I was reluctant to take. Somehow, we muddled through. But these problems highlighted the importance of appointing good judges in the first place and the limited powers a supervising judge enjoys to manage and control those whom he supervises. The importance of the independence of the judiciary was never far from my mind.

I believe that my period as judge in charge of the TCC was regarded by many as successful. That may be a fair assessment having regard to the limitations under which I was constrained to work. But much work remained to be done. Although some of the judges were very good, I was in no doubt that the court would not achieve the high reputation that was needed unless its work was done by true High Court Judges. At the end of my term in late 2000, I felt obliged to tell Tom Bingham that I was unable to recommend any judge of the court to be my successor. Thus it was that Mr Justice Forbes was appointed to succeed me.

I enjoyed much of the TCC work. As the judge in charge of the court, I was able to decide which cases I wanted to hear. This was a rare privilege and one which I was not able to enjoy again until I became Master of the Rolls in 2012. In 1999, the first claim to enforce an adjudication made under the regime established under the Housing Grants, Construction and Regeneration Act 1996 came before the court. The case, *Macob Civil Engineering Ltd v Morrison Construction* [1999] 3 EGLR 7 was one of the most important cases that I decided as a first instance judge. The regime provided a scheme for the appointment of adjudicators to make quick decisions in construction cases, which were to be binding and enforceable pending a final decision by an arbitrator or pending resolution by a settlement. The claim was for summary judgment. The defendant challenged the adjudicator's decision on the grounds that it was not a 'decision' within the meaning of the Act, since it was unlawful and invalid and that it was not binding until the challenge had been determined in arbitration. I gave judgment in favour of the claimant. I said that an adjudicator's decision was a 'decision' even if it was challenged. My decision was heralded as 'robust' in the professional journals. But I believed that a strong approach was necessary; otherwise the effectiveness of the adjudication scheme would have been undermined. I adopted the same approach in a subsequent case and it was upheld by the Court of Appeal. This general approach has survived and been applied in countless cases in the last 20 years or so. I found it very satisfying to be able to make an impact on an issue of such importance to the construction industry.

As a High Court Judge, I do not recall being asked to attend dinners, make speeches and give lectures to anything like the same extent as I was subsequently asked to do. But I do recall being invited to attend a dinner for the Royal Institution of Chartered Surveyors at the Grosvenor House hotel. I was one of the guest speakers. Boris Johnson was the other guest speaker. He was the editor of *The Spectator* magazine at the time and was much sought after as an after dinner speaker. I was quite nervous at being juxtaposed with him. He made a polished but rather pointless speech, which comprised wall to wall jokes of no relevance to surveyors. The closest he came to telling a relevant joke was to say how delighted he was to be among a large quantity of surveyors: he was probably right in thinking that there were many quantity surveyors in the audience.

Another dinner at which I was asked to speak was a City livery company annual dinner. On this occasion, I was sharing the platform with Chris Patten (now Lord Patten of Barnes) who had been a distinguished MP and member of the Cabinet until he lost his seat in the 1992 general election. He had been the Governor of Hong Kong until the transfer of sovereignty to China on 1 July 1997. He gave a very statesmanlike speech painting a broad historical picture. It was fairly serious, but far more worthwhile than Boris Johnson's speech. I found Chris and his barrister wife, Lavender delightful company.

My reference to the transfer of sovereignty of Hong Kong to China reminds me of the fact that on the Monday of the week during which the transfer was due to take place, Cherie Booth QC (wife of Tony Blair, the then Prime Minister) appeared before me in a public law case which involved several parties each represented by counsel. She asked whether I would hear her submissions first and out of sequence because she had to accompany her husband on the visit to Hong Kong for the handover. Of course, I acceded to her request. On the Friday of the same week, I had another case in which Cherie appeared following her return. She looked totally exhausted. She was an able advocate and during my career as a High Court Judge, she appeared before me on quite a few occasions. I had the sense that the official demands of being the Prime Minister's wife prevented her from preparing her cases as thoroughly as she had been able to do earlier on.

There were two other activities in which I engaged when on the High Court Bench which added to the variety of life. In 1994, I was invited by Peter Taylor to become chairman of the Ethnic Minorities Advisory Committee (EMAC) of the Judicial Studies Board (JSB) in succession to Mr Justice (Henry) Brooke and, therefore, also to become a member of the main board of the JSB. The JSB was renamed the Judicial College in 2011 and is responsible for delivering training to judges. EMAC was established to train judges to be more sensitive and better informed about matters of race. Its remit was enlarged during my chairmanship to all issues of discrimination. By a small adjustment to the acronym, but a major change to what it did, it became ETAC (the Equal Treatment Advisory Committee).

There had been considerable suspicion of and even forthright opposition to the JSB when it was first established in 1979. Many judges thought that judging could not be taught. Their view was that they did not need to be given advice on how to sum up to a jury even if they had not practised in criminal law. One leading commercial judge famously said (and was probably proud of the fact) that the first time he had ever seen a jury was when he conducted his first criminal trial as a judge. The view of many of the backwoodsmen was that good judges were innately good and had nothing to learn; and bad judges could not be improved by training. Rather pompously they said that advising judges what to do was an interference with their independence and wrong in principle. It made no difference that the training programmes were both designed and delivered by judges and that the Government had no part to play in the process.

If judicial training was generally deprecated by many of the older judges, some of them were particularly hostile to training on how to avoid causing offence to persons of different races and religions. It was not uncommon for them to say 'I am colour blind'. These self-confident judges were those who were most in need of training, because they were most likely to be actuated by subconscious, if not actual, bias.

EMAC produced a training handbook. The Lord Chancellor funded a series of 36 residential seminars which were held round the country for all full-time and part-time judges in the crown courts and for stipendiary magistrates (professional magistrates). I presided over a number of these seminars. The format was that about 40 judges and several leading members of the local ethnic communities were invited to attend lectures and discussions and on the Thursday evenings a dinner. The idea was that the judges and the members of the communities should be able to talk freely in a relaxed atmosphere. For some judges, this was the first time they had ever met someone from the communities to discuss issues of race or at all. And hardly any of the guests had ever spoken to a judge. The judges heard directly about the problems of racial discrimination. What the committee's vice-chairman Trevor Hall had to say at these seminars always caused a stir. He was black and a highly respected senior race relations consultant at the Home Office. He told the judges that he had been stopped by the police more than 40 times while driving his posh car, and not on account of any alleged driving offence. The police just assumed that a black man could not have acquired an expensive car by honest means.

In retrospect, I can see that the formula we adopted for these seminars might have appeared to be rather contrived and possibly even patronising. But I think on the whole they worked. The younger judges tended to be more appreciative than their older colleagues. But there were dangers. At one dinner in Nottingham, a Jewish Recorder was sitting next to a Palestinian guest. When the Recorder revealed that he was Jewish, the Palestinian stood up and announced that he was not willing to sit next to a Jew. News of this incident reached the ears of the Presiding Judge of the Circuit who was also present. He later wrote a stinging letter to me saying that if there was a repeat of such behaviour, he would instruct the judges on his circuit to boycott our seminars. Through gritted teeth, I wrote a letter of apology, although I thought that the Presiding Judge had overreacted and I did not see why I should have been blamed for this isolated incident.

Predictably, there was some media criticism of our programme of seminars and indeed of EMAC itself. The programmes were characterised as an exercise in political correctness. I received some media training to help me to explain what we were doing and why we were doing it. Together with a few other judges who were liable to be exposed to the media spotlight, I had some interview training from John Eidinow, a professional trainer who helped public figures, especially politicians, to learn how to deal with awkward and aggressive questions. One tip as to how to deal with a difficult question was to say: 'the real question is …' and then answer that question and not the one that the interviewer had asked. Crude and annoying for the audience, but quite effective. Other advice was not to slouch, but to lean forward and engage the interviewer with intensity and conviction. As part of the training, we were asked to speak on a subject for two minutes; then reduce it to 30 seconds; and finally distil it down to 10 seconds – excellent training for making the most of the short time that one would usually be given to put one's points across and for the production of a soundbite. After receiving this training, I never looked at television interviews in quite the same way again. More pertinently, I cannot recall a single occasion when I was actually interviewed on television and only two when I was interviewed on the radio. So the training was largely a waste of time and money but it was extremely interesting and most enjoyable.

At the end of my term as chairman of ETAC, I received a letter from Lord Irvine thanking me for my efforts. He wrote:

> I know that it has been no easy task to develop a coherent strategy in such a sensitive field especially since you and your members have been subject to pressures from external groups around the country who wish to see instant achievements.
>
> It is a tribute to your dedicated approach and your credibility in the eyes of those concerned with equal treatment issues that ETAC has developed so well from EMAC. You hand over to your successor a going concern. I am really grateful.

My involvement with the Legal Group of the Friends of the Hebrew University, Jerusalem (FHU) was something quite different. The university is a prestigious and internationally acclaimed liberal academic institution. The FHU exists to support the work of the university and the Legal Group the work of its excellent law faculty. Shortly after I was appointed to the High Court Bench, I succeeded Lord Justice (John) Balcombe as the chairman of the Legal Group. We organised occasional lectures and concerts to raise money for the law faculty. Each year, the Lionel Cohen lecture is delivered in Jerusalem by a distinguished UK jurist under the auspices of the FHU. There is also an annual dinner in London at which the lecturer is invited to speak. I gave the Lionel Cohen lecture shortly after my retirement in 2016. The rollcall of the Lionel Cohen lecturers includes many of the foremost judges, barristers and law academics of our time, some Jewish, but many not.

Some of the concerts were by famous classical musicians. But the one that stands out in my memory is the recital given in 1996 in Middle Temple Hall by Peter Taylor and Maureen Smith, who was married to Judge Geoffrey Rivlin QC, latterly the Recorder of Westminster. Maureen is a fine violinist. She had grown up in Leeds and, when she was about 17, she had been my girlfriend for a short time. This recital was in honour of John Balcombe's retirement as chairman of the Legal Group. About half an hour before the recital was due to start, I was given the shattering news that Peter was suffering from an untreatable brain cancer. This was to be announced on the BBC news later that evening. I was completely devastated. I had to introduce the musical evening and the performers harbouring an appalling secret which would not remain a secret for much longer. During the performance, I noticed that Peter made more mistakes than I would have expected. The disease was probably already having an effect on his cognitive functioning. And at the end, there was (unusually for these recitals) a standing ovation which was led by Lord Mackay. He, of course, knew. And then I had to round off the evening with some words of thanks. I found the whole evening emotionally draining and exceptionally difficult. It is etched on my memory.

Within a year, Peter was dead. He was only 66. He was very proud of his north-east roots. I was on circuit in Newcastle when he died. The Newcastle Crown Court was packed when tributes were paid to him. He had been a wonderful Chief Justice for four years. Although not a great lawyer like Tom Bingham, he was a very good lawyer. I can still hear him saying 'Don't forget common sense'. He was tough but humane, and an intensely practical man. I can still hear his resonant voice to this day.

During 2000, I began to think that I might be promoted to the Court of Appeal. I had enjoyed being a High Court Judge enormously and I had no particular desire to stop being one but I was ambitious and the challenge of the Court of Appeal was ever present. In the summer of 2000, there were several imminent vacancies.

On 5 June 2000, I received the following letter:

Dear Mr Justice Dyson,

There will be a vacancy for a Lord Justice of Appeal with effect from January 2001. I am writing to ask you if I might submit your name to The Queen for this appointment.

It would give me much pleasure to recommend your name to Her Majesty, but before doing so, I should be glad if you would let me know whether my proposal is acceptable to you.

I should be glad if, in the meantime, you would regard this matter as confidential.

Yours sincerely

Tony Blair

I had no hesitation in accepting this 'proposal'.

The letter had not been preceded by any discussion between me and the Lord Chancellor or any senior judge so far as I can recall.

9

The Court of Appeal

I F IN MY earlier life as a barrister, High Court Judges had seemed to be formidable and frightening, Lord Justices of the Court of Appeal seemed to be even more so. My appearances in the Court of Appeal had been rare and I did not know any judges of that court personally. My impression had been that all of them were extraordinarily clever and quick. If it had been suggested to me when I was a barrister that one day I would be a Lord Justice of Appeal, I would have regarded the suggestion as preposterous.

I was sworn in by Lord Irvine early in 2001 in one of the Lord Chancellor's rooms in the House of Lords. It was a very low-key private event which was over within a few minutes. I had been permitted to invite a few members of my immediate family to witness the swearing-in. I introduced them to Lord Irvine and did my best to encourage him to engage them in conversation but he seemed uninterested in doing so. Instead, he preferred to have a rather technical discussion with me about current legal issues. So my formal introduction into this august court was a disappointingly meagre affair.

All Lord Justices of Appeal become members of Her Majesty's Honourable Privy Council *ex officio*. I was appointed by Order on 14 February 2001 and the appointment was perfected when I was sworn by Her Majesty's command at Buckingham Palace on 14 March 2001. There were six of us who were sworn as members of the Privy Council at the same time. We were all somewhat nervous. Her Majesty was in sparkling form. In addition to administering our oaths, she selected the new High Sheriffs for the coming Shrieval Year. She did this by 'pricking' the appointee's name with a bodkin. Smilingly, she explained to us that the pricking tradition dates back to the sixteenth century. It seems that Princess Elizabeth I was at Hatfield House when she was required to select the new High Sheriffs. No writing implements were available, so a bodkin was used to prick the names in order to signify the appointments. Her Majesty told us this story with great charm and, almost coquettishly, she undertook the pricking exercise with evident glee.

Another honour that followed soon after my appointment to the Court of Appeal was my election in June 2001 as an Honorary Fellow of Wadham College. I had not lost my starry-eyed admiration for the academic world. I was thrilled to receive such recognition from my *alma mater*. This achievement meant a great deal to me. I had come on a long journey since my first visit to Oxford with my parents when I was about 10 years old. Perhaps I would have been less excited about going to Wadham in the first place, and then being elected as an Honorary Fellow, if I had been to a famous public school and come from a more polished and traditional English background.

But what about the experience of sitting in the Court of Appeal (which I did from January 2001 until March 2010)? This was not an unusually long period in those days, when the retirement age for judges in the High Court and above was 75 and most judges stayed on until they reached that age. The retirement age was reduced to 70 for judges who were appointed after 31 March 1995. Nowadays, it is very common for judges to retire even before they reach retirement age, in order to start a new career. The result has been that many judges are now promoted more quickly than they were before the retirement age was reduced.

I found almost immediately that there was a great spirit of collegiality in the Court of Appeal. All the judges helped each other to get through the huge workload. On substantive appeals, they sat almost invariably in constitutions of three. As a result of the increasing pressures on the court, it is now far more common for there to be constitutions of two judges. The diet of work was immensely varied covering all aspects of the law – civil, criminal and family. Although the listing officer tried to ensure that at least one of the three judges had some specialist expertise in the subject-matter of the appeal, it was impossible and, in my view, undesirable for all three judges to be specialists in the subject-matter of the appeal.

This meant that all members of the court were exposed to appeals across the full range of the law and were expected to play a full part in every appeal even if the subject-matter was one with which they were not familiar. A good example of such a case was *Inland Revenue Commissioners v John Lewis Properties Plc* [2002] EWCA Civ 1869. The taxpayer company had purchased properties to be occupied by other companies within the same group. Having granted leases of the properties, they assigned the rental income for the first six years to a bank in return for a lump sum payment. The question was whether the payment was income or capital. The court was presided over by Lord Justice Schiemann (who was a specialist planning lawyer). The other two judges were Lady Justice Arden (who had sat in the Chancery Division and had therefore had some experience of tax cases, but, by background, had been a company law specialist) and myself. I had had no experience whatsoever of tax cases at the Bar or on the Bench. My experience of VAT cases as a High Court Judge was of no assistance. Understandably, Lord Justice Schiemann asked Lady Justice Arden to draft the leading judgment. In her draft, she concluded that the payment was income. I was not persuaded by her reasoning.

Unusually before writing a judgment, I had consulted Jacqueline because, unlike the three members of the court, she was an expert in the law of taxation: this was one of the subjects that she taught at UCL. To my frustration, she did not give me a clear answer to the question whether the payment was income or capital. Nor was she able to give me a clear and simple set of criteria by which that question could be resolved. She said that it was a difficult question and there was no easy way to answer it. So I produced a draft judgment of my own in which I explained why I had reached the conclusion that the payment was capital and why I disagreed with Lady Justice Arden. Rather ambitiously, I set out some factors which I said were relevant to determining whether a payment was income or capital.

My draft judgment evoked a response from Lord Justice Arden. She amended her draft, taking account of my criticisms of her reasoning, but stood her ground: she continued to maintain that the payment was income. I was no more convinced by her second attempt than by her first. But I had to amend my draft to take account of her revised draft. Nothing daunted, she returned to the fray and amended her draft yet again, expressing gratitude to me for enabling her to improve her draft yet further. I was still not persuaded by her reasoning. But once again, I had to revise my draft to take account of her latest reasoning and explain why I did not agree with it and why I remained of the view that the payment was capital. Thankfully, the ping pong match ended there. Lord Justice Schiemann wrote the briefest of judgments saying that he agreed with me.

Such toing and froing was most unusual in my experience. I mention this case because it is a good illustration of the way in which judges who are not expert in a particular field bring to bear their general skill of legal analysis to all cases. It would probably have been better if one of the members of the court had had real expertise in tax law. But the non-specialist can sometimes bring insights to a problem which the expert is unable to do.

Another case in which I wrote the lead judgment in an area with which I had had no familiarity was *Paragon Finance Plc v Nash* [2001] EWCA Civ 1466. Paragon claimed possession from Mr and Mrs Nash for late mortgage repayments. The rate of interest was variable at Paragon's discretion. The Bank of England lowered its interest rate, but Paragon did not 'pass on' the lower interest rate. Mr and Mrs Nash argued that the interest rates were 'extortionate' under the Consumer Credit Act 1974. I wrote the lead judgment. I held that it was an implied term of the contract that the power to vary the interest rate had to be exercised in a rational and honest way. This was a point on which there had been no previous authority. In fact, I said that the bank was acting reasonably in protecting its interests and had not acted in breach of the implied term. I subsequently received a letter from Professor Sir Roy Goode QC (Professor of Commercial Law at Oxford who was an expert in the law of consumer credit) agreeing with my approach. This was an example of having to grapple with an area of the law without any specialist knowledge and relying on my knowledge of general legal principles. It was particularly challenging in that case because the other members of the court were specialists in family law (Lord Justice Thorpe) and criminal law (Mr Justice Astill). Occasionally a High Court Judge (such as Mr Justice Astill) was asked to sit as an *ad hoc* judge to make up the numbers.

During my nine years in the Court of Appeal, I sat on countless appeals. Many of them raised difficult issues of law. There were few easy cases. This was largely because it was necessary for a would-be appellant to obtain permission to appeal either from the judge whose decision they wished to appeal or more usually from the Court of Appeal itself. Permission was only given where an appeal had real prospects of success or for some other compelling reason. Much time was spent dealing with applications for permission to appeal. This was the least attractive aspect of the work of a Lord Justice of Appeal. All applications were first dealt with by a single judge on the papers. These applications kept coming relentlessly. Some of them were complex and time-consuming. If permission was refused, there was a right to renew the application at an oral hearing before one or, in a particularly difficult case, two judges. These oral applications were heard before the main work of the day. They involved much preparation. Over time, the increase in the volume of applications for permission to appeal overwhelmed the court. One of the changes that we introduced when I became Master of the Rolls was to limit the right to an oral renewal of an application for permission to appeal. This was a controversial change. It was seen as a serious erosion of the right of access to justice. But the court was overwhelmed with work and, as a result, the delays in hearing appeals were becoming a scandal. There was no money for increasing the number of judges. Something had to be done. But that is to leap ahead to the time when I was Master of the Rolls and President of the Court of Appeal. I should return to my first period in the court.

It would be tedious if I were to describe many of the appeals that I heard. Many are reported in the law reports. All of them are on various websites. I shall therefore confine myself to four cases which I believe are of general interest. The case of *Mbasogo, President of Equatorial Guinea v Logo Ltd and others* [2006] EWCA Civ 1370 arose from the failed coup by a number of persons, including Mark Thatcher (Margaret Thatcher's son), who were alleged to have attempted to overthrow the President of Equatorial Guinea. The President issued proceedings in England claiming damages and an injunction against the alleged perpetrators. The claim was dismissed by the judge at first instance. I sat on the appeal with the Master of the Rolls (Sir Anthony Clarke) and Lord Justice Moses. I wrote the part of the judgment which dealt with the question of whether the court had jurisdiction to entertain the claims. We held that, in bringing the claims, the President was doing an act which was of a sovereign character or by virtue of his sovereign authority, and for that reason the claims were not amenable to the jurisdiction of our courts.

An important previous authority that we had to consider was *Emperor of Austria v Day and Kossuth* (1861) 3 De GF & J 217. The defendants in that case had printed banknotes in London. Lajos Kossuth planned to introduce some of the banknotes into Hungary after he had overthrown the Emperor of the Austro-Hungarian Empire by revolution in 1848. The Emperor issued proceedings in our courts and obtained an injunction restraining the defendants from manufacturing the banknotes. One of the defences advanced was that the injunction should be refused because the proceedings were brought to protect the Emperor's political power and prerogatives.

The *Emperor of Austria* case was difficult to interpret. But I was excited and fascinated by it. First, I had not encountered any reference to Kossuth since 1958 when I was studying the European revolutions of 1848 for my History 'O' level examination. Secondly, any reference to the Austro-Hungarian Empire tapped into my family roots. Thirdly, I thought that it was remarkable that an English court in the early twenty-first century should be required to interpret and apply a mid-nineteenth-century legal authority. This was a very practical exposure to English legal history.

The other feature of this case that made it so memorable for me was the fact that the President was represented by Sir Sydney Kentridge QC, who by now was in his mid-80s. Sir Sydney had played a leading role in a number of the most significant political trials in South Africa during the apartheid era. These included the treason trial of Nelson Mandela and the inquest into the death of Steve Biko. He had practised at the English Bar with great distinction since 1977. He was the finest appellate advocate I encountered throughout my career at the Bar and on the Bench. His presentation of the appeal in the *Mbasogo* case was brilliant. His mastery of the legal authorities and the clarity of his exposition of the law (largely without a note) was spell-binding. It was a privilege to have witnessed it.

Two of the remaining three cases were decided by a court comprising Lord Woolf LCJ, Lord Justice Laws and myself. The first was the case of *A v B plc (Flitcroft) v MGN Ltd* [2002] EWCA Civ 337. The claimant, Gary Flitcroft, who was a married Premier League footballer, sought an injunction to prevent the defendant newspaper from publishing information concerning sexual relationships that he had had with two women who wished to sell their stories to the press. The case raised important questions about the extent of his right to privacy. The judge had granted him an injunction. We allowed the defendant's appeal. The case was an early example of our courts grappling with the weighing of a person's privacy rights under article 8 of the European Convention on Human Rights against the right to freedom of expression of the press under article 10. We said that, as mandated by section 12(4) of the Human Rights Act, it was necessary for the court to have particular regard to the importance of freedom of expression. Any interference with the freedom of the press had to be justified.

We then said that the position of public figures was different from that of private individuals. A public figure has less ground to object to intrusion into his private life, not least because his public standing may make him a role model. Our judgment continued:

> In many of these situations, it would be overstating the position to say that there is a public interest in the information being published. It would be more accurate to say

that the public have an understandable and so legitimate interest in being told the information. If this is the situation, then it can be appropriately taken into account by a Court when deciding on which side of the line a case falls. The Courts must not ignore the fact that if newspapers do not publish information which the public are interested in, there will be fewer newspapers published, which will not be in the public interest.

This statement has been criticised in subsequent judgments in our courts, I now think with some justification. It was inconsistent with the subsequent decision of the Strasbourg Court in *Von Hannover v Germany* (2005) 40 EHRR 1. The European Court said that the decisive factor in balancing the protection of private life against freedom of expression should lie in the contribution that the published material makes to a debate of legitimate general interest. Since then, our courts have addressed the issue on several occasions and have refined the correct approach to the carrying out of this difficult balancing exercise. Despite the criticisms that can be made of what we said in *A v B*, we did point the way forward in this difficult area of the law. At that time, our courts did not have much experience of handling claims for breach of Convention rights. During the following 15 years, I had to decide many such cases. A hallmark of many of them was that they involved the balancing of competing considerations. The exercise was particularly difficult if the considerations were not commensurate with each other.

The second case was *R v Secretary of State for the Home Department, ex parte Amin* [2002] EWCA Civ 390. This concerned the claim that the refusal by the Home Secretary to conduct an investigation into the death of Zahid Mubarek while he was at Feltham Young Offender Institution was a breach of the duty to investigate certain deaths that is imposed by article 2 of the European Convention on Human Rights. Mr Mubarek had been murdered by a fellow inmate with whom he shared a cell.

There had been no inquest. But there had been a police investigation and an internal examination by Feltham of its regime, both of which were conducted in private and without the involvement of Mr Mubarek's family. The killer had also been tried for murder, but the trial did not explore the wider issues relating to the death. Nevertheless, we felt that these processes were sufficient to satisfy the requirements of article 2 and allowed the appeal. So we dismissed the claim. The House of Lords disagreed: [2003] UKHL 51. Lord Bingham gave the principal speech which he concluded by saying that he could not accept that a further inquiry was unlikely to unearth new and significant facts. And how prescient that turned out to be. The subsequent Inquiry chaired by Mr Justice Keith led to a thorough report describing many serious shortcomings in Feltham which had not previously been exposed. These included the systemic racism that had led to the shocking decision that Mr Zubarek should share his cell with a known racist. Our decision, which I thought was clearly right at the time, was demonstrated to be badly wrong.

Malvine Kremsier nee Goldstein

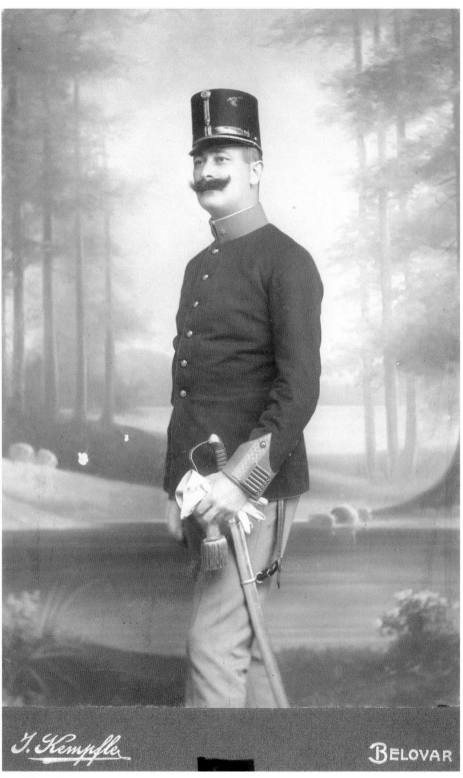

J. Kempfle   BELOVAR

Jeno Kremsier

Louis and Freda Dytch and their five children, my father second from left

As a baby

My parents, Robert and me circa 1948

Playing cricket in garden at home

At our wedding 5 July 1970

My family on my taking silk April 1982

My family after my being sworn in as high court judge, March 1993

Steven and me above Haute-Nendaz in 2006

Jacqueline and me above Haute-Nendaz in 2011

Justices of the Supreme Court 2011

Justice of the Supreme Court

After being sworn in as Master of the Rolls by Lord Judge, Lord Chief Justice, October 2012

Honorary LLD at UCL with Jacqueline September 2014

Middle Temple Coat of Arms

With Her Majesty at Runnymede 15 June 2015

With Prince William at Middle Temple 31 October 2017

Grandchildren 2018
Photograph by James Shaw

Leeds Grammar School

My portrait 2012

The final case was *R (Wood) v Commissioner of Police of the Metropolis* [2009] EWCA Civ 414. The claimant was a media co-ordinator for the Campaign against Arms Trade. He was photographed by the police on the street outside the annual general meeting of a company whose subsidiary had organised a trade fair for the arms industry. The photographs were taken to enable the police to identify potential offenders in case offences were committed at the meeting and potential offenders at the trade fair. Lord Justice Lawrence Collins and I held (Lord Justice Laws dissenting) that the taking of the photographs was a violation of the claimant's personal autonomy rights under article 8(1) of the Convention on Human Rights, but that the taking and retention of the photographs were justified under article 8(2) as being in pursuit of the legitimate aim of preventing disorder or crime. However, there was no justification for the police retaining the photographs for more than a few days: once it had become clear that the claimant had not committed any offence at the meeting, there was no reasonable basis for fearing that he might commit an offence. I mention this case partly because it attracted a certain amount of public interest as cases involving the police often do; and partly because it was a good illustration of the court working with the Convention. I greatly enjoyed human rights cases. But this was not the kind of law that our judicial predecessors had to apply. It was a far cry from lawyers' 'black letter' law and the issues were readily intelligible to the intelligent layperson.

The work of our courts generally during the early part of the twenty-first century was shaped by two major events. The first of these was the passing of the Human Rights Act 1998 which came into force on 2 October 2000. This incorporated the European Convention on Human Rights into our domestic law in a very subtle way. The interpretation of the 1998 Act took a great deal of working out, mainly by the Appellate Committee of the House of Lords (the predecessor of the Supreme Court). Our courts were required by section 2 to take into account judgments of the European Court of Human Rights (the Strasbourg Court). That court has adopted an expansionist approach to the interpretation of the Convention (describing it as a 'living instrument'). The result has been that the jurisprudence of the Strasbourg Court has had an enormous influence on the development of our own law in recent years. Many of the most important cases in which I was involved for the rest of my judicial career were human rights cases. I shall refer to several more of them in the next two chapters.

The other major event was Lord Woolf's civil procedure reforms which were given statutory effect by the Civil Procedure Act 1997 and the Civil Procedure Rules which applied to all cases commenced after 26 April 1999. The object of the reforms was to improve the efficiency of the conduct of civil litigation; wrest control of cases from the parties and place it firmly in the hands of the judges; control the cost of litigation; and generally get rid of many of its archaisms. An example of such an archaism was the word 'plaintiff' which was replaced by 'claimant'.

The reforms undoubtedly had a substantial impact on the way in which civil litigation was conducted and had many beneficial effects. But the reforms were not entirely successful. The cost of litigation continued to rise unabated. Such were the concerns about the spiralling cost of litigation that in 2009 Sir Anthony Clarke, as Master of the Rolls, commissioned Sir Rupert Jackson (a Lord Justice of Appeal) to conduct a review of civil litigation costs. The Jackson report was produced in 2010. And quite apart from the rising cost of litigation, there are many who believe that the civil procedure rules have become far too complicated and I agree with them.

Lord Woolf has been one of the giants of the legal firmament of the late twentieth and early twenty-first centuries. He is a man of great energy, vision and imagination. Now in his mid-80s, he is still working hard and in much demand. He has always been extremely kind and encouraging to me. He was Lord Chief Justice when I was appointed to the Court of Appeal. Although his civil procedure reforms did not achieve everything that he might have wished, they did effect a sea-change in the way in which civil litigation is conducted in our country. He had to face considerable resistance and, from some quarters, downright and even personal hostility which I thought was unfair and unjustified.

I need to say more about civil procedure. I was appointed as Deputy Head of Civil Justice with effect from 1 September 2003. Lord Phillips of Worth Matravers was Master of the Rolls and Head of Civil Justice at the time. I therefore became his deputy in relation to the civil justice system. I worked closely with him in this onerous role. This was my second administrative job (the first having been Head of the TCC). I never considered myself to be a natural administrator, but I have always found it difficult to say no. The most important element of this new job was being de facto chairman of the Civil Procedure Rule Committee. The titular chairman is the Master of the Rolls. But Lord Phillips made it clear that he wanted to leave the running of the committee to me. The committee, whose establishment was one of the Woolf reforms, usually meets every four weeks, and comprises judges from all levels of the judiciary, barristers, solicitors and lay persons. The work was demanding and there was plenty of it. Draft rules were prepared by professional drafters who were employed by the Government. The quality of the drafting was excellent. But no detail was too small for the hawk-eyes of the excellent hard-working committee and many improvements were made to the drafting at committee meetings.

When I was appointed Deputy Head of Civil Justice, there was still work to be done to transpose relevant pre-Woolf rules into the new rule regime. And then there was a steady stream of new legislation which required new procedural rules to govern any litigation to which it gave rise. It was also necessary to keep existing rules under review and make changes where these were considered to be necessary. An example was the rules relating to offers to settle claims. Traditionally, the only way a defendant could protect itself against having to pay costs in the event that the claimant succeeded in a money claim was to pay into court a sum which exceeded the amount the claimant was awarded at the end of the case. Initially, this system was replicated in the new Civil Procedure Rules (CPR), although they also allowed the court to order that an offer to settle was to have the same costs consequences as a payment into court. But eventually, the committee decided after consultation that it made no sense to require a defendant to make a payment into court. The rationale for the rule was not to provide the claimant with security for any judgment that it was awarded, but to enable the defendant to protect itself against costs in the event that the claimant was awarded a money judgment and thereby to encourage parties to settle their cases. So rule 36 was amended to remove any reference to a payment into court and to provide an elaborate set of rules for the making and acceptance of offers.

Many other procedural changes were made during my time as Deputy Head of Civil Justice. This is not the place to describe them in any detail. One change that I recall vividly was the introduction of hearings by telephone. There was much opposition, particularly from some of the procedural judges, to the idea of judges conducting short hearings (usually of procedural applications) by telephone conference. The opponents thought that it was essential for the judge to be able to see the whites of the eyes of the advocates. There was a real fear that the judge would find the whole process confusing and be unable to tell who was speaking on behalf of which party. Today, such objections seem laughable. But at the time they were serious and they called for sensitive handling. First, the committee made a rule authorising a trial pilot scheme in a small number of courts. Extraordinarily, this lasted a whole year. It was only when the pilot was successfully completed that the committee made rules for the introduction of telephone hearings throughout the country.

I witnessed a telephone hearing at first hand in Newcastle during one of my periodic visits to the principal regional courts. The judge heard an application in which one party was represented by a solicitor in Bristol and the other by a solicitor in Birmingham. Neither he nor I had any difficulty in identifying the advocates or working out who was speaking for whom at any given time. I could not understand what all the fuss had been about.

I regarded making regional visits as an important part of my role as Deputy Head of Civil Justice. They seemed to be greatly appreciated. I hoped that they went some way to dispelling the idea that the senior people in London had no interest in what went on north of Watford. I met the local judges and court staff as well as local practitioners. I listened to their complaints, which were usually about the lack of resources, and their suggestions for procedural improvements. Occasionally, I was able to make changes to meet their concerns. But my powers were limited.

One of the Woolf reforms was to create the post of Designated Civil Judge (DCJ). The DCJs are responsible for general civil work throughout the country and have a pastoral responsibility for the civil judiciary in their area.

Each year, a two-day conference is held at Warwick University for the DCJs. This is organised by the Deputy Head of Civil Justice. An important part of the role included managing the DCJs and attempting to deal with their concerns and complaints.

My appointment as Deputy Head of Civil Justice consolidated my reputation as a judge who decided civil procedure appeals. Throughout my time in the Court of Appeal, I heard many such cases, often with Lord Justice Brooke. He was Vice-President of the Court of Appeal (Civil). He was interested in civil procedure and often asked me to sit with him on civil procedure appeals. The Woolf reforms and the complex changes to the law relating to costs led to many appeals in which the Court of Appeal had to interpret and clarify the law in these important areas. I wrote many of the leading judgments. Many years later in December 2013, I was flattered to receive a letter from Adrian Zuckerman, the Professor of Civil Procedure at Oxford University, in which he wrote:

> The number of judgments you have delivered over the years in the field of procedure is so large that there is a good chance of coming upon one of them by opening at random the new edition of my book which I enclose.
>
> With deep admiration for the role you have played in shaping the subject.

Professor Zuckerman was the leading academic in the field of procedural law. His book *Zuckerman on Civil Procedure: Principles of Practice* is a *vade mecum* for any judge who has a civil procedure problem.

I found the increasing complexity of the law relating to costs particularly depressing. The wholesale withdrawal of legal aid in civil litigation led to alternative methods of funding. The most important of these was by means of conditional fee agreements. The consequence of these and other changes was a massive increase in the amount of litigation *about costs*. This in turn led to the emergence of a group of barristers who were costs specialists and even, in due course, to the Costs Law Reports and conferences devoted exclusively to costs.

Managing the Rule Committee was not the only function that I had to perform as Deputy Head of Civil Justice. One of the important Woolf reforms was the setting up of the Civil Justice Council (CJC). The chair of the CJC is the Master of the Rolls and Head of Civil Justice and the deputy chair is the Deputy Head of Civil Justice. The CJC comprises members of the judiciary, members of the legal professions, civil servants concerned with the administration of the courts and various laypersons who have relevant knowledge and expertise.

It advises the Lord Chancellor on civil justice and civil procedure in England and Wales. It keeps the civil justice system under review and, since its inception, has been the engine of some of the most important changes to our system. Many of the reforms to the rules on costs were the result of work done by and under the auspices of the CJC during the tenure of Lord Phillips. To give a later example, in February 2015 it published a report written by Professor Richard Susskind entitled 'Online Dispute Resolution for Low Value Civil Claims'. The report was launched by me that year when I was Master of the Rolls. It was accepted by the Lord Chancellor and formed the basis of the work on an online court that followed. The CJC conducts research and consults widely. In my view, it has been a great success. As the resources made available by the Treasury to the Department have shrunk over the years, so increasingly the Department has turned to the CJC and to the judiciary for assistance in relation to issues of civil justice. Its members are volunteers. It is a tribute to their public spirit that they are willing to work so hard for the general good, doing much work that in my view should be done by the Department.

In addition to my work on the Rule Committee and the CJC, for a time my role as Deputy Head of Civil Justice led to my being an unofficial and rather peripheral member of the inner group of the most senior judges, which was informally called 'the judicial family'. I used to attend some of the meetings of the Heads of Division who are the Lord Chief Justice; Master of the Rolls; President of the Queen's Bench Division of the High Court; Head of the Chancery Division of the High Court (Vice-Chancellor as he was then called); and President of the Family Division. I also attended their meetings with the Lord Chancellor to discuss senior judicial appointments. This was in the days before the creation of the Judicial Appointments Commission in April 2006. I now saw from the inside how appointments such as my own were made. The Heads of Division made bids for numbers to fill vacancies in their courts. And then names were discussed. That was the interesting bit for a newcomer like me. On one occasion, I spoke in support of a judge who was being considered for promotion to the Court of Appeal and who was later to become a Justice of the Supreme Court. I had long been an admirer of his work which I considered to be outstanding. But one of the Heads of Division disagreed on the ground that he was insufficiently collegiate. This view prevailed and was sufficient to lead to his rejection. Another (in my view) less able candidate was preferred. I was rather shocked by this. It demonstrated the shortcomings of the traditional method of appointing judges. The view of one senior judge could carry disproportionate weight. This is far less likely to happen under the new regime, which despite its unfortunate bureaucratic overload, is much fairer than its predecessor.

One weekend each year, the judicial family retreated from London to discuss current issues of importance. During my time as Deputy Head of Civil Justice, we went to a hotel in Minster Lovell, an attractive village in Oxfordshire. I recall one such weekend when our morning session was interrupted by a telephone call from the Lord Chancellor (Lord Falconer) to the Lord Chief Justice (Lord Woolf). On his return to the meeting, Lord Woolf told us that the Government had decided to make some momentous constitutional changes. These were to find expression in the Constitutional Reform Act 2005. The most significant of them was to reform the office of the Lord Chancellor so that the office-holder would no longer be head of the judiciary (a role now to be assumed by the Lord Chief Justice) or be eligible to sit as a judge; to create the Supreme Court in place of the Appellate Committee of the House of Lords as the highest UK court; and to create the Judicial Appointments Commission. These were breathtaking changes. From now on, it was the senior judiciary, under the leadership of the Lord Chief Justice, who were to run the justice system. I was later to discover when I became Master of the Rolls that the relationship between the senior judiciary and the civil servants was not an easy one. But for the time being, these constitutional changes did not unduly affect my life.

I retired as Deputy Head of Civil Justice in December 2006. It had been hard work to combine all the functions of that post with being a full-time member of the Court of Appeal. I was pleased to stop after more than three years and to be able to concentrate on what I enjoyed so much: hearing appeals and writing judgments.

So far I have given the impression that everything I did related to civil justice. In addition to being Deputy Head of Civil Justice, the majority of the appeals on which I had sat were civil appeals. But I also heard criminal appeals in the CACD and a variety of both criminal and civil cases in the Divisional Court. I usually sat in the CACD for a period of three weeks each term. As I have already described, I had sat in the CACD when I was a High Court Judge. As a Lord Justice of Appeal, I had to preside over the criminal appeals. At first, I found this a daunting prospect. Those who made the listing decisions ensured, at least early on, that I sat with a High Court Judge and/or a circuit judge who was experienced in criminal law. But it did not take me long to settle down to presiding in these cases. The seasoned criminal judges seemed to like my rather rigorous approach to the work. Occasionally, however, they made it quite clear that they did not agree with what they considered to be my rather 'soft' approach to sentencing. If I was outvoted by my tougher colleagues, I succumbed with good grace. There could only be one judgment.

I heard some interesting criminal appeals. One of these involved the conviction of three teenage girls for the manslaughter of Aimee, a 15-year-old aspiring ballet dancer who was set upon by the three girls. Aimee ran away, but owing to a heart condition of which not even her family were aware, she suffered a heart attack and died. We held that, because the heart condition was unknown and Aimee was an apparently healthy young girl, this was not a case of dangerous act manslaughter. I found this a difficult and very troubling case. I realised that our decision was bound to cause great upset to Aimee's family, but it seemed to all three of us that the convictions for manslaughter had to be quashed and replaced by ones for affray.

For understandable reasons those who made the listing decisions tended to give the really challenging and important criminal appeals to the judges who were steeped in criminal law. On the whole, most of the appeals against conviction that I heard were rather routine affairs involving challenges based on alleged flaws in a summing-up. Many of these were very dull and involved ploughing through a great deal of paper. But there was usually at least one interesting case during the three weeks. The combination of that and the fact that I enjoyed sitting with High Court and circuit judges some of whom I did not know was sufficient to dissuade me from asking, as some of my colleagues had done, whether I could be excused from further sitting in the CACD.

The meetings of the judicial family with Lord Falconer, to decide on judicial appointments, took place in the House of Lords. On one occasion, I had to leave the meeting because I had been summoned across Parliament Square to do jury service in what was then the Middlesex Guildhall Crown Court, in the building which is now occupied by the Supreme Court. Historically, judges and other lawyers were not eligible to serve on a jury. But with effect from April 2004, that was changed. I believe that I was the first English judge to serve. I was curious and somewhat apprehensive to see how it worked. I had decided not to tell my fellow jurors that I was a judge unless I was directly asked what I did for a living. One of my colleagues in the Court of Appeal who was summoned a little later to serve on a jury told me that, when asked what he did, he replied 'a bit of this and a bit of that'. I did not think it right to adopt such a coy approach. Fortunately, I was not asked the question by any of my fellow jurors.

On my arrival at court, I was shown an excellent video of what happens in a jury trial in a crown court. Naturally, I did not divulge that I had in fact presided over a considerable number of such trials. There followed a prolonged period of waiting for something to happen. Indeed, my abiding recollection of the whole experience was that much time was spent waiting and doing so in fairly uncomfortable surroundings.

Eventually, we were ushered into a court and together with 11 others I was selected to serve on a jury to try a man who was charged with assaulting a person in a fracas on a train. The prosecution case was that three men were involved in the incident and that the complainant was set upon by the other two. Only one of these two had been apprehended. The other man was never found. He too would have been in the dock if he had been found. The case took about two days. The only issue was whether, as he alleged, the defendant had acted in self-defence. In practice, this required us to decide, as between the defendant and the complainant, who was the aggressor. It was a straightforward case. The Recorder tried it impeccably. I did not know him, but I subsequently discovered that he had been told by one of the other judges of the court, no doubt to his dismay, that I was one of the jurors in this case. This may have contributed to the superb quality of his summing up. Quite correctly, he directed us not to speculate on why the third man was not before the court and instead to concentrate exclusively on the defendant and the complainant: the position of the third man was irrelevant. He concluded his summing up by telling us to appoint a foreman and consider our verdict.

Section 8 of the Contempt of Court Act 1981 makes it an offence to disclose any opinions or statements made by jurors in the course of their deliberations. I am, therefore, not at liberty to disclose how I was appointed foreman. Nor should I say that, in acquitting the defendant, the jury defied the clear ruling of the Recorder. In hindsight, I should probably have held out for a conviction and insisted on the jury bringing in a majority verdict. But we were not trying a grave charge and there seemed to be little point in doing so.

It was a most salutary experience to serve on a jury. First, it confirmed my view that juries will sometimes decide a case contrary to the law in the wider interests of what they conceive to be fair and just. Secondly, even in the simplest of cases, it is difficult to retain a grasp of the detail. I made a full note of the evidence. Most of my fellow jurors made no note at all: they simply relied on their memories and the general impression that they had formed. Thirdly, in this simple case, the judge was required to give the jury a large number of rather technical directions even before he reached the stage of reminding them of the salient parts of the evidence. Listening to them, I had no doubt that many of these directions went straight over the heads of most if not all of the jurors. Fourthly, the jury room was cramped and Spartan. Fortunately, we were only incarcerated in it for a short time. But it would have been unpleasant to have to spend many hours there.

Following this rather dispiriting experience, I hoped for better things in another trial. Together with a group of other would-jurors, I presented myself in the court of the Resident Judge, Judge Fabyan Evans. I had sat with him for three weeks in the CACD. That was the extent of my acquaintance of him. My name was called out. The judge looked up and said that I should stand down: 'This man is well known to me'. As I walked disconsolately away, the woman who was standing next to me in the group of would-be jurors asked: 'What you done, then?' I thought that the Resident Judge was entirely wrong to reject me and I wrote to the Lord Chief Justice (Lord Woolf) to say so. It seemed to me that Judge Evans had no reasonable grounds to refuse to allow me to serve on his jury. It was obvious that he did not want me scrutinising his work. I asked Lord Woolf to issue guidance to the judiciary to define the kind of compelling reasons that would justify refusing to allow a judge to serve on a jury. The rather vague guidance that Lord Woolf issued seemed to me to be too weak.

Not long afterwards, I was told by the crown court office that I would not be required to sit the following week. I was not given the reason. I had learnt quite a lot from my experience. When conducting criminal trials in the past, I had always tried to show consideration to juries. If I had still been a High Court Judge, I think I would have shown them even more understanding.

I enjoyed my nine years in the Court of Appeal enormously. After a few years, occasionally I started to preside in civil appeals. This was harder work than being a 'winger'. It was a convention that the presiding judge decided in advance which Lord Justice to ask to write the leading judgment. The position in the Supreme Court tends to be different. It is incumbent on the presider to ensure that there is a fair distribution of leading judgments among the judges. The presider is expected to control the pace of the appeal and make sure, so far as possible, that it is completed within the time that has been allocated for the hearing.

I cannot recall when I first thought that I might be a possible candidate for the House of Lords/Supreme Court. In 2009, Lord Clarke of Stone-cum-Ebony was coming to the end of his term as Master of the Rolls: he had succeeded Lord Phillips who had become the first President of the Supreme Court in October 2009. So there was a vacancy for the office of Master of the Rolls. By this time, the Judicial Appointments Commission was in harness. From now on, all judicial appointments were made on the recommendation of the Commission following an application by the would-be candidate. David Neuberger had been promoted to the House of Lords as a Lord of Appeal in Ordinary in 2007. He had decided to apply to become the next Master of the Rolls. I was pressed to throw my hat into the ring and agreed to do so, although I thought that David was obviously favourite to be appointed. I believe that there were no other candidates. David was duly appointed. I knew that he would be excellent as he turned out to be. I was not especially disappointed, not least because I was still struggling to shake off the post-viral fatigue (or ME) with which I had been afflicted for several months. In fact, I did not finally shake off this illness for about two years. It was hugely sapping of my energy. I was just about able to cope with work and little else. It was a very difficult time for both Jacqueline and me. The doctors were unable to explain what caused the condition or say whether, and if so when, I would recover from it. This led to a period of intense introspection and anxiety and ultimately depression. I had never suffered from depression before and have not done so since. The experience gave me a real insight into this terrible mental illness.

A few months later, there was a vacancy in the Supreme Court. Although I was not yet fully restored to good health, I decided to apply. There were several other candidates. One of them was Jonathan Sumption QC (who was later to be appointed to the Supreme Court). But there was a good deal of opposition to the idea of appointing a candidate straight from the Bar, even one as brilliant as Jonathan. In the end, he withdrew his application. I had to submit an application and present myself for an interview at the Supreme Court on a Saturday morning. I had no idea what questions I would be asked and I have almost no recollection of what I was asked. But I do recall volunteering to the panel at the end of the interview that they might be interested to know that the last time I had set foot in that building was when I served as a juror in the Middlesex Guildhall Crown Court. The fact that I mentioned it was an indication of how relaxed I was about the whole business. At all events, in due course I was told that I had been successful.

And so nine very happy years in the Court of Appeal came to a close. I was very excited about the prospect of sitting in the highest court of the United Kingdom.

I had come far from my origins in Leeds, not to mention Lithuania and Bulgaria. I had little idea of what life would be like in Parliament Square. One of the letters of congratulation that I received was from the late Justice Antonin Scalia, Assistant Justice of the US Supreme Court. He wrote that at long last I would never have to worry about being overturned by a higher court. As we shall see, that immunity from reversal was to last only 30 months.

10

The Supreme Court

M<small>Y</small> <small>APPOINTMENT TOOK</small> effect from 12 April 2010. I was the first person to be appointed to the Supreme Court who had not been a Life Peer and a member of the House of Lords. This was the result of the separation of powers which was brought about by the Constitutional Reform Act 2005.

At the outset, I was 'Sir John Dyson SCJ'. Since all my colleagues were known as 'Lord X' or 'Lady Y', this made me feel uncomfortable. It was as if I was a second tier Justice. After an unconscionably long time, it was agreed that I would be given the courtesy title of 'Lord Dyson'.

I was sworn in as a Justice of the Supreme Court by the President, Lord Phillips. The swearing-in took place in open court. It was a very formal and rather brief affair. This was in marked contrast to the more elaborate process, which includes several speeches, that is now routinely adopted when any person is appointed to a senior judicial position. I was particularly disappointed by the jejune ceremony that was followed in my case because, owing to the cancellation of flights, my daughter Michelle and her husband Jonathan had had great difficulty in returning from their holiday in Sicily to London in time for the swearing-in.

My appointment was generally well received in the legal profession. In an article in *The Times*, Frances Gibb (its legal correspondent) wrote that my appointment would be welcomed widely: 'He is both popular and talented, a construction lawyer by background with ability and a humane touch'. I received an extraordinarily large number of letters and cards congratulating me and wishing me well. It was all very exciting.

I found the atmosphere of the Supreme Court very different from that of the Court of Appeal. It made a huge difference that there were only 12 of us, as compared with the 38 members of the Court of Appeal. In the Court of Appeal, we usually sat in constitutions of three. In the Supreme Court, the default number of justices to hear an appeal was five. Most of the time, the justices of the Supreme Court lunched together in the dining-room in the court building in Parliament Square. There was no such dining-room in the Royal Courts of Justice in the Strand. Most of the members of the Court of Appeal had lunch in their Inns or a sandwich in their rooms. These differences were less trivial than they might seem. The result was that the Justices of the Supreme Court spent far more time in each other's company than did the members of the Court of Appeal.

It was something of a mystery to me how it was decided which Justice was to sit on which appeal. So far as I was concerned, there was no question of making a bid to sit on an appeal that caught my fancy, still less making a plea not to sit on an appeal that did not interest me. I believe that constitutions were proposed by the Registrar, Louise di Mambro, to the Deputy President and the President. It was they who made the final decisions.

The atmosphere in the Supreme Court was rather intense. At the beginning, I was rather lonely and felt under pressure to perform well. Even more than when I was in the Court of Appeal, I sensed that each contribution to the exchanges with counsel during an appeal and each judgment that I wrote was a test in which I would be judged by my very clever colleagues. I had the impression that at least some of them wrote judgments to impress each other and to win colleagues over to their point of view. I may have been guilty of this myself. Over time, I gained in confidence. But it did take time.

Most of the Justices kept the doors of their offices open. In this way, they were in effect issuing a standing invitation to passers-by to drop in for a chat. I certainly did. Individually, my colleagues were friendly and welcoming. I would single out for particular mention as warmly welcoming me Lord Collins, Lord Kerr and, above all, Lord Rodger.

I had first met Alan Rodger at a common law conference in Edinburgh in 1999. He was Lord President at the time. He was a brilliant Roman Law scholar as well as an outstanding judge. His judgments, lectures and academic writings were expressed with crystalline clarity. They exhibited a calm intellectual sharpness and rigour. He had a great capacity for friendship. After a short battle with brain cancer, he died on 26 June 2011. He was 66 years of age and still in his prime. I shall never forget the day when at the lunch adjournment in an appeal in which both he and I were members of the constitution, he failed to get to his feet to leave the court in the usual way. He looked around in a state of confusion as if he did not know where he was. He had to be escorted out of the court and helped to find the dining room. Everyone was shocked. He never sat in the court again. After his death, a collection of essays in his memory was published by Oxford University Press. I contributed an essay entitled 'Some Reflections on Lord Rodger's Contribution to the Development of the Common Law'.

We heard a relatively small number of appeals each year. There was little distraction from the main business of hearing these important cases which usually raised interesting questions of law. It is true that we also had to determine petitions for permission to appeal, but there were not too many of these. We decided the petitions in groups of three. The test for giving permission to appeal was whether the case raised a point of law of general public importance or there was another compelling reason for giving permission to appeal. There was a strange convention that, if one of the three considered that permission should be given, it was given even if the other two thought that it should be refused. The criteria for granting permission to appeal were somewhat elastic.

The upshot was that permission to appeal was sometimes granted when it should not have been. But for the most part, the Supreme Court only hears truly important cases.

A striking feature of the appeals is that, on the whole, the quality of the legal submissions is very high. The arguments have been tested at least twice in lower courts and have been refined and improved. I know from my own limited experience of appearing in the Appellate Committee of the House of Lords that the advocate will be anxious to be on top form. He knows that he is unlikely to be able to hoodwink five judges of the highest court. Weaknesses in an argument are likely to be exposed and quickly. The advocate needs to be prepared to deal with any point that is put to him. Sometimes, arguments surface for the first time in the Supreme Court. And some of the arguments or issues that occupied the attention of the court below may have disappeared so that the appeal focuses only on one or two key points. Occasionally, an appeal is allowed on a point which was not argued (or was barely argued) in the court below. More frustrating for the judge whose decision is upheld for substantially the same reasons as those given by him or her is the judgment which does not even acknowledge that it substantially agrees with the lower court's reasoning. I regret to say that this happens quite often both in relation to appeals from the Court of Appeal to the Supreme Court and appeals from lower courts to the Court of Appeal.

In the Court of Appeal, I had been used to the idea that, if one was not writing the leading judgment, one should only write a separate judgment for good reason. A good reason would be that one disagreed with the conclusion of the leading judgment or that one disagreed with the reasoning of the leading judgment even if one agreed with its conclusion. But otherwise, one was discouraged from writing separate judgments. Writing them was an inefficient use of the time of a busy judge. Perhaps more importantly, an unnecessary multiplicity of judgments could make it difficult to work out the *ratio* or reasoning which formed the basis of the decision.

I soon found that things were rather different in the Supreme Court. The Justices were not under pressure to the same extent as the judges of the Court of Appeal. All senior judges like writing judgments in interesting cases. Since most of the cases in the Supreme Court were extremely interesting, the Justices were keen on writing judgments in most of the cases. That is what they had been appointed to do. I recall being encouraged by one of my colleagues to write judgments if I wanted to do so, even if I had not been asked to write the leading judgment, and I neither wanted to dissent nor to disagree substantially with the reasoning of the judge who had written the leading judgment. I should say that to some extent the practice of the Supreme Court has changed more recently. Single judgments are now more common than they were when I was there.

An extreme example of the problems created by multiple judgments was *Lumba v Secretary of State for the Home Department* [2011] UKSC 12. We sat as a nine-judge court. This was unusual. It was a measure of the complexity of the case and the fact that it raised a number of difficult issues. The main issue was whether and, if so, in what circumstances a breach of public law was capable of rendering unlawful the detention of foreign national prisoners pending their deportation so as to give rise to a private law action for false imprisonment. But there were several other issues too. I gave the lead judgment. The court was split three ways and most of the judges wrote substantive judgments. The result was so complicated that the official law reporter had great difficulty in writing the headnote for the official law reports which was intended to encapsulate the court's decision and reasoning. Unusually, she asked me (as the writer of the lead judgment) to approve her draft headnote. It took three drafts before she produced a text which I thought accurately summarised what the court had decided. To some extent, this was a reflection of the complexity of the case. But her task was made more difficult than it should have been by the fact that so many judges had written judgments. One interesting feature of this appeal was the fact that the earlier decision of Woolf J in *R v Secretary of State for the Home Department ex p Hardial Singh* [1984] 1 WLR 704 as modified by later authority was agreed by the parties to the appeal as the correct starting point. I drafted my judgment on that basis. But Lord Phillips wrote a judgment saying that Woolf J's decision was wrong. I responded by adding a piece to my judgment saying that it was not appropriate to depart from a decision which had been followed for almost 30 years unless it was obviously wrong (which I did not believe it to be), still less to do so without the benefit of adversarial argument. To my relief, Lord Phillips found no support from our colleagues for his view.

The other aspect of the process adopted in the Supreme Court which was markedly different from that of the Court of Appeal was the Justices' discussion at the end of the hearing. In the Court of Appeal, there was usually an unstructured informal discussion (sometimes in the corridor outside the court). Provisional views were expressed and the judge who had already been asked to write the lead judgment went away to produce a first draft. Occasionally the judge was able to give an *ex tempore* judgment. But as cases became more complex over the years, *ex tempore* judgments became a rarity.

In the Supreme Court, it was unusual in advance of the hearing for the presiding judge to ask a particular judge to write the lead judgment. Immediately after the conclusion of the hearing, we retired to the conference room to discuss the case. Each judge was asked in turn to express his or her views. The most junior member of the court invariably went first. This placed a considerable burden on that judge because they were expected not only to say immediately how they would decide the appeal, but also to give cogent reasons for their view. This meant marshalling their thoughts within a short time. I was the junior judge in the court for more than a year. I therefore had to bat first on many occasions. It is easier to come lower down the batting order, particularly where the later judge substantially agrees with the analysis of a more junior judge and can simply say so.

I remained in the Supreme Court from March 2010 until September 2012. During this period, I sat on a substantial number of appeals which raised important points of law. This is not the place to describe many of them. I shall mention a few some of which also attracted public attention. In the case of *HJ (Iran) v Secretary of State for the Home Department* [2010] UKSC 31 the appellants were gay men from Iran and Cameroon who had sought asylum in the United Kingdom on the grounds that, if returned to their home countries, they would face the risk of persecution on the grounds of their sexual orientation. It was established that, if they were returned, they would conceal their sexual orientation in order to avoid the risk of being persecuted. The Secretary of State argued that, since their sexual orientation was therefore unlikely to come to the attention of the authorities, they could not be said to have a well-founded fear of persecution unless concealing their sexuality was not reasonably tolerable. The lead judgment was given by Lord Rodger, although I wrote a substantial judgment of my own agreeing with his reasoning in my own words. We rejected the argument of the Secretary of State. We said that to compel a person to conceal his homosexuality was to deny him his fundamental right to be who he is. This was an important decision firmly rooting the Geneva Refugee Convention in the protection of human rights. I thought that it was totally unacceptable that a person should be compelled to conceal an essential aspect of his identity, namely his sexual orientation, as the price for avoiding persecution.

We applied the same approach in the later case of *RT (Zimbabwe) v Secretary of State for the Home Department* [2012] UKSC 38. This concerned the claims to asylum by persons who were politically neutral and did not support the persecutory regime in their home country Zimbabwe, but who had to feign loyalty to the regime in order to avoid persecution for not supporting it. Their claims for asylum in the United Kingdom were rejected. I gave the lead judgment dismissing the appeal of the Secretary of State. I said that anyone who has political beliefs and is obliged to conceal them in order to avoid persecution is in a position analogous to the homosexual men in *HJ (Iran)*. The right to freedom of thought and expression protects non-believers as well as believers and extends to the freedom *not* to hold and *not* to express opinions.

The facts in *Rabone v Pennine Care NHS Trust* [2012] UKSC 2 were tragic. Melanie Rabone had a history of depression. She was admitted to a hospital and diagnosed as suffering from a severe episode of a recurrent depressive disorder. After being discharged, she agreed to an informal admission to hospital. She was assessed as a moderate to high suicide risk. Melanie requested home leave for the weekend. A doctor agreed that she could go home despite the concerns expressed by her mother. Melanie went home and was later found hanging from a tree in a local park. The father issued proceedings claiming damages under article 2 (right to life) of the European Convention on Human Rights for breach of the positive obligation to take operational measures to prevent Melanie's suicide. The article 2 claim had been rejected by the Court of Appeal. We allowed Mr Rabone's appeal. I wrote the lead judgment. I said that the NHS Trust owed the operational duty to Melanie to take reasonable steps to protect her from the real and immediate risk of suicide and that it had acted in breach of that duty. This was an important case not least because it showed the influence of the Convention on the development of our law. Such a claim would not have succeeded under the common law. I regard this as a good example of the beneficent effect that the Convention has had on our law.

The case of *Assange v Swedish Prosecution Authority* [2012] UKSC 22 attracted much public interest. Julian Assange was the subject of a request for surrender by the English authorities under a European Arrest Warrant issued by the Swedish Prosecuting Authority for the purposes of an investigation into alleged criminal offences. He challenged the warrant on grounds which included that it had not been issued by a 'judicial authority' as required by EU law and the Extradition Act 2003. In dismissing the appeal, the Supreme Court held (by a majority of 5 to 2) that the meaning of 'judicial authority' was not limited to a judge so that the warrant had been validly issued. Lord Phillips wrote the lead judgment for the majority. He gave five reasons justifying his conclusion that the appeal should be dismissed. I circulated a draft judgment in which I rejected all but his fifth reason. Lord Phillips asked me to reconsider my rejection of his four other reasons, but I refused to do so. The other members of the court who favoured dismissing the appeal joined me in rejecting all but Lord Phillips' fifth reason.

Another case in which I was not afraid to take up a position and stick to it was *In re Lehman Bros International (Europe)* [2012] UKSC 6. This was a highly technical financial services case concerning the 'client money rules' and the 'client money distribution rules' contained in chapter 7 of the Client Asset Sourcebook for the safeguarding and distribution of client money in implementation of the Markets in Financial Instruments Directive 2004/39/EC. I was a long way out of my comfort zone in this case. We were in territory in which Lord Walker was far more at home than me. He circulated a draft judgment in which he concluded that the appeal should be allowed. I was not persuaded by his reasoning and drafted a dissenting judgment with which Lord Clarke and Lord Collins agreed. Mine therefore became the lead judgment. Lord Hope then circulated a judgment agreeing with Lord Walker and criticising my draft judgment in the most intemperate language. I was taken aback by the ferocity of his attack. In his final judgment, he toned down his criticisms, but he maintained that my judgment would leave the law in disarray, saying: 'The majority's decision makes investment banking more of a lottery than even its fiercest critics have supposed'. Attacks of this kind are rare amongst our judges. It was of considerable comfort to know that two of my colleagues agreed with me.

The last Supreme Court judgment to which I shall refer was in *Al Rawi v Security Service* [2011] UKSC 34. We sat as a panel of nine Justices. They included Lord Rodger, who died before judgment was given. The question that we had to decide was whether it was possible at common law to replace the doctrine of public interest immunity (whereby a judge decides whether in the public interest certain material should be excluded from a hearing) with a closed material procedure, where the parties are excluded from a hearing in which classified material is involved. To the extent that it is possible to do so, the parties' interests are protected at such a closed hearing by special advocates. At the conference after the conclusion of the hearing, it seemed that a majority of the court considered that the common law should evolve to include provision for a closed material procedure and that legislation to achieve that outcome was not necessary. Lord Clarke wrote a judgment in support of that view. I disagreed and wrote a contrary judgment saying that only Parliament could introduce such a procedure. My reasoning was substantially supported by several other members of the court.

Sometime after we had given judgment, I was delighted to receive a letter from Professor Zuckerman in which he wrote of my judgment in *Al Rawi:*

> It is one of the best judgments I have read, in terms of articulation of principle, clarity of thought, elegance and economy of language. It left me awed and, I am ashamed to say, not a little envious. I found particularly remarkable the fine balance between the thought process behind the decision and the use of authority. So often are the judgments weighed down by frequent and lengthy quotations that one loses sight of what the writer had in mind, which cannot be said of this judgment.

During my relatively short career in the Supreme Court, I wrote a substantial number of judgments. Perhaps too many. I hope that, even where the judgment was not a lead judgment, I added something that was worthwhile. In 2013, Professor Alan Paterson (Professor of Law and Director of the Centre for Professional Legal Studies at the Strathclyde University Law School) published his book *Final Judgment: The Last Law Lords and the Supreme Court.* This was the result of many interviews and included a painstakingly thorough and insightful analysis of the judgments of the last years of the Appellate Committee of the House of Lords and the early years of the Supreme Court.

I was greatly surprised to see what he wrote about my contribution to the work of the court. He referred to me as not being known for ducking challenges and as having 'bravely' taken on the lead judgment in *Lumba* and having criticised Lord Phillips in that case as well as in *Assange.* In retrospect, I suppose it was somewhat brave to criticise the president of the Supreme Court in this way.

And then he wrote this at page 164:

> However, there can be little doubt that the most successful task leader in the Supreme Court in its first three years was Lord Dyson. His overall agreement rate with his colleagues (90%) was equalled only by Lord Collins … It might be argued that such figures are compatible both with being a task leader and with being a follower of others' leads (who by indecision or changes of heart ended up on the majority side). The latter is not Lord Dyson. Lord Dyson wasted few opportunities to tell his colleagues (senior and junior) in his judgments precisely where he did and did

not agree with them … Lord Phillips was several times on the receiving end of such forensic broadsides … Yet in four or possibly other cases his attempts to write clear and persuasive dissent were so successful that they became the lead judgment. In his two years on the Court, no other Justice succeeded in bringing over so many votes to his side after the first conference. In all, Lord Dyson gave 14 lead or single judgments (21 per cent of his cases) ranking him (whilst he was a full-time member of the Court) as the most prolific lead writer after Lords Phillips and Hope.

At page 146 of his book, Professor Paterson explained the term 'task leadership' as focusing on 'persuading a majority on the court towards a particular outcome'.

I had certainly not thought of myself as being any kind of leader during my time in the Supreme Court. Nor did I try (as others have done) to persuade colleagues to my point of view by going into their offices and seeking to convince them by oral argument. I have always tried to write clear and reasonably succinct judgments. I think that such succinctness as I managed to achieve in my judgments owed a great deal to my classical education, in particular my study of Latin. It also owed much to the fact that I always typed my judgments and never learnt to touch type.

So far I have said nothing about the Judicial Committee of the Privy Council (JCPC). The JCPC is the court of final appeal for many Commonwealth countries, as well as the United Kingdom's overseas territories, crown dependencies and military sovereign base areas. Many of the JCPC cases on which I sat were criminal appeals which raised no point of law of general importance and were rather dull. I found that the civil appeals tended to be more interesting. Justices of the Supreme Court sit on JCPC appeals. Occasionally, there is a visit overseas to hear appeals in the court of the country from which the appeals have emanated. In 2012, I went to Mauritius on one of these visits. We stayed in a smart hotel on the coast north of Port Louis. Jacqueline came with me. Sadly, the weather was appalling and there was little scope for her to enjoy the delights of that lovely island.

We sat for five days and heard about seven appeals on a variety of subjects. I found the experience fascinating, not least because the substantive law of Mauritius is civilian and not common law. One of the challenges facing the court was to produce decisions which were suitable for the local needs of Mauritius. An attempt to replicate English law precisely might be unsuitable, not to say patronising. We had one case concerning a claim for damages for personal injuries suffered by a bright young woman whose life had been ruined in a road accident. She had been planning to be a lawyer. As a result of the accident, she would be unemployable and in need of care for the rest of her life. The trial judge had assessed her damages for loss of earnings and for the cost of future care costs by plucking a figure out of the air. On any view, she would be grossly undercompensated for her loss. We were told that this was the conventional way of assessing damages in such claims. It was a far cry from the sophisticated evidence-based approach that is adopted in the courts of

England and Wales. We allowed the appeal and gave some guidance as to how damages should be assessed in such cases in the future. We did not go so far as to suggest that the English approach should be adopted in its entirety. That would require a great deal of expert evidence which might not be available in Mauritius. But we made suggestions which, we hoped, would avoid gross under-compensation in the future.

Like the other Justices of the Supreme Court, I accepted invitations from time to time to give lectures and make speeches. Some of these (and many others that I gave during my judicial career) were published in 2018 under the title *Justice: Continuity and Change*. One of the speeches which I particularly enjoyed giving was the one I gave in November 2011 at the Grammar School at Leeds (GSAL) Speech Day. GSAL had been formed by the coming together of LGS and Leeds Girls High School. Speaking in a packed Leeds Town Hall to an audience of students, teachers and parents was quite a challenge. I said in the speech that the Town Hall occupied a very special place in my heart. As I was growing up, I used to go to concerts there on Saturday nights and sit behind the timpani in the orchestra rises. It was a moving experience for me to present the school prizes in the magnificent Town Hall where I had received school prizes myself more than 50 years earlier. Earlier in the day, I had visited the school at its large new site in the green belt on the Harrogate side of Leeds. I was shown round the school by senior students who seemed far more mature and confident than I was at their age. I was particularly impressed by the music facilities, which included several practice rooms and many pianos. I spoke to some of the senior students about the Law. They were bright and asked searching questions. It was an exciting experience for me. I hope it was for them too.

In October 2011, I gave a lecture at Edinburgh University entitled 'Time to Call it a Day: Some Reflections on Finality and the Law'. I had been invited to give this lecture by Lord Reed, who shortly afterwards was to become one of the most distinguished Justices of the Supreme Court. Jacqueline and I had an enjoyable weekend in Edinburgh.

In November 2011, I gave a lecture at the University of Hertfordshire. It was entitled 'What is Wrong with Human Rights?' I said that I did not agree with those who believed that we have no need for the European Court of Human Rights. I said that their view was 'born of the arrogant belief that we know best and have nothing to learn from foreigners'. I suppose that my embrace of things European owes much to my family background. I was particularly pleased to give a lecture at one the country's less well-known universities. Oxford, Cambridge and the big constituent colleges of London University have no difficulty in attracting senior judges to speak to their students. Less successful institutions are not so blessed. This is regrettable.

Being a Justice of the Supreme Court brought a range of other privileges as well. One was an invitation to attend the address given to both Houses of Parliament in Westminster Hall on 25 May 2011 by the President of the United States,

President Obama, during his State Visit. He was introduced by John Bercow MP, the Speaker of the House of Commons, who made an excellent speech. For me, the content of President Obama's speech was unmemorable and therefore disappointing. But his language, pace and style of delivery were masterly and compensated for the lack of substance in what he had to say. He was charismatic and had the ability to play with his audience and hold their attention with apparently effortless ease.

On another occasion in 2011, the Justices of the Court were given a private guided tour of Westminster Abbey by the Dean, the Very Reverend Dr John Hall. So far as I could see, the only point of this tour was to promote friendly relations between neighbours in Parliament Square. It was a memorable event. So much of English history is manifest in the Abbey. The Dean was a brilliant raconteur and guide.

Another regular privilege was to be invited every year to the Royal Tent at one of the Buckingham Palace garden parties, but there was a price to be paid: I had to wear a morning suit. On the first occasion, I hired one. But it was tiresome and expensive to do this. I therefore purchased the outfit and wore it every year for the next five years. These were surprisingly enjoyable affairs. We were amused by the fact that the male guests were given larger tea cups than the female guests. Although making polite conversation to foreign ambassadors was often as boring for us as for the diplomat concerned, we did meet some interesting diplomats. On one occasion, I met the Hungarian ambassador, Mr Czak. He was charming and expressed interest in my central European background. He invited me to a dinner at his residence. I found his stout defence of Hungary against widespread charges of hostility to Jews, homosexuals and the Roma community as unsurprising as it was unconvincing.

It was also fun to spot famous guests and see which ones we were able to engage in conversation. I had not been very good at this kind of thing; but over time I started to improve. A degree of brazenness and a winning smile are necessary, but they cannot guarantee success. There were plenty of well-known politicians as well as distinguished leaders from various sections of national life. A surprising number of politicians were willing to talk to us. I particularly recall having a long conversation with Theresa May (then Home Secretary). She wanted to talk about the legal challenges to some of her decisions in which I had been involved. She had a remarkable memory of some of the cases and an impressive grasp of the issues. I found her very charming. The former Prime Minister, Sir John Major, admired the colour of Jacqueline's dress and was stunned by her knowledge of cricket and the names of cricketers. She has been dining out on this flattering experience ever since. And then, of course, there were the Royals. Her Majesty the Queen and the Duke of Edinburgh attended every party that we attended. They glided around the tent effortlessly, making charming conversation and spreading gold dust as they went. Each year there was also a good spread of lesser Royals. I recall one occasion when the Queen told an admiring group of guests of which we formed part that on one occasion, when it was raining, she allowed some people who were not Royal Tent guests to come into the tent to shelter from the rain. She told us that, when they had left, some of the gold-plated teaspoons had disappeared: 'rather disappointing,' she said.

There was no doubt that there was a certain cachet to being a Justice of the Supreme Court. Doors were opened which would otherwise have been closed. I have to admit that I did enjoy this. A good example was our visit in August 2011 to the Swiss Federal Supreme Court in Lausanne. We had a most interesting conversation with President Lorenz Meier in his magnificent office, overlooking the Lake of Geneva and the Alps of French Savoie. He then entertained us to a *filets de perche* lunch in a restaurant by the lake. He told us that the United Kingdom was not the only member of the Council of Europe that objected to what it considered to be the excessive interference by the Strasbourg Court in its domestic law.

By 2012, I had been in the court for about two years. I had gained in confidence, was really getting into my stride and loving the work. I was 68 years of age. Health permitting, I hoped to carry on working until my retirement age of 75. It did not occur to me to do anything else. I could have retired on a full pension in 2008 and probably started earning a great deal more money as an arbitrator. But it never occurred to me to do that. It could not have been so interesting and rewarding.

It came as a real surprise to me when in the early summer of 2012, my good friend, Igor Judge (now Lord Chief Justice) asked me whether I would be interested in becoming Master of the Rolls (MR). Of course, the office was not in his gift: we both knew that, if I was interested, I would have to make an application to the Judicial Appointments Commission. But it was inevitable that his views would count for a great deal and he was signalling to me that he would like me to become the next MR. He knew that Nicholas Phillips had to retire as President of the Supreme Court soon when he reached the age of 75. Igor had worked out that David Neuberger (who was still the MR) was the obvious person to succeed Nicholas; and had decided that he would like me to succeed David. I assume that he must have spoken to David about these moves on the chess board. But I have no idea whether he spoke to anyone else before he approached me. My first reaction was to say to Igor that I was too old for such a demanding job. He swatted that argument away. After all, he was two years older than me and the office of Lord Chief Justice was even more demanding than that of MR.

He had planted a seed in my mind and this unsettled both Jacqueline and myself. Barring unforeseen events, my future life in the Supreme Court was secure. I was making a contribution to the development of the law, although it was only when I read Professor Paterson's book that I began to realise that I had made something of a mark. So why change course?

We talked about it endlessly during the early summer of 2012. But the same restlessness and unwillingness to reject a new challenge as had propelled me rashly to move chambers in 1996 led me inexorably to decide to apply to become the MR. But the fact that it would be a new challenge was surely not a sufficient reason for taking this major decision. After all, I would be giving up sitting in the highest UK court to presiding in a lower court, the Court of Appeal of England and Wales. After I had been appointed as the MR, my good friend and colleague Brian Kerr told me that he couldn't wait to overturn me. My decisions were liable to be reversed by my former colleagues; and even where an appeal from one of my decisions was dismissed, I would not have had the last word. As against that, for the only time in my judicial career, except when I was in charge of the TCC, I would be in charge and able to choose the cases I heard and the colleagues with whom I sat to hear them. And apart from the heavy case-load, there was the challenge of discharging numerous other responsibilities which I describe in the next chapter.

But first of all, I had to succeed in my application. There was strong competition from several senior members of the Court of Appeal. I prepared my application and received some useful interview training from Dr Peter Shaw of Praesta. I duly attended the interview in the Royal Courts of Justice (RCJ) at 08.00 on the morning of 28 July 2012. The panel comprised Nicholas Phillips, Igor Judge, Chris Stephens, who was the chairman of the Judicial Appointments Commission, and two other lay commissioners. The interview started with a five-minute presentation by me on the challenges facing the Court of Appeal and how I would try to meet them. I thought the interview went quite well, except that I was completely stumped by Igor's question: what relationship should the judiciary have with Parliament? I was at home with the relationship between the judiciary and the executive, but I had not thought about its relationship with Parliament.

Despite my inability to provide a meaningful answer to this question, I emerged as the successful candidate. I was due to be sworn in at the beginning of October. I was told the result informally on a confidential basis a few days after the interview, but there was no formal announcement until well into September. This made planning for the change a rather fraught affair.

During late September, I met many of the people with whom I was to work closely during the next four years. Pre-eminent among these was Peter Farr, who was to be my loyal and wonderful private secretary for the whole of my term of office.

11

Master of the Rolls

THE MASTER OF the Rolls was initially a clerk responsible for keeping the 'Rolls' or records of the Court of Chancery and was known as the Keeper of the Rolls of Chancery. The post evolved into a judicial one. The first recorded reference to a Master of the Rolls is in 1286. So it is an ancient office. And what a wonderful title to have!

I was sworn in at 09.00 on 1 October 2012 in the court of Igor Judge, the Lord Chief Justice (LCJ). The new Lord Chancellor and Secretary of State for Justice, Chris Grayling, was sworn in before the same court at the same time. The court was packed. The LCJ's speech was brilliant and witty. I thought Mr Grayling's speech was workmanlike, but he said all the things that might be expected of a Lord Chancellor and Secretary of State for Justice. He said on this and many other occasions that he wanted our system to do more to deflect offenders from crime: 'The rehabilitation revolution is my vocation' was one of his mantras. Sadly, this revolution did not occur during his three-year term. On the contrary, the prisons were deprived of the resources that were needed to promote the rehabilitation of prisoners.

Lord Wilson of Culworth (a colleague and friend in the Supreme Court) made a typically warm and thoughtful speech in my honour. Fortunately, on this occasion I did not have to speak.

Later that morning, I attended the Westminster Abbey service to mark the opening of the legal year. I had missed very few of these during my earlier judicial career. Now as MR, I was seated between the LCJ and the President of the Queen's Bench Division, Sir John Thomas, who in October 2013 was to succeed Igor as the LCJ. There are some who deprecate the idea that the opening of the legal year should have any religious content. Intellectually, I see their point. What does religion have to do with the administration of justice in our secular age? But I have always enjoyed these occasions. They are wonderful historic events, attended by most of the senior judiciary wearing their glorious ceremonial robes. The choral singing is invariably outstanding: moving and uplifting. It is a demonstration of English tradition at its finest. I was once gently chided by a fellow Jew for singing the hymns too lustily.

After the Lord Chancellor's 'breakfast' (the reception hosted by the Lord Chancellor in the austere setting of Westminster Hall), I returned to the RCJ, changed and presided over the first of my termly Court of Appeal plenary meetings. I was rather apprehensive. I knew that the Lord Justices of Appeal had strong views and were not reluctant to express them. But I also knew that most of the 38 members of the court, who included the LCJ and some who had been judges for longer than me, wanted the meeting to be concluded as soon as possible. Although I had been warned that there were one or two troublemakers, in the event, they caused me no difficulty on this occasion and rarely did so any other time.

At 08.30 on the following day, I had the first of many (usually weekly) meetings with Igor. These usually lasted about an hour and provided an opportunity for us to share our concerns. On the whole, his concerns were graver and more wide-ranging than mine. He only spoke to me about issues on which he thought I could make a useful contribution. For example, we did not discuss issues relating to the criminal justice system. But he did speak to me about problems he was having with the Government and individual judges who had stepped out of line. He was much preoccupied with the Government's proposed changes to the pension arrangements which were causing considerable anger in the judiciary. I am not sure that I was able to make much of a contribution to his thinking and decision-making, but it may have helped him to clear his mind merely to talk issues through. I was able to air with him some of my problems. But, on the whole, these were less substantial than his. I always found Igor easy to talk to. He was very supportive and encouraging of what I was doing, whether in managing the Court of Appeal or being Head of Civil Justice.

At 11.00, I heard my first appeal. In the next chapter, I shall describe a few of the many appeals that I heard during my four years as MR. Many of them are reported in the Law Reports. All were posted on the court website. My usual sitting pattern was to hear appeals on the first three days of every week of each term, except the middle week of the long terms and the last week of most terms. As much of the administrative work as possible was crammed into Thursdays and Fridays. This meant that preparing for appeals and writing judgments had to be done in the evenings, at weekends and otherwise fitted in.

At 15.30, I met the Chief Justice of Singapore, Sundaresh Menon, who was visiting London and paid me a 'courtesy call'. I received a number of such calls from senior foreign judges from time to time. We would invariably discuss legal issues of common interest. I was to meet Sundaresh later several times. I always found him relaxed and delightful. He was also extremely successful in promoting Singapore as an international legal centre of excellence.

At 16.30, I chaired my first Civil Appeals meeting. This was attended by the Vice-President of the Court of Appeal (Civil) who was Lord Justice Maurice Kay as well as by one of the two Deputy Masters (who were Sally Meacher and Marie Bancroft-Rimmer) and other officials. These meetings were held every two or three weeks mainly to discuss the performance of the court which was closely monitored. We also decided which judges should hear 'flagged' cases, that is, cases of particular importance or sensitivity. The 'flagging' was done by the court lawyers, under the supervision of the Deputy Masters. The MR is expected to sit on more of these cases than any other member of the court, but I was always sensitive to the need not to grab too many of them.

As if that were not enough for my first day, I also sat in court for the swearing in of two new Lord Justices of Appeal (David Lloyd Jones and Colman Treacy). Igor made the welcoming speech for both of them. He took much care over these speeches. They were not at all formulaic, but were sensitively tailored to the individual.

On 4 October, I had a number of firsts. I had my first meeting as Chairman of the Executive of the Civil Justice Council. As Head of Civil Justice, I was *ex officio* chairman of the CJC as well as its Executive Council. I had already had experience of the CJC during my time as Deputy Head of Civil Justice. When he was Head of Civil Justice, Nicholas Phillips concentrated on running the CJC and largely left the running of the Civil Procedure Rule Committee (CPRC) to me. I adopted the same general approach. During most of my time as Head of Civil Justice, the senior official from the Ministry of Justice (MoJ) who attended the meetings of the CJC was Robert Wright. I found him to be an intelligent and nice man. But he was extremely cautious and unwilling to commit himself to anything of significance. He gave little away and found it difficult to give straight answers to straight questions. He always spoke of the problems facing the Department and found reasons for putting decisions off. Although I liked him as a person, I found him immensely frustrating to deal with. I had no means of knowing whether, in being so obstructive, he was carrying out the orders of his superiors or he was giving expression to a pathological indecisiveness.

Later that day, I had my first Judicial Executive Board (JEB) lunch. The JEB is chaired by the LCJ. The MR is regarded (although not officially designated) as its second most senior member. The composition of the board varied during my time, but it always included the Presidents of the Queen's Bench Division (PQBD) and the Family Division (PFD), the Chancellor of the Chancery Division (the Chancellor), the Senior President of Tribunals (SPT), the Senior Presiding Judge (SPJ) and the Chairman of the Judicial College. The JEB generally met for an all-day meeting every four weeks and once a week for an early morning meeting before court which lasted about an hour. These meetings provided a forum for discussion on a wide range of issues affecting the justice system as a whole. These included the performance of the courts; the modernisation of the courts; pay, pensions and working conditions of the judges; increasing the diversity of the judiciary, etc. Many papers were circulated in advance of these meetings. I found that papers for the four-weekly meetings often took a few hours to read. The board was, in effect, the LCJ's Cabinet.

During the afternoon I met the manager of the Court of Appeal. It did not take me long to conclude that she was quite ineffective at her job. I told her line manager that this was my view. He was fiercely protective of her. All the court officials were employees of Her Majesty's Courts Service (later Her Majesty's Courts and Tribunal Service). I had no powers in relation to her employment. But I could and should have complained sooner than I did and insisted that she was replaced.

I also met Anne Sharp, who was the Chief Executive of the JEB at the time. I was soon to discover that she was impressive and had good political antennae. Finally that day, I met Jo Gordon who was Head of Human Resources (HR) in the Judicial Office which had been set up to help the LCJ to run the system. Lawyers of my generation needed to be educated about the importance of HR. We were schooled in the unforgivingly tough Victorian world of sink or swim. Jo and her successor Joanna Peel were both good at their jobs. They knew that they had a battle to persuade the senior judges of the importance of HR. They both succeeded in changing attitudes, including my own. I know that they were impatient to make faster progress but they handled us with charm and skill and I believe that they made real advances.

On the last day of my first week, I attended several meetings. Meetings were to become a great feature of my life as MR. In my Valedictory speech in July 2016, I said: 'There is so much that I shall miss about the RCJ. I confess that I shall not miss the endless meetings. We are in the grip of an epidemic of meetings to which there appears to be no known antidote.'

The first was one of the occasional meetings between the Heads of Division and the High Court Judges Association. Apart from the MR, the Heads of Division were the LCJ, the PQBD (Sir John Thomas), the PFD (Sir Nicholas Wall) and the Chancellor (Sir Andrew Morritt). In fact, Nicholas was on leave on grounds of ill-health and sadly did not work again. These meetings gave the High Court Judges the opportunity to raise their concerns with the senior judiciary and let off steam. The LCJ bore the brunt of the meeting. From time to time during my four years, there was quite a lot of steam to let off.

Later, I met Judge Stewart QC (later Mr Justice Stewart) and District Judge Lethem. These two judges were heavily involved in the implementation of Sir Rupert Jackson's Civil Justice reforms. Although the programme of implementation was well underway when I became MR, it was far from complete. There was much work to be done and I became heavily involved in it.

I next attended my first meeting of the CPRC as MR and Head of Civil Justice. Throughout my four years in office, I was fortunate to have brilliant DHCJs who were all Lord Justices of Appeal and to whom I was able to entrust the day to day running of the CPRC: Martin Moore-Bick (for the first few months of my term); Stephen Richards for about three years; and finally Michael Briggs. In their different ways, they all took a great weight off my shoulders. I was able to delegate a great deal of the detailed work to them in the secure knowledge that I could rely on them. I usually only attended meetings when there were important or controversial issues to discuss. Although much of the work was of a rather technical nature, from time to time issues of real importance and even controversy did arise in relation to the CPR. It was important that I was present when such issues were debated.

My final meeting on that day was with the Temple Bar Scholars of the American Inns of Court. These young lawyers come from the United States every autumn and spend time in London meeting judges, barristers and solicitors and seeing our system at work. I had met them during my time in the Supreme Court. I always found them to be brilliant, lively, curious and challenging. I met them during each of my four years as MR. The meetings were invariably stimulating and enjoyable.

I had also heard appeals on each of the first three days of the week. It had been a breathless and exciting first week. It was already apparent that life as MR would be very different from life in the calmer and more reflective atmosphere of the Supreme Court. I was to discover that the pace would rarely slacken.

My second week began with a meeting with Sir Andrew Morritt to discuss civil justice issues that were of interest to him as Head of the Chancery Division. He had been a judge longer than me. In fact, I had appeared before him when I was still at the Bar. He was tall and a rather dominant figure. I was somewhat in awe of him. But he insisted on observing the protocol of meeting me in my office, because I was senior to him in the judicial hierarchy. He behaved impeccably and with great charm.

Later that week, I attended a meeting with members of the National Archive Forum on Historical Manuscripts (I shall say more about the National Archive later). I had a meeting with Lord Lester of Herne Hill QC to discuss the new defamation legislation and a meeting with Stephen Ward, who was Head of Communications in the Judicial Office of the RCJ. He had a significant role to play in advising the judiciary on its relations with the media. He emphasised the importance of notifying him of any judgments and speeches which might be controversial or which might for other reasons catch the eye of the media. The days when we could complacently say, as our predecessors had tended to do, that our judgments speak for themselves had gone. He saw part of his role as protecting the judiciary from inaccurate and unfair reporting by the media. I had only limited dealings with him during my four years as MR. It did not take me long to realise that there was little public awareness of the importance of the Court of Appeal and the work that it did. The contrast with the well-oiled Supreme Court publicity machine was striking. I told Stephen that I wanted to request an interview with Frances Gibb, the legal editor of *The Times*. He thought this was risky and counselled against it. I ignored his advice. The interview resulted in an excellent article by Frances published on 16 October 2014 under the headline, 'We are the powerhouse, the real engine room, says Dyson'. I recognised that I had taken a gamble, because I would have no control over the content of the article. But I judged that Frances was unlikely to cause real damage to the reputation of the court. In the event, the article raised the profile of the court and boosted the morale of my colleagues, for which some of them even thanked me.

The pattern of the third week was similar to that of the first two. Once again, I heard appeals on the first three days. I met Catherine Lee and another official from the MoJ. Catherine was a Director with responsibility for Civil Justice. She was promoted to be a Director General towards the end of my term. In all my dealings with her, I found her delightful, although somewhat cautious and reluctant to take tough decisions. I also met Michael Todd QC (now Mr Justice Todd) who was the Chair of the Bar. I met successive Chairs of the Bar from time to time during my term. It was important to foster good relations between the senior judiciary and the Bar as well as the Law Society. I also met Kevin Sadler for the first time. He was a senior official in the MoJ with particular responsibility for justice (including civil justice) outside London.

On the Thursday, I gave a lecture on costs at the Law Society Civil Justice Conference. Like many of the lectures that I gave on civil justice, the first draft was written by John Sorabji, my legal secretary. John is passionate about civil justice and has written extensively on the subject. He was greatly influenced by Professor Zuckerman. I wrote most of my speeches and lectures without assistance except for those on civil justice. I relied heavily on John for these, although I found that his drafts needed some editing. I was never comfortable reading what someone else had written for me: the words had to be my own.

On the Friday, I chaired my first CJC meeting. During my four years as MR, the CJC did a great deal of significant work in the field of civil justice. It responded to many consultation papers that were produced by the Government (mainly by the MoJ). It also initiated work and produced papers on a large range of topics. I always tried to be fully prepared for all the many meetings that I attended. This involved much advance reading.

Finally on the Friday, I had an introductory telephone conversation with Helen Grant MP who was the Junior Minister in the MoJ with responsibility for civil justice. Her background was as a solicitor who practised in the field of Family Law. During the following months, it became clear to me that she was passionate about gender discrimination, but had little interest in civil justice. She was very pleasant, but I found it frustrating to deal with her. I decided that, if I wanted anything done by the MoJ, it would be more profitable to raise the issue with the relevant official and, occasionally, take it up with the Secretary of State.

On the Monday of the following week, I met Diane Burleigh, the Chief Executive Officer of the Chartered Institute of Legal Executives (CILEx). I found her to be an impressive woman who fought tenaciously and to great effect to raise the profile and standing of legal executives. In the evening, I attended a dinner at the Sloane Club, hosted by Tim Jenkins, the secretary of the District Judges' Association. This was a good opportunity to meet some of the leading district judges. I was soon to discover that they are the workhorses of the civil justice system in the county courts and, outside London, in the High Court as well. Many of them felt undervalued. In my many dealings with them throughout my term as MR, I tried to show appreciation of them and their work.

On the Wednesday, I attended a Court of Appeal meeting to allocate vacation sitting weeks to the judges. This was unexciting and mundane. But it was a function that had to be performed to ensure the efficient running of the court; and it mattered greatly to the judges. After court, I met Judith March (chief executive) and Robert Heslett (chairman) of the Personal Support Unit (PSU). The PSU is a wonderful organisation which is dedicated to helping litigants in person (self-represented litigants) to cope with the stress of presenting their cases in court without the help of a lawyer. Many of those who work with the PSU are volunteers. They do not advise their 'clients' on the merits of their claims but they do take some of the terror out of the experience for them and often sit beside them in court. I am a patron. During my periodic visits to court centres around the country, I invariably visited the local PSU office and met the person responsible for running it as well as some of the volunteers. I found talking to them humbling and inspiring.

On the Thursday, I attended my first full meeting of the JEB. These meetings typically lasted from 09.00 until 15.00. They were always chaired by the LCJ. There were always a number of issues to discuss. Papers were circulated in advance of the meetings. I would typically spend at least two or three hours pre-reading. The authors of the papers usually attended the meeting to speak to their papers and answer questions. I found these meetings demanding and tiring even though I was not chairing them.

At 16.30, I had my first meeting with Chris Stephens (chairman of the Judicial Appointments Commission (JAC), whom I had previously met when I was interviewed for the office of MR. Judicial appointments are made on the recommendation of the JAC in what are called 'competitions'. During my four years as MR, I was involved in a number of important JAC competitions. These included all the competitions for the more than 20 Lords Justice of Appeal who were appointed to the Court of Appeal during my time; the replacement for Igor Judge as LCJ; the replacement for Nicholas Wall as PFD; the replacement for Nicholas Bratza as the UK judge on the European Court of Human Rights in Strasbourg; and the replacement for Sir David Lloyd Jones as chairman of the Law Commission. I always sat in a panel of five, two of whom were judges. The remaining three comprised Chris Stephens and two other lay commissioners. I found these lay commissioners most conscientious and impressive.

The competitions followed a well-established pattern. I shall describe the first of them in a little detail. They were all extremely time-consuming. They were overseen by Jeremy Brooks, a former military man who was passionate about detail and process. The first competition was to fill 10 actual or impending vacancies in the Court of Appeal. The panel was chaired by Chris Stephens. The legal members of the panel were the LCJ and myself. The candidates had to complete long, complex application forms and to submit references and two judgments (or other documents) that they had written. There were about 40 candidates. I spent many hours reading the papers prior to meeting the others in order to sift the applications down to those whom we wished to interview. The sift meeting lasted some time. At the sift meeting, we agreed on a shortlist of 20 candidates whom we were later to interview over a five-day period. At this meeting, we also agreed which panel member would cover which topic at the interview. We even agreed some of the questions and who would ask them.

The applications of all the shortlisted candidates were circulated to all members of the Supreme Court and the Court of Appeal as well as a few other senior people. Many of the comments of these consultees were invaluable. The amount of material that we had to absorb before the interviews took place was, therefore, considerable.

The interviews were stressful for the panel members, but, of course, far more stressful for the candidates. Almost all of the candidates were High Court Judges, many of whom had been appointed to the High Court before the advent of the JAC. Many had never been interviewed for anything before. We knew that some of them had been professionally coached (as I had been); but that others had probably not been coached. How to allow for the professionally trained performance? I was sceptical about the usefulness of an interview as a means of testing a candidate's skills and suitability for appointment as an appellate judge. My view was that the principal skill required of such a judge was being a first class lawyer who was able to write excellent judgments and produce them within a reasonable time. Collegiality was of some importance too. I did not see how one could learn much from an interview about whether a candidate possessed these skills. As against that, there was force in the point that, whereas the candidates were known to the LCJ and myself (because we had read their judgments and their reputations were known to us), they were unknown to the lay members of the panel. So the candidates had to be interviewed. But we tried not to be unduly influenced by a good interview performance; and conversely we tried to guard against marking down a brilliant candidate who was nervous and found it difficult to 'sell' himself or herself. I recall one particularly brilliant High Court Judge who had written some outstanding and important judgments, but who came across at interview as diffident and indecisive. When asked how he would cope with the pressure of having to write judgments expeditiously, he replied that he had real concerns about that: he hoped that he would manage, but he could not be sure. Faced with other good candidates, it is not surprising that the panel rejected this candidate more than once. He is now thriving in the Court of Appeal and coping without difficulty.

At the end of the five days of interviewing, we had long discussions before agreeing on the 10 successful candidates.

I found these competitions demanding and draining. Many criticised the complexity of the process. Some candidates thought the whole business was demeaning. I thought that the process should be streamlined and simplified. It was certainly a far cry from the 'tap on the shoulder' system from which I had benefited, but which was grossly unfair and could not be justified.

To return to the chronology, on the Friday I attended the Magna Carta Stakeholder conference in the Guildhall. As MR, I was *ex officio* chairman of the

Magna Carta Trust. This is a charity that was established in 1956. Its principal object is to perpetuate the principles of Magna Carta. A notable aspect of my term as MR was that 2015 was the 800th anniversary of the sealing of Magna Carta. The preparations for the anniversary and the many events that took place in 2015 occupied a good deal of my time. My Deputy Chairman was Sir Robert Worcester of Mori poll fame. He is an impressive man of great energy and fizzing with ideas. Without his drive, the anniversary would not have been the success that it undoubtedly was. The purpose of the conference on this Friday was to map out some of the plans for 2015.

The next week followed the pattern that was beginning to emerge: hearing appeals; weekly meeting with the LCJ; meeting of the CPRC; as well as various other meetings.

A week later, I gave the Administrative Law Association annual lecture entitled 'Where the common law fears to tread'. The theme of the lecture was to ask how far it is appropriate for judges to push boundaries and develop the common law; and when should they pull back and say that this is a matter for the democratically elected Parliament. The Supreme Court had to grapple with this issue in the *Al-Rawi* case as I have mentioned in the last chapter. I was to return to it in my Bentham Association Lecture at University College London in 2013 which was entitled 'Are the judges too powerful?' This has become an important issue in recent times which arises in many different contexts.

Jacqueline and I had both attended the Bentham lecture for many years. It was strange to be the speaker rather than the listener. I criticised the attack Lord Sumption made in one of his lectures on what he saw as the exorbitant approach of some judges to human rights issues. I explained why I believed that our judges were exercising the power given to them by the Human Rights Act responsibly and carefully. I also rejected the criticisms made in the media and elsewhere of the Strasbourg Court. I said that the court was acutely aware that it was not a representative or democratically accountable body, which was why it recognised the importance of according a margin of appreciation to the Contracting States. I subsequently met Sir Nicolas Bratza who had been the President of the Strasbourg Court. He told me that he and his colleagues were upset by what they considered to be unfair criticism of their work. He also told me that they had all read my lecture and were delighted that I had given it.

In October 2012, I attended the Denning lecture given by Lord Justice (Stephen) Sedley and accompanied part of his lecture on the piano. I am not sure that the music enhanced the lecture. But it was a striking and unusual thing to do.

I also had a meeting with Ursula Brennan (Permanent Secretary at the MoJ) and Helen Edwards (Director General of Justice at the Department). My meetings with the Permanent Secretary were infrequent. I always sensed that the most senior officials were not very interested in civil justice. They were far more focused on criminal and family justice and prisons. I tried my best to emphasise the importance of civil justice. They made the right noises, but I was not convinced that they accepted the need to promote civil justice as I thought they should.

On a Saturday early in November, there took place the first of the four Lord Mayors' Shows in which I participated as MR. The LCJ and I and a few selected judges and guests stood on the balcony at the RCJ overlooking the Strand and watched dozens of splendid floats go past in the street below. The procession culminated in the arrival of the new Lord Mayor and various Aldermen in splendid horse drawn carriages. These dignitaries made their way to the LCJ's court for the swearing in ceremony. Together with myself and a small group of selected judges, the LCJ sat on the Bench in full ceremonial kit (which included a strange tricorn hat). Earlier in the morning, we had rehearsed the ceremony. During at least one of the rehearsals, my tricorn hat, which was perched on the long-bottomed wig that I was wearing, fell off as I bowed. It clattered to the ground amidst much laughter. Fortunately, our tricorn hats remained on our heads during the actual ceremony each time. The LCJ made a speech welcoming the new Lord Mayor; I made a speech thanking the retiring (known as 'the late') Lord Mayor; and the Recorder of London (the chief judge of the Central Criminal Court or Old Bailey) also made a speech.

The following week was one of my mid-term non-sitting weeks. On the Monday evening, I attended the great annual banquet that was hosted by the new Lord Mayor in the Guildhall. The judges who were invited to this lavish affair assembled in ceremonial robes in the quadrangle of the RCJ and were driven in limousines to the Guildhall. We were escorted by police outriders who swept the traffic aside as we drove from the Strand to the City. It was quite an experience. The dinner was attended by about 500 mainly City people. There were speeches from the new Lord Mayor, the outgoing Lord Mayor, the Prime Minister, the Lord Chancellor and the Archbishop of Canterbury. Usually, the star speaker was the Archbishop of Canterbury. On the whole, I found these dinners rather boring.

The following week, I sat on a two-day appeal in the Supreme Court. I was invited back from time to time and sat mainly on public law/human rights cases. I always enjoyed going back and was warmly welcomed. But my occasional return visits did not make me regret my decision to leave. The court seemed curiously isolated. I preferred being involved in the running of the justice system and the rough and tumble of the Court of Appeal, not to mention the fact that I was in charge and could decide which cases I wanted to hear and in which cases I would write the lead judgment.

As usual, I had various meetings during this week. On the Friday, I attended my first meeting of the Judges' Council. This is a body which is representative of the entire judiciary (judges and tribunals at all levels). It usually meets three or four times each year. It is chaired by the LCJ. The MR and Heads of Division are members *ex officio*. It discusses important issues relating to the justice system of England and Wales. It was established in response to the complaint, particularly from the judges of the lower courts, that the senior judges who took the big decisions were out of touch and did not take account of the views of the rest of the judiciary. I think this complaint was justified to some extent. I did not, however, feel that my presence at these meetings was a profitable use of my time, although I felt that it was important that I should be there. I attended every meeting unless I was unable to do so.

The following week, in addition to sittings and routine meetings, I gave the annual Personal Injuries Bar Association Richard Davies Lecture. Richard Davies had been a colleague in chambers at 39 Essex Street who had tragically died in his 50s. The title of the lecture was 'Duty of care of public authorities: too much, too little or about right?' The liability of public authorities in tort had interested me for some time. I took as my starting point the Bar Council Law Reform Lecture given by Lord Hoffmann in 2009 in which he had set out arguments in favour of limiting the duty of care owed by public authorities. In my lecture, I expressed a somewhat different view.

On the Friday, I gave the keynote address at the CJC conference on litigants in person (LIPs). This was the first of what became annual events organised by the CJC at the Queen Elizabeth Conference Centre in Westminster. Each conference was superbly chaired by Robin Knowles QC (later Mr Justice Knowles). They were attended by many 'stakeholders' who were contributing significantly to making life easier for LIPs. They included lawyers, representatives of local authorities, other public bodies and many voluntary organisations. The massive reduction in the availability of legal aid had led to a substantial increase in the number of LIPs using the courts. They needed help in understanding the law and the justice system; and the judges needed help in coping with litigants who were not legally qualified and for most of whom conducting a case in court was a strange and terrifying experience. Lord McNally (a Minister of State for Justice until December 2013) also spoke at the conference. It was clear to me that there was a pressing need to share information and to co-ordinate the various initiatives that were being pursued throughout the country. Shortly afterwards, I appointed Mrs Justice (Sarah) Asplin (now Lady Justice Asplin) as the LIP Liaison Judge. She was a great success.

The following week, I had about 12 meetings. This was rather on the high side, but not especially uncommon. The next week was the final week of my first term as MR. In addition to the usual fare of sittings and meetings, I had my first meeting with officials to discuss government plans to reform judicial review. Chris Grayling was very keen to make it more difficult to bring judicial review proceedings. There had been a big increase in the number of judicial review claims in the courts in recent years. He noted that most of the claims failed. He felt strongly that this was a terrible waste of public time and money: many of the claims were funded by legal aid and, he said, it was unacceptable that public authorities were spending so much time defending them. This was an issue that was to occupy a good deal of my time in the coming months. In the end, I was able to persuade him to water down some of his proposals, but not by much.

I entertained my staff as well as the Vice-President of the Court of Appeal (Civil) and the DHCJ to a Christmas lunch in the George, a nearby pub. I did this in each of my four years. These were happy occasions which, I think, were much enjoyed by my hard-working staff.

By the beginning of 2013, Stephen Richards had replaced Martin Moore-Bick as DHCJ. I was delighted and greatly relieved that Stephen had agreed to take on the job. Nobody else had offered to do it. It was well known that chairing CPRC meetings was immensely demanding and not very exciting. Stephen was an outstanding judge and chaired the CPRC brilliantly, although, unlike Rupert Jackson and Michael Briggs for example, I felt that he did not have a real passion for civil justice.

On 28 January, Stephen and I met MoJ officials to discuss the issue of extending fixed recoverable costs. Throughout my four years, I tried to persuade the Government that the fixed recoverable costs regime should be extended beyond its current limited scope. It seemed to me that an obvious way of tackling the scandal of the excessive costs of civil litigation was to award the successful party a reasonable sum that was fixed by the rules. I always recognised that the challenge would be to determine the amount of the reasonable sum for different kinds of case. My ideas were not rejected either at this first meeting or on subsequent occasions when I raised the issue. Rather, I was told each time that the Government had its own priorities and extending fixed recoverable costs was not one of them. It was only towards the end of my term, when Michael Gove was Lord Chancellor and Secretary of State that we made a breakthrough. This was largely as a result of an initiative by Professor Zuckerman who met Mr Gove and was evidently more persuasive than I had been.

On 30 January, Stephen and I had our first meeting with Chris Grayling. I told Mr Grayling how important civil justice was and how frustrating it was for me that it had to play Cinderella and be in the shadow of her sisters, Crime and Family law. He said that he understood this, but in all my conversations with him, I was never convinced that he believed that access to civil justice was an important social good or that he really appreciated the importance of the rule of law. My impression of him was borne out by his policies and actions. It is true that the MoJ was constantly under pressure from the Treasury to cut costs and find savings. But I felt that this provided Mr Grayling with an excuse for not doing things that he did not want to do anyway. His successor Mr Gove was under the same pressures from the Treasury. But he showed a greater willingness to find ways of improving access to justice. On a personal level, I got on with Mr Grayling very well. But I had a struggle even to persuade him to accept my recommendations for appointments to the CPRC and the CJC, all of which he had to approve. He was suspicious of appointing individuals who had what he called an 'agenda'. In the end, I believe that I gained his trust and he did always approve the individuals I recommended. I learnt early on that he was a serious Euro-sceptic. He was critical of the Strasbourg Court. He told me more than once that his Government was determined that the United Kingdom should withdraw from the European Convention on Human Rights. So far as I was aware, withdrawal from the EU was not government policy at that time and his anti-European stance did not represent the Government's view. Following the EU referendum in 2016, his views about the EU were to become part of mainstream government thinking.

In mid-February 2013, I chaired my first meeting of the National Archive Advisory Council at the splendid National Archive building in Kew. The Advisory Council is an independent body which advises the Secretary of State for Culture, Media and Sport (previously the Lord Chancellor) on issues relating to access to public records and represents the public interest in deciding what records should be open or closed. It has 15 members including historians, archivists and retired diplomats. It is chaired by the MR. The main item on the agenda at these meetings was whether to recommend acceding to the requests of government departments not to release documents to the National Archive or into the public domain. Eligible grounds were that they were sensitive in one or more respects specified by statute. These included that the documents contained unflattering expressions of opinion by officials or ministers about heads of government, ministers or officials of allegedly friendly states which might damage relations with them; their release might be detrimental to national security interests; they contained confidential information about the health of individuals; or they concerned members of the Royal Family.

One of the most interesting discussions concerned the question whether documents which formed part of the archive of Lord Denning's 1963 Inquiry into the so-called 'Profumo Affair' should be released. Lord Denning had given an undertaking to all the witnesses to his Inquiry that their oral and written evidence would never be disclosed to the public. Many years later, Lord Mackay of Clashfern, when he was Lord Chancellor, modified the undertaking and reduced the length of the embargo to 100 years. The Advisory Council was now asked to consider whether to advise the Lord Chancellor to relax the embargo yet further. The case for maintaining the status quo was presented by an official from the Cabinet Office. His argument was that, as a matter of principle, the undertaking had to be honoured, since otherwise witnesses would not be willing in the future to give their evidence in an uninhibited and frank manner. He assumed that the request to withhold the documents would be accepted by the Council without demur. But the members of the Council were not persuaded. The official tried again at the next meeting. Once again, the members were not persuaded. On the third occasion, following a careful, balanced and well-argued report from the Treasury Solicitor (Sir Paul Jenkins QC), a compromise was reached. Paul Jenkins succeeded me in 2018 as Treasurer of Middle Temple. Tragically, he died only a few weeks after taking office. He was wickedly gossipy and great fun. But behind the colourful façade lay an astute man with a sharp mind. His death was a great loss to Middle Temple and everyone who knew him.

It was unusual for the Advisory Council to refuse a request to withhold a document from the National Archive or to release it to the National Archive as a closed document. Although I had no doubt that the members of the Council were doing their job conscientiously and well, during my term as MR, I became increasingly concerned that it might be at risk of legal challenge by judicial review. There were occasional articles in the media about the secret activities of this 'shadowy' organisation. From time to time, I received letters from (sometimes distinguished) people complaining that decisions that certain documents should not be put into the public domain were not justified.

The National Archive is a remarkable institution and the Advisory Council does important work. Chairing the Council was a curious function for the MR to perform in addition to the other more mainstream activities. Nevertheless, I was pleased to do it. Most of our quarterly meetings were held at the National Archives building in Kew. It houses more than 120 miles of documents.

Shortly after I retired, Jacqueline and I were given a guided tour by an official and two of the archivists who work at Kew. We had told them before our visit that we would like to see any naturalisation certificates that they held of our grandfathers and any other documents relating to our families as well as some documents relating to the history of the Jews in England and a selection of the National Archive's many other historical documents. The most interesting family document that we were shown was the naturalisation certificate of Jacqueline's French paternal grandfather issued in 1912 together with all its supporting documentation.

But that is to jump far ahead. On 17 February 2013, I flew to Luxembourg. I led a delegation of UK judges to participate in a one-day conference with the Court of Justice of the European Union (CJEU). Our team included Lord Neuberger, Lord Mance, Lady Justice Arden and several High Court Judges. The CJEU delegation was headed by the President of the Court (Justice Skouras) and included Justice Schiemann (the UK judge) and UK Advocate-General Eleanor Sharpston. We discussed various topics relating to the CJEU. These included the issue of how the court could streamline its processes and what approach national courts should adopt to making references to the CJEU on questions of EU law. It was clear that, to the evident frustration of some of his colleagues, Justice Skouras was resistant to reforming the court's way of doing things and that there would be no changes while he remained at the helm.

In the following week, once again there were several meetings of the kind that were now becoming routine. I should mention my first meeting with Jillian Kay, who had succeeded Anne Sharp as the chief executive of the Judicial Office. Jillian remained in this important post for three years. Although quiet and unassuming, I soon discovered that she was quite steely and determined. Sometimes, she would stand her ground in the face of occasionally strong opposition from senior judges. I rarely disagreed with her.

In the last week of February, among the people I met was Dr Sam Rugege. He was the Chief Justice of Rwanda. I was to meet this charming and impressive man again in June 2016 at a conference in Krakow about international war crimes.

On 15 March, I went to Birmingham University to give the annual Holdsworth Club lecture. My title was 'Compensation culture: fact or fantasy?' The inspiration for this lecture was the perception, fuelled by frequent statements in the media and by some government ministers, that the country was in the grip of a compensation culture, whereby any accident would result in payment of compensation however unjustified. Claims for alleged whiplash injuries were a particular problem. There was no doubt that something of a whiplash industry had arisen in recent years and the Government was rightly trying to do something to curb it. This was the kind of challenge that appealed to Mr Grayling. I explained in my lecture that our courts were alive to the problem and suggested that the judges were swift to reject unmeritorious claims: if there was a compensation culture, the judges were not responsible for it. After the lecture, I judged a students' moot (a legal debate). My fellow judges were two QCs from the Birmingham Bar. This was the only time that I gave a lecture and judged a moot on the same day: it was hard work.

On 20 March, there was a meeting of the JAC panel that was charged with the task of recommending a replacement for Igor as LCJ. The panel comprised David Neuberger, myself, Chris Stephens and two other lay commissioners. The competition took the usual form. The candidates were Heather Hallett, Brian Leveson and John Thomas. There was considerable media speculation about the outcome and much press support for Heather. The prospect of the first female LCJ excited a great deal of comment. After considering the extensive written material that we had and taking account of the interviews that took place in July, we were unanimously of the view that John was the best candidate. When our recommendation was accepted by the Lord Chancellor, the Prime Minister and Her Majesty, I had the unenviable task of going to see the unsuccessful candidates and consoling them.

On 12 April, Jacqueline and I flew to Cape Town for the biennial Commonwealth Law Conference. Igor and Judith Judge also attended it. Igor was keen that I should be there. Senior judges from most of the Commonwealth jurisdictions were present. In addition to senior judges, there were also many lawyers from Commonwealth countries. I gave a rather boring speech on some aspects of civil procedure. Civil procedure is a necessary and important subject on which I gave many speeches during my judicial career. But I often found it difficult to excite my audience. On the other hand, Igor made a brilliant speech at the end of the conference. His condemnation of apartheid was not original, but it was expressed very simply and in the most moving and inspiring language. His was the only speech to evoke a standing ovation. Overall, I did not think that to spend a week away from my desk on this visit was the best use of my time. I declined the invitation to go to the next conference two years later, even though that would have involved travelling no further than Glasgow.

During the following week, I met the Chief Justice of Sri Lanka who presented me with some very special tea. It was not until 2018, after I had retired, that we visited Sri Lanka. Our two-week visit included some wonderful walking through tea plantations in the central highlands and attending a reception given by the High Commissioner to mark the seventieth anniversary of the independence of Sri Lanka (at which we met many of the great and the good of Sri Lanka as well as Prince Edward).

The MR is *ex officio* a member of the Worshipful Company of Drapers, which is one of the oldest of the City livery companies and occupies magnificent buildings in Throgmorton Avenue in the City of London. I was not made a liveryman until after I had retired, when I took part in a formal ceremony for that purpose. The Company does admirable charitable work, which includes maintaining the early nineteenth-century Queen Elizabeth alms houses in Greenwich which are home for about 30 elderly people from the area. Once a year, I had lunch at the Drapers Hall with the Master and several senior members and officers of the Company and then went with them on what was called a 'visitation' to Greenwich. The visitation started with a short service that was conducted by the local vicar in the charming chapel. I then made a short speech. This was followed by tea at which I walked from table to table talking to the residents. Some were very old. Most of them had interesting stories to tell about their lives, including their experiences of wartime London. I suspect that I may have looked a little like a member of the Royal Family as I moved (I hope seamlessly) from table to table. I enjoyed every one of these visits, not least because, although it may seem immodest to say so, I had the impression that they were one of the highlights of their year. The Masters and most of the other senior members of the Company are well connected and seem to be very much at home in the life of the City of London. The Master in 2013 was Lady Victoria Leatham, a member of the Cecil family. She had been born and brought up in Burghley House, near Stamford. I rather relished the fact that, although my background was so different, I was entirely comfortable in their company.

May was a busy month. In addition to the usual activities, I attended my first State Opening of Parliament as MR. I was always thrilled to be present on these occasions and conscious of the history and tradition with which they were suffused. The senior judges all sat rather uncomfortably perched on the Woolsack in the House of Lords waiting for a very long time until the Royal Party arrived in the Chamber. Eventually, the Party arrived resplendent in their robes. Page boys were responsible for ensuring that the Queen's heavy white train was placed in the perfect position. One year, to great consternation, a page boy fainted. This did not seem to affect the Royal Party, which included the Duke of Edinburgh and the Duke and Duchess of Cornwall. They gave the impression of not even having noticed and continued to sit stony-faced without a flicker of movement. I found it quite stressful having to sit absolutely still almost within touching distance of the Queen. I was fearful that I would sneeze or cough. After a long wait, we could hear the approaching rabble of the MPs coming from the House of Commons. Then Black Rod knocked loudly on the door of the Chamber and the MPs trooped in. From this apparent chaos emerged the Queen's speech which was produced to her by the Lord Chancellor out of what looked like a rather homely woollen sack. She then read the speech in which she set out the measures that her Government intended to introduce in the next session of Parliament. And then it was all over. The Royal Party left the Chamber as perfectly as they had entered it. It was like a wonderful piece of theatre.

Later in the month, I took part in my first London Legal Walk as MR. This is a six-mile walk which starts at the RCJ, runs through the Royal parks as far as the western end of the Serpentine in Hyde Park and returns by a different route to the RCJ. Many thousands of lawyers take part. Together with the LCJ, I had to pose for photographs in Carey Street with teams from many firms of solicitors, barristers' chambers and other groups of lawyers. It is always a happy event which raises well over £500,000 for various legal charities.

On 7 June, I attended the first of the lunches to which I was invited annually by the President of the Law Society in the lovely eighteenth-century house at 60 Carey Street. This was a small lunch attended by about six members of the Law Society and myself. There is a strong now largely historical link between the Law Society and the MR. Until recently, the MR used to admit all new solicitors to the profession, by admitting them to the roll of solicitors; and also used to deal with all challenges to decisions of the Law Society of a disciplinary nature. The latter are now dealt with by an independent tribunal. The only relic of the former is that one day each year, the MR admits a group of about 60 new solicitors to the roll. There are approximately 12 admissions each year. Most of them are presided over by the President of the Law Society.

The admission of new solicitors to the roll was one of the most enjoyable duties that I had to perform. They were very much family occasions. I made a short speech which was later to form the basis of the speeches I made in 2017 when, as Treasurer of Middle Temple, I called student members of the Inn to the Bar. I shook every new solicitor by the hand and made a point of speaking briefly to each of them individually. The range of their backgrounds was huge; and the range of the practices in which they were working as trainees was also strikingly large. Most of them were not doing commercial work in large city practices. This may have been because those solicitors were working so hard that they did not have the time to be admitted to the profession in person: the process could be done administratively. After the ceremony, I joined the new solicitors and their supporters for tea and further conversation. This was always a most satisfying day and a refreshing break from the endless diet of appeals and meetings.

Later in June, I attended the annual Cranworth dinner at Downing College, Cambridge and made the after dinner speech; gave a speech at a seminar for the district judges of the South-East Circuit; and attended the annual dinner of the Medico-Legal Society and made the after dinner speech there too. There was a profusion of dinners and speeches. I crafted all my after dinner speeches by myself.

On 20 and 21 June, I attended the annual conference of the designated civil judges (DCJs) at Warwick University. I attended this conference every one of my four years. The DCJs are essential to the effective working of civil justice out of London. The conference started with a dinner on the Thursday night. The following morning, I gave a keynote address in which I summarised the principal issues of the day. Although I did not feel that there was any hostility to me personally, I was conscious of the anger of the judges about the growing problems created by the reduction of resources and their sense that the Government did not really care about civil justice. My speech was followed by other speeches and then, most usefully, a discussion in which the judges could air their grievances and make constructive suggestions as to how to improve matters. MoJ officials, but no ministers, were present and witnessed the discussions. This was important and some useful changes did result from them, although, as usual, the lack of resources was a seriously limiting factor.

July is always a particularly busy month since it precedes the long vacation in August and September when many of the courts are closed. 1 to 3 July were largely taken up with preparing for and holding the interviews with the candidates for the competition to replace the LCJ.

On 4 and 5 July, I attended the annual conference of the Australian Bar in Rome where I gave a speech on civil justice. I met Justice Susan Kiefel of the High Court of Australia. She is now the Chief Justice of that court. We were to meet again in Brisbane the following year when she heard another speech from me on civil justice and expressed amazement that I had been able to make the subject so amusing (I think this was meant to be a compliment). I did not get much benefit from my visit to Rome. It was a good example of what a Swedish judge once described to me as 'judicial tourism'. Some judicial and legal visits are professionally useful; many, like this one, are not.

Later that month, I attended a dinner for some Canadian Supreme Court Judges that was held in our Supreme Court. One of these, Rosalie Abella, had become a friend. Our paths crossed a number of times. I also attended the annual party of the Technology and Construction Bar Association (of which I had become the president).

On the 12th, I paid a visit to the civil courts of Birmingham. I made regional visits from time to time to important civil justice centres outside London. These included Manchester, Liverpool, Leeds, Newcastle, Oxford and Bristol. I met the DCJs and court managers and tried to find out what was going well and where the problems lay. I was then shown round the offices and introduced to the listing officers and many of the other officials who are essential to the working of the courts. Having met the officials, I met some of the wonderful people who run the PSU to whom I have already referred when describing my visits when I was DHCJ. I think everyone I met really appreciated these visits just as they had appreciated the visits I made when I was DHCJ. In retrospect, I think I should have made more such visits. But my desire to sit on many appeals limited the amount of time I could spend on other matters.

These meetings were followed by lunch with the local civil judges and occasionally a visiting High Court Judge. In the afternoon of each visit, I conducted a meeting to which local solicitors and barristers were invited and from which the local judges were excluded. In this way, I hoped that the local lawyers would be able to speak freely about the quality of the service that was being provided by the courts and to identify aspects of civil procedure rules and process which they thought could be improved. I found these sessions useful. I was able to make some changes as a result of what I learnt.

Occasionally, I encountered opposition and even real aggression. I recall some judges expressing their strong disagreement with the tough line that I had advocated should be taken on the issue of whether judges should grant relief from sanctions to a party who had failed to comply with a court order or a rule. I had set out what I considered to be the correct approach in the case of *Mitchell v News Group Newspapers Ltd* [2013] EWCA Civ 1437. I subsequently softened it a little in *Denton v TH White Ltd* [2014] EWCA Civ 906. The judges said that the *Mitchell* approach would lead to a denial of justice to litigants and that they intended to ignore it and carry on in the traditional more relaxed and forgiving way. I considered that this defiance of a decision of the Court of Appeal was deplorable and I told them so.

In essence, I had said that a party should not usually be granted relief from the consequences of a default which was more than trivial unless there was a good reason for the default. The consequences of a default could be very serious. In some cases they could be that a claim was struck out or a defendant was debarred from defending the claim. The traditional approach to dealing with a failure to comply with a rule or court order was to excuse the defaulting party on condition that he paid the costs occasioned by the default. This approach had led to a sloppy litigation culture which I believed it important to correct. The decision in *Mitchell* was very unpopular in some quarters. Articles were written which were fiercely critical of it. But many welcomed it as providing much needed discipline in the way in which civil litigation was conducted.

In a symposium to mark my contribution to the administration of civil justice held in Oxford on 14 November 2014, Stephen Richards described the judgment in *Denton* as 'very far from a capitulation to pressure from the profession. On the contrary, I regard as a fine example of judicial realism, skill and subtlety, effecting a brilliant adjustment of *Mitchell* with the aim of overcoming the problems without losing the emphasis on compliance with the need for a change of culture'. This was a flattering assessment which I greatly welcomed. I should say that in 2017, the Supreme Court said in *BPP Holdings Ltd v Revenue and Customs Commissioners* [2017] 1 WLR 2945 that the 'refinements' of *Mitchell* in *Denton* were 'largely clarifications'. Eventually, the situation calmed down. And so after a rather difficult birth, my approach to this important issue came of age and is now generally followed. The result has been an improvement in discipline and efficiency in the conduct of civil litigation.

But to return to July 2013, I received an honorary degree from the University of Essex. I was later to receive honorary degrees from University College London (UCL) and the University of Leeds. I was thrilled to receive these degrees. I have remained starry-eyed about academia all my adult life although, having been an academic for many years, Jacqueline thinks this is faintly ridiculous. At the University of Essex, we were escorted to the ceremony by my good friend the late Professor Anthony King, who was a leading political scientist. I was introduced by another good friend, the late Professor Sir Nigel Rodley, who as I earlier described had been my contemporary at Ingledew College in Leeds. He introduced me in a warm and generous oration. In my response, I said that our teachers at Ingledew would have been incredulous to see the two of us together at this degree ceremony. Over the years, Nigel and I had enjoyed many conversations about human rights law. On 30 January 2014, I gave the annual University of Essex/Clifford Chance lecture whose title was 'The extraterritorial application of the European Convention on Human Rights: Now on a firmer footing. But is it a sound one?' I was supportive of the expansive approach that the court was adopting to its jurisdiction. Nigel chaired the lecture and expressed approval of it. But there are many who take a different view.

On 26 July, I gave the Valedictory address for Mr Justice (Colin) Mackay. I had been asked to do this instead of Igor, who usually did the Valedictories for all High Court Judges and above, because I knew Colin well. He had been my right-hand man when I was head of chambers. He was an excellent High Court Judge. I believe that I captured his rather complex character in what I said. These speeches are important and I took considerable care with them.

On 30 July, I gave the Valedictory address from the Bench in the huge Lord Chief Justice's Court 4 to mark Igor's retirement. The court was packed (including the balcony) and it was a very moving occasion. I was quite nervous. I wanted to strike the right note and I worked hard to produce a fitting speech. I believe that he was a great LCJ and said so. I also teased him gently about his lack of IT skills. I touched a raw nerve there, because for months after he retired, he made a point of telling me how at home he now was with mobile phones and emails. Despite this sensitivity, he and his family seemed pleased with my speech, although I understand that his mother rather bridled at being described as 'formidable'.

So I had managed to get through my first year without too much difficulty. But I had found it harder work than I was expecting. This was partly because I insisted on hearing a large number of appeals, many of which were difficult and of general importance. I did this partly because for me deciding cases was the best part of the job; and partly because I thought that, if I was perceived by my colleagues as having become for the most part an administrator, I would lose credibility in their eyes.

On 2 September, I was awarded an honorary LLD by UCL. The other hono-
rand was Sir Malcolm Grant who had just retired after 10 years' successful
tenure as President and Provost of the college. Dame Hazel Genn QC (Dean
of the Law Faculty) proposed me and gave a wonderful oration. In the evening
there was a dinner in college at which I spoke. Ever since Jacqueline had been
working at UCL, I had formed a deep attachment to the place. I was thrilled to
be honoured in this way.

On 1 October, John Thomas was sworn in as the new Lord Chief Justice in
Court 4. I gave a speech welcoming him. I worked closely with him during the
next three years until I retired in 2016. He was a brilliant LCJ who fizzed with
energy, ideas and reforming zeal. He did not interfere with my running of the
Court of Appeal or the way I discharged my duties as Head of Civil Justice,
although he made suggestions from time to time, most of which I adopted.
I also sought his advice occasionally as he did mine. I believe that we had a very
good relationship.

On the same day, Brian Leveson was sworn in as the PQBD as successor
to John. I also worked closely with Brian, who was an excellent PQBD. I had
the unenviable task of assuaging Lady Justice (Heather) Hallett, who had also
applied for this position. Following so soon after her failure to be appointed
LCJ, it was understandable that her failure to be appointed PQBD was a disappointment which she found difficult to bear.

In the second full week of the new term, I went to Leeds. I gave a lecture to
the local branch of the Council of Christians and Jews entitled 'Religion and
the Law'. I had last seen some of the people who attended the lecture more than
50 years earlier. It was as if a curtain was drawn back and I was peering into the
small Jewish community to which I once belonged. My impression was that little
had changed.

The following morning, I gave the Mustill lecture, which is a biennial lecture
sponsored by the North East Branch of the Chartered Institute of Arbitrators.
The title of the lecture was 'Arbitration after the Brussels 1 Reform'. As I said
earlier, Michael Mustill was an *alumnus* of Ingledew College. He was a proud
Yorkshiremen and particularly attached to Nidderdale where he had a home. He
had been one of the leading commercial lawyers of the late twentieth century
and a great judge. He had retired from the Appellate Committee of the House
of Lords in 1997 and had gone on to have a distinguished career in academia and
as an international arbitrator. He was the co-author of *Commercial Arbitration*.
He knew a great deal more about arbitration then I did. To my surprise and
somewhat to my dismay, when I rose to deliver my lecture, I saw Lord and Lady
Mustill sitting in the front row. Although he was in poor physical health (he died
the following year), I could see that he was listening intently to what I was saying
and he made a most insightful contribution during the question time after the
lecture. He was complimentary and charming to me. He later wrote a letter to
me saying that the lecture was 'quite outstanding and it was a great honour to

me that my name should be associated with it'. He said that there was 'quite a literature now on this awkward topic, most of it very poor. Yours was a golden exception'. I cannot pretend that I was not delighted to receive this letter from such a great lawyer and such an authority on the subject.

Later in the month, I flew to Hong Kong to participate in a conference hosted by Hong Kong University to discuss issues about media law. This was not a subject in which I yet felt particularly at home, although during my four years as MR, I heard quite a number of privacy and defamation cases some of which were high profile. I gave a lecture entitled 'Advances in Open Justice in England and Wales'. I expressed the view that all appeals should be televised (and not merely those in the Supreme Court) and that, with certain exceptions, all trials should be televised. This was somewhat bold because this idea, even if subject to exceptions and protections, did not command much support. The conference was attended by academics, practitioners and judges, mainly from the Far East and Australasia, but also from the United Kingdom. One of the speakers was a brave human rights lawyer who was attempting to practise in mainland China. He movingly described the difficulties that he faced and the harassment to which he was subjected by the authorities. At the end of his talk, the audience burst into applause. He was listened to in stony silence by a group of academics from a Chinese university. One evening, Geoffrey Ma, the Chief Justice of Hong Kong, hosted a dinner in my honour at his magnificent official residence at the top of the Peak on Hong Kong Island.

On my return to London, I had a meeting with Professor Richard Susskind who was the IT adviser to the LCJ. He had been saying for a long time that our IT systems were not fit for purpose. He was later commissioned by the CJC to write a report which led to the recommendation by Lord Justice (Michael) Briggs that an online court should be established. Despite the fact that I am something of a technophobe, I fully supported Richard's work and Michael's report.

On 1 November, I presided over the Court of Appeal annual away day. We discussed the business of the court and the problems which the court was then facing. The pressures on everyone resulting from the ever increasing volume of new cases had led to a growing backlog and greater delays. The away day gave the members of the court a good opportunity to ventilate their concerns and put forward ideas as to how to improve matters. We were later to take some radical measures to try to improve the situation. The general consensus was that these away days were worthwhile, not least because they were good for bonding. In previous years, they had been held in a smart London hotel. But this year, the financial squeeze had caused us to relocate to an altogether less attractive venue: a dismal room in the offices of the MoJ. A number of my colleagues protested about the venue. Their principal ground of complaint was that, since government departments were parties to so many of the appeals that we had to decide, we should not be seen to be holding our meeting in a government building. I thought this was a ridiculous reason for objecting to the venue. But in subsequent years, we held the meetings in the Rolls Building (a court building). We were never able to return to the smart hotel.

A few days later, I had my first meeting with Shailesh Vara MP who had taken over from Helen Grant as minister responsible for civil justice. I was to meet him a few times until he was replaced by the excellent Lord Faulks QC. On a personal level, I found Shailesh very charming. But so far as I could tell, he was ineffectual. He was unwilling or unable to engage with me on issues which were of real concern to me and many others, such as the proposed reforms relating to judicial review and, especially, the proposed massive increase in court fees (the fees payable for issuing proceedings). The most controversial of these was that the fee payable for proceedings to recover a sum in excess of £10,000 was to be increased to 5 per cent of the value of the claim (up to a ceiling of £10,000). I argued that the increased fees were likely to drive potential litigants away from the courts, particularly small and medium-sized enterprises. This would result in a serious denial of access to justice and would not lead to the hoped-for increase in revenue which was the declared object of the proposals. I made all these points to Shailesh, but he failed to give me a reasoned response. I found this very frustrating. I suspected that he had no real power. But when I raised all my concerns with Chris Grayling, I made very little headway with him either. I thought that it was shocking that the Department had undertaken the most exiguous research into the likely impact of the proposals.

The increased court fees were duly introduced by the Government in March 2015. In January 2016, together with Sir James Munby (PFD) and Sir Ernest Ryder (Senior President of Tribunals), I appeared before the Justice Select Committee of the House of Commons which was examining the issue of the increase in court fees. I was outspoken in my criticism of the increases. I told the committee, 'We have warned of the real dangers [of denial of access to justice] and we also warned that the research carried out by the government ... was lamentable'. The chairman of the committee, Robert Neill MP, was clearly surprised that I had used such strong language, but I said that I stood by it. There was a great deal of media coverage of what I said.

To return to November 2013, I gave a speech at the biennial dinner in the Guildhall for Nightingale House (the care home for elderly Jewish residents) a charity that my family has supported for decades. We have rarely missed these dinners. They are attended by about 500 people. Jacqueline's uncle's family has been heavily involved with Nightingale for years. It was quite an honour to be asked to give this speech, which is often given by leading national figures (not necessarily Jewish).

Later in the month, I gave the keynote address at a conference on construction adjudication held by the Adjudication Society. It was extraordinary how the Housing Grants, Construction and Regeneration Act 1996 had given rise to so much case law, as well as textbooks, articles, work for the lawyers and now a society. I had hoped that the early jurisprudence (including my own decision in *Macob v Morrison*) would have sorted things out. Clearly not.

I spent the first part of the following week in Cardiff. On the first day, I met the Counsel General of Wales (Theo Huckle QC) and was given a tour of the Welsh Assembly. On the following three days, I sat on appeals with two of my colleagues. The cases were not particularly interesting or difficult, but they were Welsh. The political pull of the Welsh factor is such that the court usually sits in Cardiff twice a year.

On 3 December, we attended the annual Diplomatic Reception at Buckingham Palace. We had not attended the previous year because I did not want to attend yet another official function and I inexcusably refused the invitation without consulting Jacqueline. For this treasonable conduct, I was rightly reprimanded by her. My mother and grandmother would both have been outraged as would many others. So we attended the reception in each of my remaining years. It is a 'white tie' event attended by ambassadors, senior politicians and other grandees. It gives the guests an opportunity to explore some of the magnificent rooms of the palace. The guests are assigned to one of two huge rooms. They wander around in their assigned room looking for famous people with whom to exchange a few words. We met some interesting people both from home and abroad. After a while, members of the Royal Family enter and make their customary tour, pausing here and there to make polite conversation. The food was good and a desultory number of couples took the opportunity to dance to an excellent band in a huge hall.

A few days later, I visited the court in Leeds and made my standard tour. On the 10th, I attended a meeting to discuss cost budgeting. This was one of the most important of the Jackson reforms and was designed to reduce the cost of civil litigation. It was proving to be very unpopular with the legal profession but I supported it. It was an issue that was to occupy a good deal of my time during the following months.

The next term started in the now familiar way with the court plenary meeting followed by other meetings. On 23 January, I spoke at the annual dinner of the Denning Society in the lovely Lincoln's Inn Old Hall. At the dinner I sat between Sir Martin Nourse (a former judge of the Court of Appeal) and Lady Hazel Fox QC, Lord Denning's stepdaughter and a distinguished international lawyer. Another guest was Professor John Gurdon (Nobel Prize winner) who had been our son Steven's PhD supervisor at Cambridge. Lord Denning was one of my most famous and illustrious predecessors as Master of the Rolls. He held the office for 20 years until he retired at the age of 83. He used to sit on appeals five days a week and was often able to give *ex tempore* judgments. Today, *ex tempore* judgments in the Court of Appeal are collectors' items. He was a brilliant (and sometimes rather controversial) lawyer who made some important contributions to the development of our law. Even a man of his brilliance could not have held the office for anything like 20 years today. His administrative duties were minimal: there were far fewer Lords Justice of Appeal to manage; and he was not Head of Civil Justice (all the administrative responsibilities for running the justice system being discharged by the Government rather than the judges).

The law was much less complex: for example, EU law had infiltrated our law to a far lesser degree than it has today and the European Convention on Human Rights had not been incorporated into our law.

On 6 February, I attended the Global Law Summit dinner in the Mansion House. The event was entitled 'One year to go' and marked the fact that the Magna Carta commemoration was now imminent. The dinner was attended by Chris Grayling who had decided to use the 800th anniversary of Magna Carta as a reason for showcasing London as a centre for legal services and the promotion of the rule of law. I spoke at the dinner and expressed my amazement and gratitude that the Treasury had provided £1 million to fund Magna Carta activities, including educational projects in schools, round the country. It was amazing since the country was in the grips of austerity. We had been told by the Ministry that there was no money for anything. I sat next to Philip Hammond MP, then Secretary of State for Defence. He later became Foreign Secretary and later still Chancellor of the Exchequer. His connection with Magna Carta was that he was the MP for Runnymede and Weybridge. We had a wide-ranging discussion. He was critical of the recent Supreme Court decision in *Smith v Ministry of Defence* [2013] UKSC 41 which had held that the MoD could in principle be sued in negligence for failing to provide soldiers with adequate equipment. He said that this showed a complete lack of understanding of the practicalities and the difficulties facing the military and the government. He offered to meet me in order to educate me and explain why the decision was so bad. I did not take up the offer.

Later in the month, I had a difficult meeting with the SPJ and the PFD and officials to try to agree a fair allocation of judicial resources as between civil and family work. The civil/family issue was a constant sore throughout my four years. Family work was taking an increasing proportion of resources at the expense of civil work. I was always having to fight for civil. One of the problems was that for children cases a 24-week limit had been imposed on the period between the date of issue of proceedings and the hearing date, and the number of children cases was constantly increasing. At our meeting, we agreed a real-location of judge sitting days as between civil and family cases but this did not really solve the problem. The increase in civil judge sitting days was achieved in the main by an increase in part-time judge sittings. The result was that a higher percentage of part-time judges sat on civil cases than on family cases. On the whole, part-time (deputy) judges are less experienced and get through the work less efficiently than full-time judges. The civil justice system continued to fare less well than the family justice system.

Early March was taken up with meetings as usual. I met Lord Faulks QC, the new Minister of State for Justice with special responsibility for civil justice. At last, a minister had been appointed who had a real understanding of civil justice. We had a good working relationship throughout the rest of my term of office. He resigned after the appointment of Liz Truss in July 2016 as Lord Chancellor in succession to Michael Gove. I had the impression that he was not always in sympathy with government policy, but he was never disloyal. He was very supportive of me on issues such as the extension of the fixed recoverable costs and changing the procedural rules to help the Court of Appeal to cope with the increasing pressures that it was facing as a result of the inexorable increase in work.

On 14 March, I met Sadiq Khan MP, the shadow Lord Chancellor, who later became the Mayor of London. He was delightful, relaxed, informal and chatty. I was unable to judge whether he had any seriously considered policies. He may have done, but the dominant impression he gave me was of bright and breezy friendliness. He had not yet been subjected to the stress of holding office and exercising real power. All of that changed when he became the Mayor.

For the rest of the month, I attended a number of meetings and dinners. These included a meeting over dinner with other senior judges and Dean Spielmann, the President of the Strasbourg court; another all day CJC conference; the annual district judges' conference; a conference attended by members of our Supreme Court and Court of Appeal and senior judges of the Irish Republic (at which, as usual, we discussed issues of human rights and EU law); a dinner at the Mansion House hosted by the City of London Solicitors; a meeting at the Institute of Government with the LCJ and Mr Justice Cranston; a meeting with Lord Neuberger; and a meeting with Justice Randy Holland who was an Associate Justice of the Supreme Court of Delaware.

On 14 April, I participated in the annual swearing in of the new QCs. It was a particular pleasure for me to swear in our son-in-law, Jonathan Hall who had developed a most successful practice as a junior barrister. His practice as a Silk was to take off rapidly.

The following month, we had one of many meetings that took place to discuss reforms to Her Majesty's Courts and Tribunal Service (HMCTS). The LCJ was the driving force behind this major project. He was ably assisted by the new chief executive of HMCTS, Natalie Ceeney. My main interest was in the reforms in so far as they affected civil justice, but I also had a supporting role in relation to the general reforms. This modernisation project was to take up a good deal of my time.

On 24 May, I was the guest of Professor Andrew Burrows QC at the Chichele Dinner at All Souls College, Oxford. This is a very grand affair held in the magnificent Codrington Library. On one side, I sat next to Professor Tony Honoré (who with Professor Herbert Hart had written *Causation in the Law*). He was 93 at the time. It was truly humbling to have the privilege of talking to such a brilliant person. On the other side, I sat next to the Warden, Sir John Vickers with whom I had a conversation that was fascinating (at least for me) and covered a wide range of subjects. He is not a lawyer, but he was disconcertingly au fait with many of the current legal issues. I was unable to match this with an ability to talk, intelligently or at all, about economics and banking.

On 7 June, I took part in a conference on Magna Carta and religion and gave the closing address. Although 2015 was still months away, there was already a great deal of Magna Carta activity. Magna Carta was intruding into my life with increasing momentum. It would continue to do so until the end of 2015.

In July, I received an honorary LLD from Leeds University. This was particularly thrilling for me because the university is only a few minutes' walk away from the former site of Leeds Grammar School. My fellow honorands included Sir Patrick Stewart (actor), Sir Andras Schiff (pianist) and Professor Michael Arthur (now Provost of UCL, formerly Vice-Chancellor of Leeds University). The ceremony was conducted in the Great Hall. Fanny Waterman and my brother were in the audience as, of course, was my ever faithful and ever supportive Jacqueline. The degrees were conferred by Lord (Melvyn) Bragg who made an excellent speech. I shared with him not only a love for the Lake District, but also the fact that we were both *alumni* of Wadham College, Oxford. After the ceremony, together with the Schiffs, we went by taxi to our hotel out of town in Lawnswood. Andras, who is surely one of the greatest pianists of our time, was jokey, giggly and almost child-like. Apart from music, his great passion seemed to be football. Later we returned to the University for a dinner at which I made a speech. I enjoyed talking to Lord Bragg. This was a memorable and enjoyable day. The following day, we caught an early train back to London. By 10.30, I was back in court to carry on with the appeal that I had been hearing the previous day.

In the last week of term, I made a short Valedictory speech to a full court to mark the retirement of Peter Hurst. Peter had been the Chief Taxing Master and Chief Costs Judge since 1992. I had worked with him a good deal for many years, first when I was DHCJ and later when I was Head of Civil Justice. He has undoubtedly contributed more to the development of the law and practice relating to costs than anyone I can think of. I was delighted to be able to say this publicly.

September was marked by a wonderful lecture tour/holiday to Singapore, New Zealand and Australia. We had never been to any of these countries. We started in Singapore where we were met at the airport and whisked to the VIP lounge to await our baggage. We were then driven to our very posh hotel. This gave us a rare insight into the treatment accorded to real VIPs. I had been invited to give the 2014 Distinguished Speaker lecture in the lecture theatre of the splendid Supreme Court building. The title was 'The limits of the common law'. It bore some similarity to parts of my lecture 'Are the judges too powerful?' We were well looked after for the rest of our brief stay in Singapore. We were shown some of the advanced technology deployed in their courts which made me both envious and ashamed of the primitive methods we were still adopting at home. We visited the beautiful Botanical Gardens and had lunch at the National University of Singapore. One of the hosts was a tax law professor who had been an LLM student of Jacqueline's at UCL. We were entertained to dinner in restaurants on successive nights by Chief Justice Menon and his wife and Attorney General VK Rajah and his wife. They were all charming and very good company.

We then flew to Queenstown, New Zealand. We spent two nights in a lovely hotel overlooking the lake and attended the World Bar Conference. The participants were advocates and judges from all over the world, including from the United Kingdom. I gave the keynote address entitled 'Advocates as protectors of the Rule of Law'. Chief Justice Menon and Sian Elias (Chief Justice of New Zealand) spoke too. There were also inspiring speeches from advocates who practised, with difficulty, in countries whose human rights record was poor. One of these was a remarkable human rights lawyer from the Philippines who described some terrifying experiences. Not for the first or last time, I realised how fortunate we are to live in the United Kingdom where the rule of law is respected and not questioned by our political leaders. We had a little time for sightseeing and a most enjoyable dinner that was hosted by Sian Elias and her husband Hugh.

We then flew to Sydney where we stayed for nine days. I gave two lectures in Sydney. One was at the New South Wales University. The other was at the Australian Appeal Judges' Conference. They were both on civil justice-related subjects. We met a number of delightful senior judges including Tom Bathurst (Chief Justice of New South Wales), James Allsop (President of the Federal Court of Australia) and Margaret Beazley ((President of the New South Wales Court of Appeal). We were disappointed with the cultural fare that Sydney had to offer, although the Museum of Art contains some lovely indigenous works of art. But we were bowled over by the physical beauty of the city and its setting.

From Sydney, we flew to Melbourne where we stayed for six days. Although it is less strikingly beautiful than Sydney, we preferred it. It is culturally more lively and interesting. We walked a lot, including past the iconic Melbourne Cricket Ground, into the magnificent botanical gardens and along the Yarra River as well as in the city itself and its lovely arcades. One evening, we had dinner at the home of Carol Gordon, who is a relation of Jacqueline's. This was a welcome relief from dinners with judges.

The main lecture that I gave was at Melbourne University. I gave an adapted version of the lecture that I had given to the Council of Christians and Jews in Leeds on Religion and the Law. The Dean of the Law School, Professor Carolyn Evans, greeted us on our arrival and said that she was delighted that I had chosen this topic. I soon discovered that she had written extensively on the subject, and was the author of the leading Australian textbook on it. I had no idea that this was the area of her particular expertise. If I had known, I am sure that I would have chosen a different subject. I managed to get through the lecture and some searching questions, after which there was a dinner. After the main course, the Dean suggested that, since the discussion after the lecture had been so lively and interesting, we should continue with it before the next course was served. So I was still not out of the woods.

We had accepted an invitation by Marilyn Warren (Chief Justice of Victoria) to attend the annual conference of the Supreme Court Justices of Victoria in a hotel about an hour's drive away from Melbourne up the Yarra Valley. After the dinner, I spoke about my life in the law. The judges were very welcoming and the atmosphere was extremely friendly. We found that we had a great deal in common and bonded well. My European background has tended to lead me to underestimate the importance of the Commonwealth, the power of the common law and the strength of our shared values. After my talk and some questions, the music began. One of the judges played the guitar and performed like an ageing rock star. I had not encountered anything like this before.

We stayed until lunchtime the following day. There were some excellent presentations. The most interesting one was from a leading and most impressive tax lawyer who had given up advising on tax and was now devoting himself to doing *pro bono* work for the indigenous people who live in the Northern Territories. I had no idea that there were so many problems and so much deprivation in that State.

From Melbourne, we flew to Brisbane. We stayed in the magnificent Governor's House for four days as guests of Paul and Kay de Jersey. Paul, who had been the Chief Justice of Queensland, was now the Governor. The large nineteenth-century house is set in many hectares of land. We had a palatial bedroom and staff to attend to our every wish. I gave only one lecture in Brisbane. This was the grandiosely named 'AIJA Oration'. My lecture was a slightly revamped version of one of the lectures I gave in Sydney. It was given in the magnificent Banco Court of Chief Justice of Queensland. The attendees included Justice Susan Kiefel who said that, for a lecture on civil procedure, she had found it surprisingly entertaining. Without a sprinkling of irrelevant jokes, it is difficult to introduce levity into a lecture on civil procedure. After dinner, we were invited to dinner in a smart restaurant overlooking the river. To my embarrassment, the current Chief Justice had not been invited, although he had attended the lecture and allowed it to be given in his court. His appointment had been deeply unpopular because it was thought that he was not up to the job. Most of the judges had apparently boycotted his swearing in. He subsequently resigned. This was a most brutal business.

On our last day, we were driven by the husband of Justice Michelle May, who was a judge of the Family Court of Australia, Appeal Division, to their ranch about 100 miles north up the valley of the River Brisbane. Michelle was unable to join us because she was sitting in court. Her husband was a retired judge and one of their daughters came too. We were driven round the estate and saw kangaroos in the wild; and we walked along a stretch of the river. This was a wonderful day out: the only time we truly escaped from cities on the whole tour.

The tour was a great success. This was our first and, I suspect, will be our only visit to the Antipodes. We met large numbers of wonderful people: lively, fun and above all friendly. I had given seven lectures. This was by far the longest and most tiring of all the professional visits that I made as a judge. Writing lectures was very time-consuming. The fact that almost all of them were posted on one website or another meant that one had to have a certain insouciance to deliver the same lecture more than once. In the pre-internet days, nobody would know how many times a speaker gave the same lecture or made the same speech. So it was hard work. But for the most part, these visits and lectures were enjoyable. Sometimes I wondered whether they were a worthwhile part of the job of being a senior judge. I believe they were. Judges and lawyers from other countries still have great respect for our law and our judges and lawyers. They seem to enjoy meeting us and discussing the burning issues of the day. I was always struck by the fact that so many of the problems that we were facing beset other countries too.

October marked the beginning of my third year as MR. I was now becoming used to the plenary meetings of the court. The senior Lord Justices who were older than me and had been pillars of the court for so long had now retired. It had become a younger court and although these meetings were not totally relaxing affairs, I felt very comfortable and at home when chairing them. I had to get used to the idea of being one of the oldest judges in the Court of Appeal.

Early in the term, because the LCJ was unavailable, I gave the Valedictory address for Lord Justice Maurice Kay who had been a calm and supportive Vice President. I enjoyed crafting speeches of this kind. I have always been hopeless at telling jokes, not least because I usually fluff the punchline. But I am able to tell anecdotes in a way which evokes titters rather than guffaws. Like most Valedictories, this was a warm and happy occasion.

Later in October, I had a meeting to discuss the vexed issue of revising the guideline hourly rates for solicitors' fees which were used by the costs judges as a basis for the assessment of costs in litigation. The published rates had been published many years earlier and had been updated each year in line with inflation. My predecessor had set up a committee to recommend new rates based on the reasonable cost to solicitors of doing the work. The committee received evidence and produced a report with recommendations. In the end, I concluded with regret that the evidence did not support the recommendations and I rejected them. My decision was not popular with the profession, which was hoping for a substantial increase. Neither the Government nor the Law Society was willing to fund the research that would be necessary to produced reliable figures. The result was that, over time, the existing guideline hourly rates ceased to have much relevance. All of this took a great deal of my time. It was certainly not exciting, but it was important.

In November, I had a meeting with Lady Justice (Jill) Black to discuss the possibility of re-routing some appeals in family cases from the Court of Appeal to the High Court. I spent a great deal of time on this issue, in particular negotiating with Sir James Munby who was supportive of the idea. The problem was that the Court of Appeal was being flooded with a large number of mainly hopeless family appeals and the burden of dealing with them was becoming intolerable. I had tried to tackle the problem by persuading Lord Justices who were not family law specialists to take on some of the applications for permission to appeal, some of which were extremely time-consuming. But the problem had persisted and was getting worse. In the end, we did manage to divert a certain class of family appeals to the High Court. This required the approval of the ever helpful Lord Faulks QC as well as rule changes and it helped to some extent.

On the 14th, I went to Oxford for the civil justice symposium held in my honour to which I have referred earlier. It was organised by Professor Adrian Zuckerman to mark my contributions to civil justice. He had persuaded a number of distinguished judges to give papers (Lord David Neuberger, Lord Brian Kerr, Lord Justice Stephen Richards, Lord Justice Rupert Jackson, Lord Justice Michael Briggs and Mr Justice Vivian Ramsey) and had invited other distinguished people to sit and listen. The papers were subsequently published in an edition of the *Civil Justice Quarterly* (2015). The symposium was followed by a small dinner held at University College, Oxford at which John Sorabji and I spoke. It was a great honour for me.

A few days later, a Magna Carta reception was held in the Speaker's House in the House of Commons. One of the Deputy Speakers hosted the event and spoke as did I. The Magna Carta commemoration events were now well under way.

Later in the month, I met Kate Briden for the first time. She had taken over from Dave Thompson as the person in charge of the Royal Courts of Justice. I found her more helpful and constructive than her predecessor. She fully understood the pressures under which the Court of Appeal was struggling and was later to introduce changes that went some way to alleviating the situation.

On 1 December, together with Sir James Munby (President of the Family Division) and Sir Jeremy Sullivan (Senior President of Tribunals), I gave evidence to the House of Commons Justice Committee on the impact of the reforms introduced by the Legal Aid, Sentences and Punishment of Offenders Act 2012 (LASPO). The committee was expertly chaired by the Right Honourable Sir Alan Beith MP. The main focus of its enquiry was on the effect of the withdrawal of legal aid brought about by LASPO and the consequent increase in the number of self-represented litigants. This was my first appearance before a parliamentary committee. I was a little apprehensive. I had seen other parliamentary committees in action on television and knew that some MPs used the hearings as an occasion for political grandstanding. My concerns were immediately allayed. We were treated with politeness and respect by all the members of the committee. I tried to describe the effects of the reforms with reasonable objectivity. I was asked whether I thought that the cuts in legal aid had led to miscarriages of justice. I replied: 'It would be extraordinary if there had not been some cases which would have been decided the other way had the litigant been represented by a competent lawyer'. This led to the headline in *The Guardian* 'Cuts in legal aid leading to miscarriages of justice'. The committee produced an impressive, carefully researched and compelling report which was very critical of the Government. It concluded that the reforms were failing to achieve three of its four stated aims. Although I had been a little nervous at first, I enjoyed the experience.

On 12 January 2015, we both attended a big Magna Carta auction dinner in the Guildhall. Later in the month, a reception was held in Middle Temple for Louis Blom-Cooper QC to mark the launch of his latest book. It was a real pleasure for me to speak in praise of this great man, then approaching his nine-tieth birthday. I referred to his boundless energy and his inspiring enthusiasm. I described the only occasion when I was led by him at the Bar. This was in the case of *Lamb v Camden* which I have already described in chapter seven. Although his physical health was poor in his final years, he never lost his memory or his sharpness of mind or sense of excitement. When he died in September 2018, he was writing his latest book. He enriched the lives of many, including me.

Later in the month, I chaired a session of the Global Law Summit which was held at the Queen Elizabeth Centre in Westminster. This was an all-day event that was the culmination of the Lord Chancellor's plans to use the Magna Carta anniversary to promote London as the leading centre for international law. Later, I had a meeting with Sir Mark Sedwell, the Permanent Secretary of the Home Office. He wanted to discuss civil justice issues of particular inter-est to the Home Office. Foremost among these was immigration. Immigration and asylum cases formed a substantial part of the diet of the Court of Appeal's work. Many of the applications for permission to appeal were hopeless, but a significant number were not. It was important not to lose sight of the fact that some of the asylum claims raised issues of life and death.

In March, I had meetings with Robert Bourne, the new President of the Law Society and Catherine Dixon, the new Chief Executive of the Law Society; I made an after-dinner speech at the Trinity College Oxford Law Society; and attended a preliminary meeting of the panel convened by the Judicial Appoint-ments Commission to recommend a new Chair of the Law Commission. The format of this competition was very much along the lines of the competitions for senior judicial appointments. Following interviews of some strong candidates, we recommended Lord Justice David Bean. Our recommendation was accepted by the Lord Chancellor.

I had already commissioned Lord Justice Michael Briggs to make recommen-dations to me for the reform of the way in which the Court of Appeal discharged its civil justice business. The court was being swamped with work and the time between the issue of the notice of appeal and the hearing date had become unac-ceptably long. As a result of the reforms that he and his working group later proposed, a number of important reforms were introduced before I retired.

Later in the month, I made a visit to the Civil Court Centre at Newcastle; I gave a talk entitled 'How my classical education has affected my life' at a recep-tion to mark the launch of Classics for All, which is a charity whose object is to promote the teaching of Classics in state schools; attended the annual dinner of the Association of District Judges; and gave the Keating lecture. This is an occasional lecture given in honour of the memory of Donald Keating QC, the

Head of my first chambers. I was very pleased to be asked to give this lecture because it was yet more proof that I had been forgiven for leaving chambers all those years ago. In fact, in their marketing they had claimed me as one of their own. The title of the lecture was 'The contribution of construction cases to the development of the common law'. I was delighted to see so many of my former colleagues in the audience and especially pleased to see some members of Donald's family too.

The pace did not slacken. In April, we attended a banquet at the Mansion House and I gave a Magna Carta speech at the Law Society entitled 'Delay too often defeats Justice'. On the 24th, we went to Dublin for the Fourth British/Irish Commercial Law Forum. The focus of the event was Magna Carta. To our great surprise, we were met at the airport by the UK ambassador to the Irish Republic, Dominick Chilcott and were driven in his official car to our hotel. In the great hall of the Inns of Court where we dined, I gave a speech entitled '800 years of Magna Carta – the commercial rule of law in the 21st century'. To my further surprise, the ambassador attended the dinner and listened to the speech. During the day, we were given a guided tour of Trinity College and went to an exhibition on literary Dublin. The weekend culminated in a reception for the participants in the Forum which was hosted by the ambassador at Glencairn House, his beautiful official residence in the hills south of the city.

In May, Lord Justice Jackson gave the annual Harbour Litigation Funding lecture. The subject of his lecture was costs management and, in particular, costs budgeting, which were proving to be one of the most controversial of the Jackson civil justice reforms. I gave a speech strongly supportive of the reforms.

Later in the month, we went to Jersey for two days. I had been invited to give a lecture entitled 'The English experience of access to justice reform'. My lecture was largely a repeat of one I had previously given. I accepted the invitation rather unashamedly because I had not previously been to Jersey and wanted to visit it. We were taken to a chamber concert in the delightful miniature opera house. On the Saturday, we hired a car and drove round the western part of the island. We visited the 'tunnels' which had been constructed by the Germans during the Second World War in order to house their military hospital; and we walked along the north and west coasts, inspecting the formidable pill boxes that the Germans had built. This visit was a delightful interlude and provided welcome respite from my gruelling and relentless schedule.

On 4 June Michael Gove MP, who had succeeded Chris Grayling as Lord Chancellor, telephoned me for an introductory conversation. I had dealings with him from time to time during the following 12 months until the change of Government following the resignation of the Prime Minister, David Cameron. I found Michael very charming and almost unnaturally courteous and polite. I did not spend sufficient time with him to be able to assess how deep the seam of his charm was. He was clearly most intelligent and very quick to get to the point and understand issues even those of which he had had no prior notice.

He gave me the impression that he really understood that it was important to have a system of justice that was not only efficient, but was also fair and just. Unlike his predecessor, he seemed genuinely to believe that it was important for the rule of law to have a strong independent Bar. He expressed what appeared to me to be genuine concern about the effects on the justice system of the cuts that had been made to legal aid and the poor remuneration of lawyers who engaged in publicly funded work. He was clearly troubled about the effect of the freeze on judges' pay since the banking crisis of 2008 and the reduction in the benefit of judicial pensions on the morale of the judiciary and the ability to recruit sufficient new judges of the right quality. In the summer of 2016, he accompanied the LCJ and me to a meeting with Greg Hands MP, the Chief Secretary to the Treasury, at which we explained the gravity of the pay and pensions problems. Mr Hands explained that the Government was concerned that, if judges were treated as a case worthy of special treatment, other senior public servants (like generals and permanent secretaries) would also ask for special treatment. We argued that the judges were truly in a different category from any other group. My sense was that Mr Hands was persuadable. After the meeting, Michael Gove said that he believed that there would be a good outcome for the judges. But sadly for us, Michael was replaced as Lord Chancellor on 11 July 2016 by Liz Truss MP. In my view, that was a great pity.

Her tenure of that office, which lasted only until 11 June 2017, was to prove disastrous. Not the least of her shortcomings was her failure to discharge the statutory duty to protect the independence of the judges when the judges of the Divisional Court of the High Court were pilloried by some of the media as 'enemies of the people' for their decision in *R (Miller) v Secretary of State for Exiting the European Union* [2017] UKSC 5. The judges had held that the Government was wrong to say that it was not necessary to obtain the prior approval of Parliament before giving notice of withdrawal from the EU under article 50 of the Treaty of Lisbon. The critics of the court's judgment said that the judges were seeking to undermine the will of the people as expressed in the referendum. This was a disgraceful misrepresentation of a decision which did no more than resolve a question of statutory interpretation. The judges could not have stated more clearly that they were saying nothing about the merits or demerits of Brexit. At first, Liz Truss said nothing to defend the judges from this attack. Eventually, in response to widespread criticism for her failure to say anything, she said:

> I think it is dangerous for a Government minister to say 'this is an acceptable and this isn't an acceptable headline', because I am a huge believer in the independence of the judiciary and am also a very strong believer in the free press.

I was not alone in thinking that most of her predecessors would have immediately stepped in to defend the judges far more robustly than this. The response suggested to me that she was more concerned to avoid upsetting the media than to perform her statutory duty of protecting the independence of the judiciary. It is highly regrettable that in recent times, the Government seems to have regarded the office of Lord Chancellor and Secretary of State for Justice as being relatively unimportant. Sadly, there are few votes in Justice. It is deeply unsatisfactory that in the less than three years that elapsed between May 2015 and January 2018, no fewer than four ministers held the office. These were Michael Gove (May 2015–July 2016); Liz Truss (July 2016–June 2017); David Lidington (June 2017–January 2018) and David Gauke (January 2018–present).

In the first part of June, I had attended the annual dinner of CILEx (the Chartered Institute of Legal Executives) and gave an after dinner speech. There was more interviewing of candidates in the next competition to fill the latest vacancies in the Court of Appeal. I went to Paris to take part in a Colloque of the Comité Franco-Britannique-Irlandais on Freedom of Expression and Privacy Rights. As the title suggests, there were delegates from the United Kingdom, France and the Republic of Ireland. Each speaker spoke in his or her native tongue. It was assumed, not always realistically, that everyone understood English and French. I gave a short paper in English. The contributions were summed up magisterially by Jean-Marc Sauvé, who was the Vice-President and de facto Head of the Conseil d'État. He spoke slowly and clearly in measured cadences of impeccable French which would probably have satisfied even the great General de Gaulle. The Colloque was poignantly timely because it was held in the shadow of the terrorist attack on the Paris office of the satirical magazine *Charlie Hebdo* on 14 January 2015 in which 12 people were murdered and 11 injured. The attack was by Islamists and had been in response to a publication which had lampooned Islam. The Colloque was held in one of the magnificent courts of the Cour de Cassation on the left bank of the Seine close to the Conciergerie. This was a part of Paris in which I had spent much time as a student during my three months' stay there in the spring of 1961. In the evening, we were entertained to dinner at the Conseil d'État.

On 15 June, the 800th anniversary of the sealing of the Magna Carta finally arrived. Setting off at about 06.00, we travelled in a mini-bus with a number of other judges from the Royal Courts of Justice to Runnymede. Although members of the Royal Family were not due to arrive until 09.50, we could not risk being late. In the result, we arrived ridiculously early. It was freezing cold. By the time proceedings were underway, between 4,000 and 5,000 people were present at the famous meadow close to the river Thames. The VIPs included Her Majesty the Queen and several members of the Royal Family, including Prince William; David Cameron, the Prime Minister and a number of other Cabinet ministers; Justin Welby, the Archbishop of Canterbury and a number of bishops, deans and other Church of England dignitaries; as well as many overseas visitors including Loretta Lynch, the US Attorney-General. The proceedings were not well organised by Surrey County Council. I had to push myself forward so as not to miss my place in the small procession of people who went on to the stage that had been constructed for the occasion. This hardly helped to settle my nerves. The procession included Her Majesty and the Duke of Edinburgh, the Prime Minister and the Archbishop of Canterbury who all took their seats on the stage.

As chairman of the Magna Carta Trust, it was my responsibility to welcome everybody. I walked to the front of the stage: the rear was occupied by the London Symphony Orchestra which had been playing an interesting selection of classical music. I took up my position in front of the lectern waiting to be introduced by the County Council official. I had been told that the introduction would be my cue to speak. After what seemed like a very long time, during which I looked round in vain for the official, it became clear that there would be no introduction after all. So I started to speak. I had been allotted three minutes for my speech and was told that the Prime Minister and Archbishop had been allowed four minutes each for theirs. I had worked hard to craft my speech and tried to make almost every word count. Towards the end, I said that Lord Denning had gone so far as to describe Magna Carta as 'the greatest constitutional document of all time, the foundation of the freedom of the individual against the arbitrary authority of the despot'. I concluded: 'With those words ringing in our ears, it now gives me great pleasure to invite the Prime Minister to speak'. I had not intended to imply that the Prime Minister was a despot even in jest. But that is how my words must have been interpreted because there was much laughter around the meadow. Many told me that it was the only joke of the day.

At the conclusion of the third speech, I went over to Her Majesty and escorted her to the commemorative plaque which she unveiled. She was charming to me as were the others. Together with the Prime Minister and the Archbishop, I descended from the stage and made polite conversation to various church dignitaries and local authority officials. From Runnymede we were driven to the Royal Holloway College, Egham. We were shown its wonderful collection of nineteenth-century English art before having lunch. Once again, I was seated next to Phillip Hammond.

We then returned to the Royal Courts of Justice and my Cinderella experience was at an end. I wonder what my mother and grandmother, both of whom were starry-eyed about our Royal Family, would have made of all of this. Although the 800th anniversary commemoration had its tedious episodes, overall I count myself as having been very privileged to be given such a prominent part to play in it.

Later in June, we attended a garden party hosted by the Archbishop of Canterbury and Mrs Welby in the gardens of Lambeth Palace. We had not been there before. We were overwhelmed by the size and beauty of the gardens, situated as they are so close to the centre of London. We knew hardly any of the other guests. This was not surprising, since most of them seemed to have a connection with the Church. Everyone to whom we spoke was extremely friendly.

Later in the month, I attended a reception and dinner at Grays Inn in honour of Beverley McLachlin, the brilliant Chief Justice of Canada. I had met her in 2008 on the judicial visit to Ottowa that year. I was to meet her again in New York City in June 2018, by which time we had both retired. On this later occasion, together with US Associate Justice Stephen Breyer, the two of us were members of a panel that had been asked to discuss the importance of the independence of the judiciary for the maintaining of the Rule of Law.

On 23 June, I had one of several lunches with editors of national newspapers. They were hosted by the LCJ in his room. They gave a real opportunity for off the record discussions between the Lord Chief, the editor concerned and myself. The guests included the editors of the *Financial Times* (Lionel Barber), the *Times* (John Witherow), the *Sunday Times* (Martin Ivens), the *Guardian* (Kathryn Viner), the *New Statesman* (Jason Cowley) and the *Spectato*r (Fraser Nelson). I found the discussions fascinating. For the most part, the editors were impressive, frank and friendly. They understood the judges' role in our constitution and seemed to think that, on the whole, the judges were doing a difficult job rather well. I think they appreciated our frankness with them. I felt that such meetings were likely to increase the editors' respect for the judiciary and understanding of what they do. But during my time as MR, the LCJ did not invite any of the editors of the more popular newspapers. Perhaps he should have done. Meetings with them might have been less fruitful. I doubt whether Paul Dacre (then the powerful and influential editor of the *Daily Mail*) would have been deflected from his criticisms of liberal judges who decided cases against the Government or from his view that what is in the public interest is what interests the public, which, in any case, is wrong as a matter of law.

In July, I gave a lecture in Cambridge to Canadian judges and lawyers, which was based on the BAILII lecture that I had given the previous year on 'Criticising judges; fair game or off limits?'; I had my first meeting with the new President of the Law Society; and attended a dinner to mark the retirement from the Bench of Sir Jeremy Sullivan (Senior President of Tribunals). It was events like the retirement of Jeremy that brought home to me how long I had been a judge. He first became a judge when he was appointed a High Court judge in 1997. I can still recall his appearances before me when I was a High Court Judge and he was a leading and most impressive planning QC. As a colleague in the Court of Appeal, he made quite a show of looking forward to retirement and a life of leisure in which he could indulge his passion for trains: he had a small-gauge railway track and trains at his home in deepest Buckinghamshire. I was not looking forward to retirement. I still loved hearing appeals and deciding cases, although the rest of the job was somewhat relentless and had its *longueurs*.

As always, the Long Vacation came as something of a relief. In September, we went to Lincoln, which was one of the Magna Carta cities. The visit had been arranged by Lord Cormack whom I had met at a Magna Carta event.

We were looked after by the High Sheriff of Lincolnshire who escorted us round the castle and the Magna Carta museum. We were then given a guided tour round the magnificent cathedral by the Dean, Philip Buckler. He showed us the plaque which commemorates the 18 Jews who were killed as a result of the 1255 Lincoln Blood Libel. In the evening, we were entertained to dinner in the Deanery.

In October, I started my fourth year as Master of the Rolls. On the 13th, I gave the Oxfordshire High Sheriff lecture in the Examination Schools in Oxford, a building I had not entered since 1966 when I took my Finals. The audience comprised academics, judges, practising lawyers and students from the university and from various schools (including from state schools who had been bussed in from London). I had proposed to give a lecture on the so-called 'compensation culture', illustrated by cases about accidents at school. The Under-Sheriff was happy with that. Late in the day, I was told that the librarian of the Bodleian Library was coming to the lecture and was planning to bring one of the three manuscripts of the Magna Carta held by the library (dating from 1217). I was asked whether I could introduce a Magna Carta theme into the lecture. I agreed to do so with reluctance because I had already adapted my Holdsworth lecture and little more work remained to be done. So I came up with the improbable title of 'Magna Carta and the compensation culture'. The title was the easy bit. Weaving in something about Magna Carta that did not sound too contrived was more difficult. At the end of the lecture, I took questions, as I usually did. One of the best questions was asked by a 12-year-old girl from a state school in Lambeth.

From the lecture, we moved to the Deanery of Christ Church Cathedral where I was presented with some lovely white leather gloves by the Dean at the Ceremony of the White Gloves. This was followed by choral evensong in the cathedral. From there we were driven to the High Sheriff's beautiful old house in Adwell, a village not far from Stokenchurch. After a most enjoyable dinner, we were driven home.

Later in the month, I participated in an all-day seminar with the judges of the Strasbourg court on issues of European Convention of Human Rights law. On the 27th, I attended a preliminary meeting of the panel that had been convened to recommend three candidates one of whom would be chosen by the Parliamentary Assembly of the Council of Europe to be the UK judge to replace Paul Mahoney on the European Court of Human Rights. Dame Rosalyn Higgins QC chaired the panel. Apart from myself, the other members were Lord Reed (UK Supreme Court), Sir Richard Heaton (Permanent Secretary of the Ministry of Justice) and Baroness Onora O'Neill (a Cross Bench member of the House of Lords and a philosopher who had been Principal of Newnham College, Cambridge). Although initially I was daunted by this high-powered group, I found them all friendly and easy to get on with. On a subsequent occasion, we were to shortlist the candidates for interview and later still to interview the shortlisted candidates. We had little difficulty in agreeing the three names to put forward. One of these, Tim Eicke QC, was eventually appointed.

On the 30th, we had our annual away day. This was the first meeting at which we had a plenary discussion about some of the reforms that Michael Briggs and his working group had put forward to try to relieve some of the pressures that were besetting the court. Eventually, proposals that were to be accepted included reducing the scope for applying for permission to appeal and increasing the number of appeals which were to be heard by two, rather than three, Lord Justices. Neither of these proposals commanded universal support. Chairing the discussions was quite a challenge.

On 5 November, we went to Plymouth and stayed the night in the beautiful home of Lady Astor at 3 Elliot Terrace on Plymouth Hoe. The view from our bedroom overlooking Plymouth Sound was spectacular. Lord Denning had stayed there several times. The visitors' book contained a number of entries which he had written in his beautiful handwriting. It was clear that he had a deep affection for the place. I had been invited by the Plymouth Law Society and Plymouth University to give the annual Pilgrim Fathers lecture. The title of my lecture was 'The Globalisation of Law'.

The month was packed with meetings of the usual variety as well as hearings. What was very much out of the ordinary, however, was our visit to Malaysia.

I had been invited to give the twenty-ninth Sultan Azlan Shah Law Lecture in Kuala Lumpur. This is an annual lecture which is given by leading jurists from the common law world (mainly the United Kingdom) in honour of HRH Sultan Azlan Shah who was a distinguished judge in Malaysia before he became the monarch of the State of Perak in 1984. He was succeeded by his son, HRH Sultan Nazrin Shah who was proclaimed the thirty-fifth Sultan of the State of Perak in May 2014. The title of my lecture was 'Is judicial review a threat to democracy?' Unsurprisingly, my theme was that, far from being a threat to democracy, judicial review is important for the promotion and maintaining of the rule of law and that it provides an effective mechanism for challenging decisions of public bodies to ensure that they are lawful. I was careful not to say anything about the state of affairs in Malaysia. But the audience was able to draw its own conclusions from what I said about the importance of judicial review in the UK justice system.

The visit to Malaysia was without question the most lavish of all the visits we made. We stayed four nights in an extraordinarily large suite of rooms at the Mandarin Hotel in Kuala Lumpur; were driven around the city and its environs in a chauffeur-driven car with support from a police outrider to sweep aside the traffic that was in our way; and we visited the Federal Court, which looks like a mosque. Throughout our stay in Kuala Lumpur, we were acutely aware of how Islamic a state it is.

We were looked after by Visu Sinnadurai, who in effect acted as the agent of the Sultan. Visu was most helpful but he seemed rather nervous, as if he expected that something would go wrong. He probably had good cause, because we were unfamiliar with the customs and protocols that have to be followed whenever the Royal Family is involved in an event. That is why he insisted on a dress rehearsal for the lecture which I was to give in the grand ballroom of the Mandarin Hotel. One of the customs is that women should not cross their legs when sitting. When I entered the ballroom with the Sultan and took my seat on the stage before giving the lecture, I noticed to my dismay that Jacqueline was sitting cross-legged in the front row facing the stage. In full public view, I gesticulated to her to uncross her legs. Eventually she got the message. There were about 1,500 people in the audience including politicians, judges, lawyers and students. As I left the ballroom following the lecture to go to the reception, I was mobbed by hundreds of students, many of whom were equipped with iPhones and wanted photographs. I sensed that there was a real interest in judicial review and human rights. Many people whom we met were openly critical of the Government, in particular of the Prime Minister who was said to be corrupt and of the judiciary, some of whom were said to lack independence.

After the reception, the Sultan hosted a splendid dinner in a private room at the Shangri-La Hotel. Other guests included the Chief Justice and senior judges. After the dinner, there was a karaoke event with an excellent live band. I had been warned that this was coming and had been told that it would be impolite to refuse to perform. I had never taken part in a karaoke before and had therefore practised hard. I sang the Beatles' 'Hey Jude' and enjoyed it enormously. The Sultan sang 'Delilah' with great gusto. Those in the know said that this showed that he was happy and that he had approved of the lecture. When I said to him that I hoped it had not created too many waves, he said that it had only created a few ripples. I found both the Sultan and his wife, Tuanku Zara Salim, utterly charming and relaxed.

After Kuala Lumpur, we were flown in the Sultan's private jet to Langkawi, a tropical paradise island in the north of the country, where we stayed in great luxury at the Four Seasons Hotel. On the plane, we were looked after by the Sultan's stewardess. The plane remained at the small Langkawi airport until we flew back to Kuala Lumpur three days later.

The hotel was by the beach. It had a wonderful swimming pool and all the things that luxurious seaside hotels are meant to have. We were not frequent habitués of five-star hotels by the sea or anywhere else. But we had no problem at all in adapting to this environment for three days. The highlight was a private boat trip with a naturalist guide up some nearby mangrove channels and creaks. We learnt a lot about mangroves as well as other local flora and fauna.

We then flew back to Kuala Lumpur and from there to London. This was an amazing visit, and all for one lecture. The rest of the year was filled with the usual mix of meetings and pageantry.

In January 2016, I attended a meeting with Natalie Ceeney to discuss issues relating to HMCTS. It was becoming increasingly clear that she was frustrated by the insistence of the Department on micro-managing the work that she was doing, including the modernisation reforms on which she was working. In the end, I believe it was this that caused her to resign. I also had one of my meetings with the Chair of the Bar Council, Chantal-Aimee Doerries. We discussed civil justice issues, such as the proposal for an online court for small cases and the extension of the fixed costs regime. She expressed grave reservations about both, because she thought that they would lead to a loss of work and reduced earnings for young barristers. She seemed to me to be acting rather like a shop steward who was representing the interests of the Bar, without any understanding that the world was changing. I told her that the Bar would have to accept that changes were coming. In the end, Michael Gove accepted the need for an online court and an extension of the fixed costs regime.

On a Saturday at the end of the month, I spoke at the TECBAR (Technology and Construction Bar Association) annual conference. The main thrust of what I said was that successful QCs practising in the field of construction law should seriously consider a judicial career. I tried to persuade them of its attractions. They listened politely and thanked me profusely, but I did not sense that I made much of an impact on them. They were earning too much money. Some of them said that they were unwilling to be subjected to the stressful and time-consuming process of applying to the JAC. This conference was not the most exhilarating event in my judicial career, but I felt it important to do everything that I could do to maintain the high quality of our judiciary.

I had much more fun on the evening of 11 February 2016. Nobody had told me that the Master of the Rolls is *ex officio* a Commissioner for the Reduction of the National Debt. This body (of which I had never heard) is a statutory body of the UK Government whose main function is the investment and management of government bonds. The other Commissioners are the Chancellor of the Exchequer, who was then George Osborne, the Governor of the Bank of England, the LCJ, the Speaker of the House of Commons, three Deputy Governors of the Bank of England and the Controller and Auditor-General. The body was formed in 1786 and had last met on 9 July 1860 when William Gladstone was Chancellor of the Exchequer.

We had been invited to a meeting of the Commissioners in Committee Room A in the Cabinet Office and a dinner at No 11 Downing Street. Once I had established that this was not a hoax, I accepted the invitation. As the date approached, I became increasingly nervous. I wondered what I could contribute to a discussion about the investment and management of government bonds. By chance, I later learnt the purpose of the event. The reconvening of the body was to be a purely symbolic event in honour of Sir Nicholas Macpherson, who was retiring as Permanent Secretary to the Treasury. The first item on the agenda was to approve the minutes of the meeting of 9 July 1860, which we duly did. This was followed by an interesting presentation about the evolution of the national debt since 1860, the signing of a commemorative document and dinner. George Osborne presided over the meeting and the dinner in a most charming, relaxed and amusing way. The conversation flowed easily at dinner. Although it included expressions of view about the pros and cons of negative interest rates, it was by no means restricted to such monetary matters. This was an altogether delightful and memorable evening.

Later in February, I went to Dublin to take part in a UK/Irish conference held at the former Guinness family home in Phoenix Park. This is a magnificent house where visiting dignitaries stay. The subject of the conference was EU law. The participants were the now familiar senior judges from our jurisdictions.

Into March, and more meetings. On the 14th, I gave a keynote speech at a conference on commercial law at Leeds University that had been arranged jointly with one of the leading universities of China. I had been invited by Professor Roger Halson. The previous evening, Jacqueline and I and some of the leading lights from the Leeds University School of Law had dinner with some of their important guests from China. The conversation at dinner was extremely hard work.

At the beginning of May, we went to Krakow in Poland for three days. I had been invited to take part in an event to mark the seventieth anniversary of the Nuremberg War Crimes Trials and the eightieth anniversary of the Nuremberg Race Laws. On the first day, a conference was held at the Jagiellonian University which was founded in 1364 and is one of the oldest surviving universities in the world. There were speeches from eminent scholars and Edward Mosberg, an Auschwitz survivor. I participated in a panel discussion with Rosie Abella (Supreme Court of Canada), Dorit Beinisch (former President of the Supreme Court of Israel) and Sam Rugege (Chief Justice of Rwanda). The discussion was moderated with elan by Professor Alan Derschowitz (former Professor of Harvard Law School). Irving Cottler (former Minister of Justice and Attorney General of Canada) also spoke.

On the second day, we went to Auschwitz to take part in the March of the Living. This is an annual walk from Auschwitz to Birkenau by more than 10,000 young people who come from all over the world. We were given a brief tour of Auschwitz before embarking on the two-mile walk. The walk culminated in speeches and music at Birkenau, close to the site of the partly destroyed gas chambers and crematoria, where my great uncle Otto and his wife from Berlin and Jacqueline's great uncle Gaston from Marseille were murdered in 1943. The vitality and noise made by the young made it difficult to reflect on the enormity of the crimes that had been committed there. I understood that the somewhat carnival nature of the event was sending a strong message that Hitler had failed in his mission to exterminate the Jewish people. But this did not seem to be the right place to hold a carnival. Nevertheless, the visit was moving and memorable. I had never previously been to Auschwitz.

Later in the month, I spoke about the Law to sixth form girls at St Albans' School for Girls. I had done the same thing earlier at my old school and was to do it again in 2018 at Cheltenham Ladies College. I enjoy trying to excite and inspire the young. They all responded superbly when we discussed some current legal problems.

In June, we had the sift meeting and three days of interviews for the competition to fill the latest Court of Appeal vacancies. I attended the Service of Thanksgiving to mark the ninetieth birthday of HM The Queen in St Paul's Cathedral. This was followed by a reception at Guildhall. Later in the month, I attended my last Designated Civil Judges' conference. I remember this mainly because it coincided with the news that the outcome of the referendum was that the United Kingdom was to leave the EU. Attendees at the conference commented that I appeared to be visibly shaken by this news when I made my usual keynote address at the start of the conference.

Although I did not officially retire until the beginning of October, July was in effect the last month of my judicial career. I attended my last annual Mansion House dinner hosted by the Lord Mayor for the judges. I had missed very few of these since I was appointed as a judge in 1993.

On the 21st, Liz Truss was sworn in as the new Lord Chancellor. I was sorry to see Michael Gove go after little more than a year. I believe that he had a real understanding of justice and could have made significant improvements despite the financial constraints under which he was having to work. I had one working telephone conversation with Liz Truss which seemed to go well. She seemed to be sympathetic to the points that I was making, but I retired before I was able to see how things would work out. In the event, at least from the judges' point of view, her term of office proved to be something of a disaster. She did not last long.

The 26th was the occasion of my Valedictory in the LCJ's court. The court was packed. It was a very moving occasion for me. John Thomas spoke as did Lord (David) Pannick QC and a former President of the Law Society. Our entire immediate family was present, including my brother, Robert. So far as I could tell, the five grandchildren all behaved impeccably. My speech was not the usual self-deprecatory, witty, classic English type of affair. It was unashamedly serious, emotional and rather intense. Perhaps the millennia of persecution of the Jews do leave their mark. What I said included:

> I have thought how lucky I have been to live in this great country. I wonder what my father's parents would have made of today. They came from Lithuania at the turn of the 20th century. They were both 19 years of age. They had had little education and little money. They were hoping to go to the US, but could not afford to get any further than Leeds. And my mother came from Bulgaria in 1939 at a time when most people in this country had probably not even heard of the place. Her mother spent six months in Bergen Belsen in 1944. Something that she could hardly ever bring herself to talk about. I wonder what she would have made of today too. I keenly regret that my parents are not here today. Even at my age, I would have liked to bring them my achievements for their approval.

> It is on an occasion like this that I feel a deep gratitude to this tolerant country for allowing my forebears to settle here and giving me and my family the opportunity to flourish here. I fervently hope that the events of recent weeks have not put that tolerance at risk. I am fearful that it is being put under strain by the xenophobia and

dangerous forces of hate that have been unleashed in some quarters. I have faith in the fair-mindedness of the British people and believe that their tolerance will continue to shine through. But as a fall-back position (and it is always good to have a fall-back position) I may have an escape route. I think that, thanks to my mother, I may be entitled to apply for a Bulgarian passport.

I can still think of no better place to live than in this country. I am proud to have been able to give something back to it. Maintaining the Rule of Law is as important as it has ever been. Perhaps even more so today, as the Executive arrogates to itself more and more powers. I hope that I have been able to make a modest contribution to maintaining the Rule of Law in my 23 years as a judge. I have been hugely privileged to have had a wonderful career.

After thanking the many people who had helped and inspired me, I concluded:

I have left the hardest bit to the end. I have made many decisions in my life, but far and away the best and most important was to ask Jackie to marry me all those years ago. I knew she was the girl for me almost immediately and we were engaged within a few weeks. My professional life has been very exciting and stimulating. But I have been happiest when in her company, just doing the simplest of things. She has been my rock of support and my life mate. I have been so fortunate. And so fortunate to have a wonderful family, all here today. One of my grandsons has said that Grandpa has an interesting job and Grandma just tags along. How cruel children can be. Anyway, it's not true: I mean the bit about tagging along.

I do not intend to retire to cultivate my garden. I plan to be quite busy. But I do hope to be able to spend more time with her.

I am astonished and humbled by how many have come to say good bye today. I thank you all so much.

In his Law Diary for the *Times*, Edward Fennell wrote:

Is Lord Dyson, outgoing master of the rolls, the most popular judge? His farewell this week in the Lord Chief Justice's court was packed with at least 200 senior judges and lawyers, including three former lord chiefs. Lord Pannick QC, on behalf of the Bar, said: 'one of the reasons why Lord Dyson has been a great judge is because [he] is not only a great judge … he is an accomplished pianist – and has other interests including family; his wife Jackie, was his 'own personal court of appeal'.

In the evening, we held a party in the garden of the Middle Temple. We had invited many colleagues and friends. David Neuberger spoke with characteristic warmth and generosity. Our daughter Michelle spoke too. Many commented on how well she spoke. We were both very proud of her. I made a very short speech in reply.

So it was that I reached the end of my exciting and rewarding judicial journey. There were more rewards and excitements to come. But none could match my 23 years as a judge for satisfaction. I am conscious that in the description that I have given in this chapter, I have not referred to any of the appeals that I heard. What I have said so far may give the impression that I spent four years attending endless meetings, talking to famous people and going on trips, sometimes to exotic and faraway places, where I was often given almost regal treatment. I must now correct this impression. In fact, I sat on appeals in the Court of Appeal three days a week most of the time (as well as returning to the Supreme Court from time to time to hear appeals there) and spent a good part of most weekends reading the papers for the next appeals and writing judgments. I regarded the appeals as the most important part of the role that I performed. For me, it was also the most interesting. Although I had to try to acquire the skills of an administrator and a manager, I regarded myself first and foremost as a judge. Having the opportunity to play a part in shaping the law was a huge privilege as well as an intellectual challenge.

12

Master of the Rolls: Memorable Cases

I T HAS BEEN difficult to select a few of the many appeals that I heard for mention here. All of them were important for the parties concerned. Many of them were important because they raised significant points of law or were of some national interest. I found almost all of them challenging and interesting. That is because, as Master of the Rolls, I was expected to hear important appeals and that is what I chose to do. I could have made life easier for myself by taking fewer cases. That is what some of my colleagues urged me to do. But there seemed to be so many interesting and important appeals and I wanted to hear many of them. I was like a child who had too many tempting toys to play with. As with my selection of cases that I heard in the Supreme Court and in the lower courts, for the most part I have avoided the judgments which would only be of interest to lawyers. Instead, I have chosen a few of those that caught the public eye at the time and were of more general interest.

An early appeal was *R (T) v Greater Manchester Chief Constable* [2013] EWCA Civ 25. We held that a blanket statutory requirement on individuals who applied for jobs working with children to disclose convictions, even for offences and cautions that were long spent under the Rehabilitation of Offenders Act 1974, was disproportionate and amounted to a breach of the right to respect for their private lives under article 8 of the European Convention on Human Rights. Our decision attracted a good deal of media interest and support. T had been given a police caution in connection with the theft of two bicycles many years earlier when he was 11 years old. The fact that he was so young at the time of the caution and the offences were so relatively minor made this a very striking case to test the legislation. We allowed T's appeal and granted a declaration that the legislation requiring disclosure of cautions in all cases was incompatible with article 8 of the Convention.

In the first part of 2013, we heard a number of very high profile appeals. These included *Othman (Abu Qatada) v Secretary of State for the Home Department* [2008] EWCA Civ 290. The UK Government regarded Abu Qatada, who was once described as Osama bin Laden's right hand man, as a serious threat to national security. He had been served with a deportation notice. The Home Secretary appealed against the decision of the Special Immigration Appeals Commission (SIAC) that Abu Qatada could not be deported to Jordan to face a retrial for alleged terrorism offences because there was a real risk that he would suffer a flagrant denial of justice in Jordan. SIAC had held that there was a real risk that statements by his former co-accused would be admitted in evidence at the retrial. It was common ground that these statements had been obtained by torture. We acknowledged that Abu Qatada was regarded by the UK Government as a danger to national security and that there was a general feeling that his deportation was long overdue. But we dismissed the appeal because there was a real risk that his right to a fair trial guaranteed by article 6 of the European Convention on Human Rights would be breached if he were deported to Jordan to face trial. Our decision was very unpopular with the Government, the Opposition and many others. People could not understand why we could not get rid of this obviously dangerous man. If he ran the risk of having an unfair trial in Jordan, they argued, that was his problem. These criticisms of our decision troubled me. But I had no doubt that the decision was right. The United Kingdom was a party to the Convention and could not, directly or indirectly, cause an individual to be subjected to an unfair trial or to suffer a real risk of a flagrant denial of justice. In the end, a government-to-government agreement was reached that the evidence obtained by torture would not be relied on at the retrial. Abu Qatada did not challenge this and he was eventually deported.

A high profile case of a very different kind came to the court courtesy of Boris Johnson. The name of the case was *AAA v Associated Newspapers Ltd* [2013] EWCA Civ 554. The claimant, a child, asserted that her privacy rights under article 8 of the Convention had been breached by a piece in the *Daily Mail* which speculated that she had been the child of an extra marital affair between her mother and Boris Johnson, who was then the Mayor of London. Her claim had been rejected by the judge and we dismissed her appeal. The mother, Helen Macintyre, had tried to keep secret the identity of the child's father. The *Daily Mail* had argued, amongst other things, that it was in the public interest to name Mr Johnson as the child's father because 'it went to the issue of recklessness and whether on that account he was fit for public office'. We held that the story was 'a public interest matter which the electorate was entitled to know when considering Mr Johnson's fitness for high public office'. It was also relevant that Ms Macintyre had revealed the paternity of the child on other occasions, including in an interview she gave to a journalist for the *Tatler* magazine. The *Daily Mail* celebrated this 'significant ruling' as a great victory. Stephen Glover wrote an article lauding the judgment. He wrote of his 'amazement' because he had assumed that 'the higher judiciary shared the view of certain high-minded newspaper editors, the pressure group Hacked Off and most politicians that what a public figure does in private is entirely his or her own business, provided it is legal'. For me, it was an unusual and not altogether welcome experience to have one of my decisions praised by the *Daily Mail*. Drawing on article 8 of the Convention and the jurisprudence of the Strasbourg Court, our courts were starting to develop the law on the right to privacy. During my four years as Master of the Rolls, I was to hear several appeals in this important area of law.

In July 2013, I heard two important high profile appeals. The first was a challenge by residents' groups and 15 local authorities to the London to Birmingham section of the HS2 high speed rail project. A description of the highly technical issues is not appropriate in this book. We rejected the challenge.

The second was *R (Nicklinson) v Ministry of Justice* [2014] UKSC 38 and *R (on the application of AM) v Director of Public Prosecution* [2014] UKSC 38. Mr Nicklinson (until his death sometime after the High Court hearing) had suffered from 'locked in' syndrome. He wished to end his life but was unable to do so without assistance. Assisting a person to commit suicide is a criminal offence under section 2 of the Suicide Act 1961. Mr Nicklinson applied to the High Court for a declaration that it would be lawful for a doctor to assist his suicide or that section 2 was incompatible with article 8 of the Convention on Human Rights. His claim was rejected by the High Court. On appeal, we held first that the time had not come for the common law to be developed to recognise a defence of necessity to murder in certain cases of euthanasia, such as where a doctor gave effect to the settled wish of a competent person to end his life. That was a matter for Parliament. Secondly, we said that the blanket statutory prohibition on euthanasia and assisted suicide was not a disproportionate interference with an individual's rights under article 8. By a majority, the Supreme Court agreed with us on this.

The second appeal was that of an individual who used the pseudonym Martin. Mr Martin wished to end his life by travelling to the Dignitas clinic in Switzerland. He sought an order that the Director of Public Prosecutions amend the 2010 'Policy for Prosecutors in Respect of Cases of Encouraging or Assisting Suicide' so that carers and other responsible individuals who were not family members would not be prosecuted for assisting Mr Martin's suicide. Mr Martin had a measure of success in this challenge: we held that the policy was not sufficiently clear and precise to be lawful. Although the Supreme Court agreed that the policy was insufficiently clear, they held that it was for the Director of Public Prosecutions (rather than the court) to review it and decide what changes to make to it.

Assisted suicide is an issue on which opinions are sharply divided. Most people have a view about it. It raises fundamental moral questions of the greatest importance. My view as a private citizen is that assisted suicide should be permitted, subject to stringent safeguards. But that did not influence my conclusion that, as a matter of law, decriminalising assisted suicide was not a matter for the judges. The facts of these two cases were tragic. I have already touched on Mr Nicklinson's situation. Mr Martin was now 48 years of age. He had suffered a severe stroke from which he would never recover. He was unable to speak and virtually unable to move. He was unable to take his own life. He had tried to starve himself to death, but his attempt had failed in the most distressing circumstances. None of the members of his family or close friends could bring themselves to accompany him to Switzerland. His only hope was to enlist the help of a carer or other stranger. But no such person was willing to help for fear of being prosecuted for assisting him to commit suicide: the policy did not clearly state that there would be no prosecution in such circumstances. The plight of both Mr Nicklinson and Mr Martin was desperately sad. Regrettably, I did not think that the judges could help them.

Later in 2013, we heard another appeal which attracted much public attention. The case of *Black v Wilkinson* [2013] EWCA Civ 820 concerned the question whether a person who provided bed and breakfast accommodation in her home had unlawfully discriminated against a gay couple in refusing to provide them with the double bedroom which one of them had booked. The reason she had given was that, as a devout Christian, she objected to sexual relations outside marriage: at that time, homosexual couples could not marry each other. The gay couple claimed that her refusal amounted to unlawful discrimination on the ground of their sexual orientation and was contrary to the Equality Act (Sexual Orientation) Regulations 2007. We upheld the challenge. We said that it was a case of indirect discrimination because the defendant's policy put homosexual couples at a disadvantage as compared with heterosexual couples on the ground of sexual orientation, since the former could not marry but the latter could. The significance of the distinction was that direct discrimination could not be justified in law; whereas indirect discrimination could be justified. The defendant sought to justify her discrimination by reference to her religious beliefs. We held that, in deciding whether the legislative interference with a person's right to freedom of religious expression was proportionate and justified, the balance came down in favour of protecting a person against discrimination on the ground of sexual orientation. We said that, in deciding proportionality, the court should give great weight to the fact that, after wide consultation, the matter had been carefully considered by the legislature, which had produced a scheme giving priority to religious belief only in certain narrowly defined circumstances. There was no appeal from our decision. But it was considered by the Supreme Court in the similar case of *Bull v Hall* [2012] EWCA Civ 83, CA. In that appeal, the majority held that the case was one of direct discrimination. The minority held that it was a case of indirect discrimination. All held that, if it was a case of indirect discrimination, it was not justified.

I mention this case in a little detail because it was a good example of the many cases that I heard which called for the court to balance competing considerations and to weigh different rights against each other. In a way, the bed and breakfast cases were less difficult than some, because the fact that Parliament had considered the issue was a factor of considerable weight. But even that could not be decisive. A frequent example is the balancing of one person's right to private life under the article 8 of the Convention against another person's right to freedom of expression. Conducting this kind of balancing exercise inevitably draws the judges into the political arena to some extent. Our predecessors would have been shocked to be asked to make value judgments of this kind.

In 2014, we heard the appeal in *R (Evans) v Attorney General* [2015] UKSC 21. Mr Evans, a journalist employed by the *Guardian* newspaper sought disclosure under the Freedom of Information Act 2000 (FOIA) of correspondence sent by the Prince of Wales to various government departments. The Upper Tribunal decided that Mr Evans was entitled to disclosure of certain correspondence, including correspondence on environmental issues, on the ground that it was in the public interest for there to be transparency as to how and when Prince Charles sought to influence government. The Attorney General issued a certificate under section 53(2) of FOIA stating that he had, on 'reasonable grounds', formed the opinion that the government departments were entitled to refuse the requests for disclosure. The effect of such a certificate would be to block the disclosure ordered by the tribunal. We held that it was not reasonable for the Attorney General to issue a section 53(2) certificate merely because he disagreed with the decision of the tribunal. Something more was required, such as that there had been a material change of circumstances since date of the tribunal decision or that the decision was demonstrably flawed in fact or in law. In the present case, the Upper Tribunal had reached its decision after a six-day hearing during which it had heard evidence and argument. The tribunal had considered all the material, its decision had not been appealed and the Attorney General had not suggested that it contained any errors of fact or law or that its conclusion was unreasonable. Unsurprisingly, the media were excited by this case. They wanted to know how far Prince Charles was trying to influence government policy, and how effective his lobbying was. This raised important political issues with which we were not at all concerned. The question for us was purely legal: was the Attorney General, on the facts and on the proper interpretation of section 53(3) of FOIA, entitled to veto the decision of the tribunal? Although the arguments before the Supreme Court were given a more constitutional focus than they were before us, the Supreme Court essentially agreed with our reasoning.

Another high profile case that we heard in 2014 concerned the case of Janet Tracey (*R (David Tracey) v Cambridge University Hospitals NHS Trust and Secretary of State for Health*) [2014] EWCA Civ 822. Janet Tracey broke her neck in a car accident soon after she had been diagnosed with terminal cancer. The case centred on a 'Do Not Resuscitate' (DNR) notice that had been placed on her hospital bed without consulting her or her family. We held that Mrs Tracey's right to respect for her private life under article 8 of the Convention had been violated by the hospital trust in failing to involve her in the process which led to the DNR notice. I said that a decision to place a DNR notice on a patient's records has the potential to deprive the patient of life-saving treatment. There should be a presumption in favour of patient involvement and convincing reasons are needed not to involve them. As I said: 'A decision as to how to pass the closing days and moments of one's life clearly touches on a patient's personal autonomy, integrity, dignity and quality of life'. According to an article in the *Guardian*, nearly 70 per cent of people die in hospital and 80 per cent of them die with DNR notices in place. It is, therefore, not surprising that our decision attracted a great deal of attention. The case was not about a right to demand to be resuscitated, but about the right to know how DNR decisions are made and the right to be consulted before they are made. So far as I am aware, the media coverage was favourable. It was understandable that doctors might wish to take DNR decisions in what they consider to be obvious cases, for example, where the patient is close to death and the doctors believe that the pain that is inevitably caused by resuscitation cannot be objectively justified. But this cannot justify a failure to consult the patient or, where that is not possible, a close relative. I believe that this is now well understood by the medical profession.

In December 2014, we handed down judgment in the case of *R (Gudanaviciene and others) v The Director of Legal Aid Casework and The Lord Chancellor* [2014] EWCA Civ 1622. As part of a programme to reduce the legal aid bill, the Government introduced the Legal Aid, Sentencing and Punishment of Offenders Act 2012 (LASPO). It included a provision that certain civil legal services would qualify for legal aid only if the Director had made an exceptional case funding determination. Such a determination would be necessary to avoid a breach of the right of access to justice which is guaranteed by article 6(1) of the Convention. Section 10 of LASPO required the Director to have regard to the Guidance given by the Lord Chancellor.

This appeal concerned six immigration cases which had been joined together as they raised common issues about exceptional case funding under section 10. In substance, the appeal was a challenge to the Guidance. We held that the cumulative effect of certain passages in the Guidance was to misstate the effect of the relevant jurisprudence of the Strasbourg Court and to undermine the rights that it protected. Although the Guidance correctly identified many of the particular factors that should be taken into account in deciding whether to make an exceptional case determination, their effect was substantially neutralised by the strong steer given in certain passages. These passages sent a clear signal to the caseworkers and the Director that the refusal of legal aid would amount to a breach of article 6(1) of the Convention only in rare and extreme cases. There were no statements in the case law (including the Strasbourg jurisprudence) which justified such a parsimonious approach.

Following our judgment, the Guidance was modified. I mention this decision because it was one of many in which legal challenges were made to policies or decisions where the Government had pushed right up to, and sometimes beyond, the boundary of lawfulness in what it considered to be the public interest, for example, in order to save money, protect the people of this country or keep a firm grip on immigration and asylum applications.

An example of an appeal concerning a challenge to such a policy was the case of *Lord Chancellor v Detention Action* [2015] ECWA Civ 840, where what was under review were draconian rules whose object was to ensure that asylum appeals were dealt with speedily. The Lord Chancellor had made so-called Fast Track Rules which were applicable to appeals to the tribunal against refusals by the Home Secretary of asylum applications. We held that these rules were unlawful because they were ultra vires the Tribunals, Courts and Enforcement

Act 2007 under which they had purportedly been made. Section 22 of the Act provided that the power to make rules was to be exercised with a view to securing that the proceedings were handled quickly and efficiently, but so as to ensure that justice was done in the particular proceedings and that the system was accessible and fair. I said that asylum appeals were often factually complex and difficult and that the safeguards introduced by the rules were insufficient to overcome the unfairness inherent in a system which required asylum seekers to prepare and present their appeals within seven days of the decisions under challenge. The Fast Track Rules were systemically unfair and unjust. They failed to strike the right balance between speed and efficiency on the one hand and fairness and justice on the other. They were weighted too heavily in favour of the former and needed adjustment. Precisely how they were to be adjusted was a matter for the Tribunal Procedure Committee and Parliament and not the court.

I regret to say that the cases of *Gudanaviciene* and *Detention Action* both bore the hand of a Lord Chancellor who was willing to sacrifice justice on the altar of cost-saving. I was pleased to be able to play a small part in redressing the balance.

The appeal of Mrs Long (*R (Long) v Secretary of State for Defence)* [2015] EWCA Civ 770 raised very different issues. This was a memorable and sad case which attracted some public attention. Mrs Long brought a claim seeking a further investigation into the death of her son, Corporal Paul Long, who was one of six British soldiers of the Royal Military Police (RMP) who were murdered by members of a crowd at a police station in Iraq in June 2003. The claim was brought on the basis that the United Kingdom had not discharged its obligation under article 2 of the Convention to investigate the death of a member of one of its armed forces. We held that there was an arguable breach of the substantive article 2 duty to protect the right to life, so as to trigger the duty to investigate a death in certain circumstances. This arose from the practice of the RMP of not requiring its forces to be equipped with an iridium telephone when they went on patrol. Had Corporal Long's patrol been equipped with an iridium phone, there was a real prospect that the deaths could have been avoided. But we decided that any investigative duty had been discharged by previous inquiries.

I recall this case very well. Mrs Long sat on the front bench below me throughout the two-day appeal, impassive and dignified. I concluded my judgment by saying:

> I am only too aware of the anguish that she continues to suffer over the death of her son on that fateful day in June 2003. It is entirely understandable that she wishes to leave no stone unturned in her quest to discover precisely how the RMP soldiers were not provided with iridium phones when they should have been. But for the reasons that I have attempted to give, I am satisfied that, as a matter of law, she is not entitled to any further investigation into this tragic affair.

Like the appeals of Mr Nicklinson and Mr Martin, this is a good example of a case where I would have wished to follow my instincts of sympathy and found in favour of the appellant. But I had to show resolve and follow the dictates of the law.

The case of *R (Miranda) v Secretary of State for the Home Department* [2016] EWCA Civ 6 arose from the detention of Mr Miranda at Heathrow airport when he was stopped and questioned and items taken from him, notably encrypted storage devices. He was the partner of Glenn Greenwald, a journalist who had been working for the *Guardian* newspaper. Mr Miranda had been carrying encrypted material in order to assist his partner's journalistic activity. The material comprised 'highly classified' documents which had been stolen by Edward Snowden from the National Security Agency of the United States. Agreeing with the Divisional Court, we held that the exercise of the stop power given by Schedule 7 to the Terrorism Act 2000 had been lawful. We rejected the argument that the use of the stop power was an unjustified and disproportionate interference with the right to freedom of expression. The files that Mr Miranda was carrying were a threat to national security: compelling national security interests outweighed Mr Miranda's right to freedom of expression.

But in disagreement with the Divisional Court, we declared that the stop power conferred by Schedule 7 was incompatible with article 10 of the Convention on Human Rights as regards journalistic material, in that it was not subject to adequate safeguards against its arbitrary exercise. It would be for Parliament to provide such protection. The most obvious safeguard would be some form of judicial or other independent and impartial scrutiny conducted in such a way as to protect the confidentiality in the material.

This was a case about where the balance should be struck between supporting national security and defending journalists' right to freedom of expression. The issues were rightly considered to be of great importance for our democracy. Our decision was the subject of a great deal of press comment. Unsurprisingly, it was welcomed by the media as an important victory for the freedom of the press. Rosie Brighouse, legal officer at Liberty, said: 'This judgment is a major victory for the free press. Schedule 7 has been a blot on our legal landscape for years – breathtakingly broad and intrusive, ripe for discrimination, routinely misused. Its repeal is long overdue.'

In *Harb v HRH Prince Abdul Aziz bin Fahd bin Abdul Aziz* [2016] EWCA Civ 556, we heard an appeal against a decision of Mr Justice Peter Smith. The substantive issue in the case was whether an enforceable agreement had been made by which the Prince had undertaken to pay Mrs Harb £12 million and to transfer two properties to her. The appeal attracted much attention. This was principally because one of the grounds of appeal was based on the behaviour of the judge. It was alleged by the Prince that there had been an appearance of bias by Mr Justice Peter Smith against the Prince's counsel and therefore against the Prince himself. The basis of this allegation was a letter that the judge had written to one of the heads of Blackstone Chambers complaining about an article written by Lord Pannick QC, who was a member of the same chambers as the Prince's counsel. The article had been very critical of the judge's conduct in other cases. In the letter, the judge had said that Lord Pannick's article was 'quite outrageous' and that it 'has been extremely damaging to Blackstone Chambers within the Chancery Division'. He also said that he had strongly supported Blackstone Chambers over the years 'especially in Silk applications' and concluded 'I will no longer support your Chambers; please make that clear to members of your Chambers. I do not wish to be associated with Chambers that have people like Pannick in it.'

I had no doubt that the judge's behaviour was totally unacceptable. Indeed, in a subsequent letter to the claimant's solicitors, he accepted that he should not have written the earlier letter. It seemed to me that we had no choice but to express our disapproval in strong terms. If we had not done so, we would rightly have been accused of protecting one of our colleagues. I reflected long before writing this:

> It is difficult to believe that any judge, still less a high court judge, could have [written the letter]. It was a shocking and, we regret to say, disgraceful letter to write. It shows a deeply worrying and fundamental lack of understanding of the proper role of a judge ... In our view, the comments of Lord Pannick, far from being 'outrageous' as the judge said in the letter, were justified. We greatly regret having to criticise a judge in these strong terms, but our duty requires us to do so.

I did greatly regret having to write in such terms. Predictably, the press had a field day with it. The judge was already the subject of a complaint to the Judicial Complaint Investigations Office arising from his conduct in the earlier *British Airways* case. I felt rather sorry for him, but I had to put personal feelings to one side and do what I saw as my duty. In fact, the appeal was allowed on the grounds of shortcomings in the way in which the judge dealt with the evidential issues in the case. Despite our criticisms of the judge's conduct, we did not uphold the allegations of apparent bias.

The last case I shall mention is *Belhaj & Another v Straw & Others* [2014] EWCA Civ 1394. Mr Belhaj was an opposition commander during the Libyan armed conflict of 2011. He alleged that he and his pregnant wife had been abducted from China to Libya where they were tortured by the Gaddafi regime. Their claim was brought against the Foreign Secretary and named Foreign Office officials for a series of common law offences in connection with their alleged involvement in the abduction. In the High Court, it had been held that the claims were not barred by state immunity under the State Immunity Act 1978, but were barred by the act of state doctrine. We agreed with the judge on the state immunity issue, but held that the claims were also not barred by the act of state doctrine, because they fell within a limitation to the application of the doctrine on grounds of public policy in cases of serious violations of international law and fundamental human rights. We reached this conclusion because the allegations were of particularly grave violations of international law and fundamental human rights; there was a compelling public interest in the investigation by the English courts of these allegations; and unless our courts were able to exercise jurisdiction in this case, the allegations would not be investigated and the claimants would be left without any legal recourse or remedy. It required a degree of boldness to reject the arguments advanced on behalf of the Government that the claims should be struck out. I was pleased that I was not sitting on my own to decide this important case. The Supreme Court dismissed the Government's appeal.

13

On Being a Judge

UNTIL SHORTLY BEFORE I was appointed an Assistant Recorder in 1983, it had never occurred to me that I might want to become a judge, still less that I might become one. But when I was approached by someone in the Lord Chancellor's Department in those pre-Judicial Appointments Commission days, I saw no reason not to accept the offer of an appointment as an Assistant Recorder. It would be a new experience and an exciting challenge. It committed me to sitting no more than four weeks a year. In the first instance, it was a three-year appointment. It certainly did not commit me to a career as a full-time judge.

I had appeared in two jury trials early in my career at the Bar. That was the extent of my experience of juries and criminal trials in the Crown Court. Shortly before my first case as a judge, I had attended a short judicial training course. I recall being instructed by the High Court Judge who was running the course that we had to be tough when it came to sentencing: 'harden your hearts and stiffen your sinews' was his rallying call. This was clearly aimed at people like me who that judge, like other seasoned criminal judges, regarded as unreliable softies with bleeding hearts. For many years, sentencing policy, whether emanating from decisions of the Court of Appeal, the Sentencing Guidelines Council (or its successor the Sentencing Council) or legislation, has ebbed and flowed between encouraging severe punishment ('prison works') and promoting the rehabilitation of offenders. The general trend has been for sentencing to become more severe. When I started sitting as a judge, the idea of 'the short sharp shock' or the 'clang of the prison gates' had taken hold. We were encouraged to pass short custodial sentences for the less serious offences. This idea was later to be discredited on the grounds that a short sentence serves no useful purpose. It merely introduces offenders to bad people; it gives no opportunity for the prison authorities to undertake any rehabilitation; and a custodial sentence disrupts and destroys an offender's employment. But in the 1990s, the short custodial sentence was the favoured disposal in many cases.

The first time I passed a custodial sentence on a defendant was an awesome experience for me. The word 'awesome' is overused these days. It no longer connotes shock or dread. But in my early days as a judge, I felt a real sense of awe each time I deprived a defendant of his liberty and consigned him to a period of incarceration in a prison. Before becoming an Assistant Recorder, I had visited Wormwood Scrubs as part of my training. Prisoners rightly enjoy certain basic human rights, but being locked up in a prison is an unpleasant experience. Inevitably, I gradually became used to imposing custodial sentences and the sense of awe dissipated. I always found the most difficult sentencing decision was whether to pass a custodial sentence at all. Deciding on the length of a custodial sentence, although sometimes difficult and always important, caused me far less anxiety. Over time, even the decision whether to impose a custodial sentence became less stressful.

Gradually, I became more confident in managing jury trials. But although it became easier, I continued to find them quite demanding. The potential pitfalls presented by a small criminal trial are no different in principle from those presented by a major murder trial. The rules of evidence are taken seriously in any criminal case. By the late twentieth century, the rules of evidence that had been crafted by judges over many years had almost disappeared in civil cases. But they were usually applied with rigour in the criminal courts.

I never quite overcame the feeling of my heart sinking when counsel popped up to make an application (usually in the absence of the jury). There seemed to be no limit to the ability of counsel to make challenging and sometimes ingenious applications. And usually, a decision had to be made immediately. It was a rare case in which one could enjoy the luxury of taking time to reflect or consult other wiser and more experienced judges and ask for a helping hand. This could be quite stressful. In the early years, I sensed that some counsel knew that I was not an experienced criminal lawyer and occasionally tried to intimidate or bamboozle me into making a decision in their favour. Judicial training was still relatively in its infancy in those days. The Handbook published by the Judicial Studies Board (which later became the Judicial College) containing specimen directions on how to direct a jury on various issues did not exist when I started. These directions reflected what had been said by the Court of Appeal Criminal Division over the years. The Handbook was updated regularly and I found it of invaluable assistance. Failure to observe the directions could lead to the quashing of a conviction by the Court of Appeal. In the result, conducting a jury trial felt to me like participating in an assault course and negotiating traps and pitfalls. Having a conviction quashed through failure to give the jury proper directions would lead to a huge waste of public money. It would also be professionally embarrassing. There was therefore every reason to take great care to give all the directions that courts had said were necessary and not to make mistakes. It seemed to me that many of these directions were unnecessary and betrayed a lack of trust in the jury system. This was somewhat ironic, since some of the judges who had propounded the need for these directions were the most passionate in their praise of our jury system. But I did not allow my scepticism about the necessity for many of these directions to influence what I did in court. I tried to be meticulous in giving the directions. The arrival of the Handbook was a godsend for me.

After I became a High Court Judge, I started to try very serious criminal cases on circuit. In many ways, I found these easier than my early small trials.

I was more experienced and therefore more confident. The heavy criminal cases were usually conducted by skilled counsel, who were unlikely to make bad points or, usually unwittingly, mislead the court by failing to help the judge to make correct rulings and give the jury appropriate directions in the summing up.

I was fortunate never to try a fraud case. Fraud cases can involve much paper and take a long time. I was also lucky not to try many sex cases. Most of the criminal cases that I tried as a High Court Judge were murders. I was absorbed and fascinated by the awful and often sad stories that unfolded through the mouths of the witnesses. It was difficult to believe that people who seemed so ordinary and unassuming in the witness box could behave so unspeakably towards their victims. Sometimes, I was glad that the essential questions of credibility and fact were being decided by the jury and not by me. On the whole, my experience was that juries were tough, not easily taken in by a villain's good performance in the witness box and took their duties very seriously.

But most of my judicial career was spent as a judge trying civil cases, deciding public law claims against various public law bodies in what is now known as the Administrative Court and, for 15 years, as an appellate judge.

I am often asked whether I preferred being a judge to being a barrister. I enjoyed both greatly. Traditionally, there has been an assumption that the best barristers make the best judges. Presumably, that is why historically the senior judges have usually been appointed from the ranks of the most successful barristers. This conventional route into the senior judiciary is now followed less often, partly because increasing numbers of successful barristers do not wish to become full-time judges.

But the assumption that the best barristers make the best judges is highly questionable. The most important attributes of a good judge are patience and fairness; integrity; being a good lawyer; having good judgement and common sense; and producing judgments which are clear and well-reasoned within a reasonable time. The sole aim of judges should be to reach a decision which they honestly consider to be correct in fact and law. They should not mind which party wins. Although they will naturally want to have regard to the 'merits' of the case and find in favour of the 'good guy', they should not distort the facts or the law to ensure that the 'bad guy' loses. Nor should they deliberately make findings of fact with the aim of making their decision appeal-proof.

One of the dangers that a judge at any level should guard against is the risk of becoming desensitised by excessive exposure to the same kinds of case, such as applications for permission to appeal by litigants in person, especially in the fields of family law or asylum and immigration law. After several years of dealing with such applications, which are often very long and sometimes written in barely legible manuscript, it is difficult to apply the same degree of care that one applied when dealing with such a case for the first time. And yet, it is essential to do so: the issues at stake in these cases could hardly be higher for the persons involved.

Another danger in appellate cases is the risk of overlooking the fact that a large number of cases involve a complaint by a real person of some wrong that is alleged to have been done to him or her. It is easy to forget this when one is immersed in a mass of documents and legal authorities. Many of the cases that I have described above involved complaints of suffering or injustice. The victims' stories come to life when they give their evidence in the witness box at a trial. Sometimes, it is difficult to fully appreciate the human dimension of a case solely on the basis of the documents and hearing the advocate's submissions. It is not often that an appellate judge has eye to eye contact with the claimant. That is why the sight of Mrs Long sitting in the front row during her appeal regarding the death of her son made such an impact on me that I felt moved to mention it in my judgment (see chapter eleven).

A good civil barrister needs to be a good lawyer and all barristers need to have good judgement and integrity, which includes not doing anything to mislead the court. But barristers want to win their cases. They *do* mind if their clients lose. Advocacy is an exciting business. There is a thrill in persuading a judge to accept one's submissions or in securing an acquittal before a jury or in destroying a witness by a successful piece of cross-examination, although this may be an unedifying spectacle. It is therefore not surprising that not all good barristers make good judges. It is surprising that it should ever have been assumed that they do. I know some senior judges who were extremely successful barristers, but were not good judges. They found it difficult to cast aside their barristers' robes and let the advocates get on with presenting their cases without undue interruption from the Bench and without the judge descending into the arena. Sometimes, a judge may be justified in intervening in the interests of justice, for example, where the barrister is out of his depth and is not putting an obvious point. But a good judge will do this only occasionally and in a clear case. Such interventions are more likely to be justified on behalf of a litigant who is acting without legal representation.

I believe that I was a competent civil barrister. My strength lay in building a cross-examination or a submission calmly step by step and making my points succinctly and clearly. I would not have been an effective jury advocate, probably because my approach would have been too intellectual and rigorously analytical. Nor would I have had the ability to woo a jury with magical charm and the colourful language that I have seen deployed spell-bindingly by the best criminal advocates.

I found being a judge immensely satisfying. I enjoyed not having the pressure of having to try to win a case for a client. The only pressure I felt as a judge was to try to arrive at the right answer by a fair process (it was particularly important that losing parties should feel that they had had a fair hearing) and to express my reasons well. I always tried to write judgments which were no longer than were necessary. It helped that I always typed my judgments and, not being a touch typist, typed rather slowly. In recent years, there has been an unwelcome trend towards judgments which are unnecessarily long. There are a number of reasons for this. One is that many judges worry that, unless they deal with every detail, they will be criticised for overlooking a point that they have not covered and their judgment will be reversed on appeal. Another reason is that the use of the computer has encouraged judges to copy and paste long passages from documents including other judgments. This is far easier than writing a few sentences summarising their effect.

No judge likes to have his or her decision overturned. I have never believed those macho judges who say otherwise. If they really mean that they do not care whether their judgments are reversed on appeal, they are likely to be bad judges. They should care if their judgments are overturned, although I accept that much depends on the reason given for the appeal being allowed. If it is because the appeal court has changed the law, or there has been a change of circumstances since the original hearing (including the introduction of new points into the case), then the judge should not mind that his or her decision has been reversed. But if the appeal is allowed because the judge acted unfairly or made perverse findings of fact, then that should be a matter of concern.

Early in my career as a High Court Judge, I was told by an experienced Court of Appeal judge not to worry about being reversed. Even the judgments of the very greatest judges are overturned from time to time. Appellate judges do not keep a log of judges whose judgments they overturn. They are too busy working on their appeals. It is only an egregiously bad judgment that is likely to remain lodged in the memory of an appellate judge.

When Court of Appeal judgments of mine were overturned by the Supreme Court, whether they had been given by me as a Lord Justice of Appeal or as Master of the Rolls, I was always interested to know why. Sometimes, the shape of the case and the arguments had changed considerably so that the difference of outcome did not reflect on my performance at all. Other times, I was persuaded that the reasoning of the Supreme Court was to be preferred to my own. Yet other times, in difficult cases where the arguments were finely balanced and there was much to be said on both sides of the argument, I was not particularly troubled that the Supreme Court reached a different conclusion from my own. There were many such cases and they often generated dissenting judgments in the Supreme Court. Finally, there were cases where I was unpersuaded by the Supreme Court's reasoning and remained of the view that my decision was correct. But the law does not recognise the correctness of a decision that has been reversed unless it is rehabilitated by a subsequent decision of the Supreme Court. Otherwise, the decision is of no interest to anyone except perhaps some academic who is in search of an article to write.

But even as Master of the Rolls, regardless of the circumstances, I was happier to have my decisions upheld rather than reversed by the Supreme Court. I have earlier referred to the letter I received from US Justice Scalia when I was promoted to the Supreme Court saying that one of the attractions of the Supreme Court was that one's decisions would no longer be vulnerable to reversal by a higher court. But even judgments of the Supreme Court are at risk. The Supreme

Court sometimes revisits issues that it has determined in an earlier appeal and changes its mind. The reasoning of individual judgments may also be rejected in subsequent cases. A dissenting judgment is likely to be criticised expressly or at least by implication in the majority judgments. And academic lawyers have a field day criticising all judgments at all levels. So Justice Scalia overstated the position: even the Supreme Court is not a safe haven.

Little is known in the outside world about the process of appellate judging. The Supreme Court sits in panels or constitutions of five (by far the most usual), seven, nine and most rarely 11. Most appeals to the Supreme Court raise important points of law: the more important the points, the larger the panel. The usual routine is that immediately after the conclusion of an appeal, the Justices retire to discuss the case and to express their provisional views. Occasionally, the issues are so difficult that there is no point in expressing even provisional views until there has been further time for reflection. But that is rare. The expectation is that, having had the benefit of studying the written material before the hearing and of testing submissions during the course of oral argument, the Justices will have been able to form some provisional views by the end of the hearing. I have already mentioned the convention that, at their post-hearing discussions, the Justices are called upon to express their views in order of their seniority. It seems that the thinking behind this convention was that, if the senior members of the court spoke first, the junior members would be cowed and inhibited, and unwilling to express a view contrary to those of their senior colleagues. I have always believed that this convention is unwarranted. It pays scant regard to the independence of spirit of the junior members of the court. In my view, the more flexible approach that is usually followed in the Court of Appeal of allowing a free discussion to see whether a consensus emerges is to be preferred. After each Justice of the Supreme Court has expressed his or her provisional view, one person is given the responsibility of writing the lead judgment. The most senior Justice on the panel may ask for a volunteer, or may ask a particular Justice to write it or may decide to write it himself or herself. A majority view may emerge from the discussion. It may also be clear that one or more of the Justices has a different view. It is not unknown for a Justice to write and circulate what he or she conceives is likely to be a dissenting judgment even before the draft lead judgment has been written and circulated. This is sometimes done in a naked attempt to influence the other members of the court to change the views they had provisionally expressed at the meeting. Although persuasion is the stock in trade of the barrister, it seems that the desire to influence and persuade is also never far from the surface of the judicial mind either. I suspect that the reason is that a judge who has reached a conclusion after thinking hard about a point wants the product of his work to have some significance. It is of little comfort to a judge to know that his dissenting judgment may become tomorrow's orthodoxy. So he wants to try to persuade colleagues to his point of view. Some judges even go into the rooms of their colleagues in an attempt to lobby support for their opinions. I never did this myself and it was rarely done to me.

I tended to rely on the power of the written word. Occasionally, when all the draft judgments had been circulated, it was clear that, unless something was done to try to deal with the multiplicity of opinions expressed, the outcome would be chaotic, confusing and bad for the law. In such a situation, the presiding judge of the panel would convene his colleagues and attempt persuade them to agree to make compromises in the interests of keeping the law as clear and simple as the circumstances permitted. Such attempts were not always successful.

Things in the Court of Appeal were rather different. We usually sat in panels of three. The presiding judge identified the person whom he wished to write the lead judgment before the appeal was heard. The argument against doing this was that the other members of the court might be less diligent in their preparation than they would be if they knew that they had to write the lead judgment. This is an insult to the professionalism and assiduity of the members of the court. In my experience, all members of panels prepare thoroughly for the appeals on which they sit. After the conclusion of the argument, the judges discuss the case in a relaxed and unstructured manner. At the end of the discussion, the judge who has been asked to write the lead judgment goes away to write the judgment. From time to time, there are dissenting judgments in the Court of Appeal. There are also supporting judgments which reach the same conclusion as the lead judgment, but there are relatively few of these. This is partly because, in view of the pressure of work, judges tend not to want to write a supporting judgment unless, although they agree with the conclusion of the lead judgment, their reasons are significantly different. There is no point in writing a judgment to the same effect as the lead judgment, even if you believe that your style and language is superior to that of the lead judgment. Judgments are not English language essay competitions.

On the whole, I found sitting with other judges in an appellate court more enjoyable than sitting as a first instance judge on my own. It helped to relieve the stress of judging. It was reassuring to know that the collective knowledge and wisdom of a panel of judges increased the likelihood of finding the right answer. But there were downsides. Sitting on one's own, one can dictate the pace and direction of the hearing. The presiding judge of an appellate court can also do that, but there is little scope for the other members of the panel (the 'wingers') to do so. This can be frustrating for the wingers. Even worse is the fact that the judge who has agreed to write the lead judgment may take a long time (in a bad case, several months) to produce the fruits of his or her labours. It does not take long to forget the details of a case. One tended to know who the serial offenders were. If one of these was to write the lead judgment, I would usually make a note of my thoughts immediately after the conclusion of the argument. This would be a useful aide-memoire to which I could have recourse when I eventually received the draft lead judgment.

I am sometimes asked what difference oral advocacy makes to the outcome of a case. This is a question worth asking not least because of the eye-watering fees that are paid to many barristers. In most civil cases, the court is provided with written submissions in advance of the hearing. In a complex case, these can be very long. The judge should therefore be familiar with the broad outlines of the case before he goes into court; and will often have mastered much of the detail. That is why such care is now taken by the advocate over the preparation of the written submissions. So the judge will often have a provisional view of what he or she considers to be the right answer. But my experience was that good oral advocacy did make a real difference in some cases and persuade me to change the view that I had provisionally formed after studying the papers before the hearing. And in the really difficult cases, I had often not formed a provisional view at all.

Outstanding advocates can be very persuasive. I found that they could lead you seductively step by step to a conclusion which you knew instinctively could not be right, but where the less able opposing advocate was not good enough to expose the flaws in the argument. Where that occurred, I had to go away and work the answer out for myself.

Really bad advocates present a different challenge to a judge. I rarely had difficulty in preventing an advocate from repeating himself. I found that a firm 'you have already made that point, and I have understood it' usually sufficed. More problematic is the advocate whose submissions are incoherent. It seemed to me to be incumbent on the judge to summarise the principal submissions of the parties in the judgment and then deal with them. It is difficult to record the submissions if one does not understand them. Conscious of the fact that all parties are entitled to a fair hearing, I would try to express in what I considered to be a more coherent form the point that I thought the bad advocate was making and then deal with it. This is a tricky exercise because it is unfair to the other party to do too much to improve the bad advocate's submissions.

One of the features of being a judge for which I was not prepared and for which I had received no training was how to cope with public criticism from the media and elsewhere. So far as I am aware, my early experiences of small cases as an Assistant Recorder did not expose me to public comment of any kind. The first time I realised that judges are vulnerable to criticism which may be unfair was when as a High Court Judge I was attacked by the press and Michael Howard in 1995 for my decision in the IRA prisoners case of *Norney* (see chapter eight). Although my decision was plainly correct and was not appealed, I was heavily criticised, sometimes in intemperate language. This experience led me to think more carefully how I might present decisions which were likely to attract public criticism, without allowing a fear of criticism to influence their substance. I knew that the media were subject to tight deadlines and would often not have the time or inclination to read an entire judgment. One of the techniques that I developed was to write a concluding paragraph, headed 'Conclusion', which summarised the reasons for my decision. This was likely to be seized on with gratitude by a busy reporter. It saved him from the burden of having to read the judgment in detail and reduced the risk of an inaccurate report of its meaning and effect. And so it was to my considerable satisfaction that newspaper reports often quoted from my concluding paragraphs in sensitive cases. It was the same idea that led the Supreme Court to publish press summaries in all of its cases. When I was Master of the Rolls, I too drafted press summaries in certain high profile cases which I knew would be a particular interest to the media. Judges from earlier times would have been horrified to see how their successors now accommodate the media. Their view would undoubtedly have been that a judgment spoke for itself and that any summary would have impaired its integrity. That approach seems naïve and quaintly arrogant to modern eyes.

It is trite to say that our system demands that, save in exceptional circumstances, proceedings are conducted in open court. During my professional life, there has been much discussion about whether to televise court proceedings. I have always been less worried about introducing television into our criminal courts than many of my colleagues. I have had experience of being in courts whose proceedings are televised. This is done in every appeal in the Supreme Court and increasingly in the Court of Appeal too. The fears that the behaviour of judges or advocates would be influenced by the presence of cameras have proved to be groundless. I found that I concentrated so much on counsel's submissions that I was totally oblivious of the presence of the camera. I accept, however, that jury trials give rise to considerations which do not apply in civil litigation.

Judges have to be prepared for public criticism and need to be tough and should try to develop a reasonably thick skin. But the skin should not be too thick. A judge should respond positively to fair criticism and be prepared to admit that he may be wrong. I have already referred to the case of *Mitchell v News Group Newspapers Ltd* [2013] EWCA Civ 1437 (see chapter eleven) in which I said that the courts should adopt a less forgiving approach to granting relief to parties for failure to comply with court orders, rules and practice directions. This marked a major change from the traditional more lax attitude evinced by the courts, which in turn had led to a less efficient and strict way of conducting civil litigation. I was heavily criticised for this by many in the legal profession (especially solicitors) as well as some judges and legal commentators. I was taken aback by the trenchant tone of the criticism. I was upset by stories that I heard that solicitors were having nervous breakdowns out of fear that, in the new climate, their claims would be struck out for failure to comply with time limits. But I believed that a major change of litigation culture was required and that a harsh decision such as *Mitchell* was the only way to achieve this. On reflection, I thought that I might have expressed myself in terms that were a little too uncompromising. In the later case of *Denton v TH White Ltd* [2014] EWCA Civ 906, I slightly toned down the severity of *Mitchell*. This seemed to take the heat out of the issue and a significant change of culture was achieved. But the *Mitchell* saga was not a pleasant experience for me.

Judging at any level can be quite stressful. I have often been asked whether worrying about a judgment kept me awake at night. I did sometimes lose sleep. This was more likely to be because I could not relax as a result of prolonged intense mental activity than because I was racked with angst, although I do generally have a tendency towards anxiety. I certainly did not worry about the enormity of some of the decisions that I had to make, and I doubt whether many judges do. They are far too busy trying to work out the right answer to be wracked with worries of that kind. I think there must be a close analogy with surgeons here. Surgeons often know that the lives of their patients are in their hands and that a mistake can lead to death. I do not believe that surgeons reflect on the enormity of what they are doing when they carry out an operation. They are too busy concentrating on doing a good job.

Almost all the senior judges I know enjoy judging. They may complain about their working conditions, but they love the work. It is intellectually satisfying and it really matters. Resolving disputes fairly and persuasively is a rewarding thing to do. It is critical to maintaining the rule of law and keeping our democracy in good working order. To have the opportunity (as I did) to nudge the law along a little is a great privilege. I could not have wished to have a more exciting or worthwhile career.

14

No Longer a Judge

WHEN I RETIRED as a judge in October 2016, I was not at all sure how I wanted to spend the remaining precious years of my life. I knew that I wanted to be fairly busy. A life of nothing but holidays and bridge, which I would have had to learn to play, would not have satisfied me. Attending a course on some aspect of history or music remains a possibility. I wanted to spend more time with Jacqueline and the family. But the grandchildren were already in their teens, or almost so. They had very busy lives as did our children and their spouses. I was approached by a few chambers to see whether I would like to join them as an arbitrator and mediator. One of these was my old chambers, 39 Essex Street (now known as 39 Essex Chambers). I decided to go back to them, although they were hardly recognisable to me. There had been 33 members of chambers when I went on the Bench in 1993. There were now more than 130 members. They occupied huge premises at 81 Chancery Lane which looked little different from large modern offices that could have been anywhere. I decided to go back there because I knew I would be welcomed by some of my old friends as indeed I was. One of these, Nigel Pleming QC, went so far as to invite me to share his room, which I did and which I have enjoyed doing. I suspected that, if I were to join one of the other sets of chambers that were interested in me, I might have a more successful next career. But I could not be sure. And many people told me that I would become very busy wherever I went. I did not want to be overwhelmed with work. I had already had enough of that, although I did want to be reasonably busy.

So I went back to 39. It took some time before I started to get work. I knew that it was ridiculous to be anxious about not having enough work but I was. Having decided to continue working, I wanted to make a success of it. I knew that I was rather old to be planting my flag in the world of international arbitration after an interval of almost 25 years; that I had not had a great deal of experience of commercial law, as opposed to construction law; and that there were large numbers of competent experienced arbitrators, including growing numbers of ambitious retired senior judges, who were competing for the same work.

It was something of a blow that the senior clerk, David Barnes, left chambers before I had become established. His excellent successor, Lindsay Scott, had to spend most of her first year reorganising chambers. But she advised me that I had to be seen in the marketplace, and should attend and speak at conferences and network with enthusiasm. I took her advice and did all these things. In particular, I networked away, handing out my cards with abandon like everyone else. I found this less difficult and less objectionable than I expected.

Over time, I started to receive arbitral appointments, some with seats in London and others with seats abroad. I made it clear that I wished to spend as much time in London as possible, although I would not object to an occasional case abroad. I believe that I could have been appointed to serve as a judge on a foreign court. But I was not interested in following that path.

In addition to construction, commercial and sports arbitrations, I have done some advisory work. I also did one fascinating mediation in an intractable dispute between wealthy elderly parents and their children. The parents had given many valuable assets to the children. Their behaviour towards each other had given rise to much acrimony and bitterness. Some of it was played out in the press. Litigation ensued and, despite the valiant but vain efforts of myself and my co-mediator, an ugly trial in the glare of publicity seemed inevitable. Eventually, however, the case was settled shortly before the trial date. I doubt whether our efforts contributed much to the settlement.

I also undertook two large and rather unusual projects. The first was an Inquiry on behalf of the London Borough of Lewisham into whether members or officials of the Council had acted improperly in relation to a proposal to redevelop a large site in New Bermondsey. The site included 'The Den' which is the football ground of Millwall Football Club. I conducted the Inquiry with the assistance of Catherine Dobson who is one of the most outstanding of the younger members of chambers. I heard evidence in private over a few days and published my report in November 2017. I had only participated in one Inquiry before (the Hillsborough Inquiry before Lord Justice Taylor in 1989) and had never conducted one myself. I found it challenging and enjoyable. The proposed developer was a privately-owned company registered in the Isle of Man. Its two shareholders were also registered in offshore tax-havens. Doing business with such a company was too much for many of the left wing councillors of Lewisham. For that reason, they opposed the idea root and branch. Other councillors, who were desperate to see the much-needed redevelopment take place, took a more pragmatic view. In my report, I exonerated all the officers and members of the wrongdoing that had been alleged against them. My report was criticised almost line by line by Millwall Football Club but no legal challenge followed.

The second project was advising the Republic of Cyprus on the reform of their civil procedure rules. These rules are based on the England and Wales rules which were published in 1958. The modernisation of the Cypriot civil justice system is long overdue and the reform of its rules is an important part of the process. I agreed to lead a small group with the assistance of, among others, David di Mambro (an English barrister with great experience of drafting rules) and Marcos Dracos (a barrister who practises in London and Cyprus).

Reforming the rules is a major undertaking. We took the current England and Wales Civil Procedure Rules as our starting point, but simplified them greatly and adapted them to the particular needs of Cyprus. The whole modernisation programme is being orchestrated by George Erotokritou, a delightful and shrewd former judge of the Supreme Court of Cyprus. The modernisation project is being funded by the EU. From time to time, our group visited Cyprus to explain to leading judges and lawyers what we were doing and to encourage them to be receptive to reform. There is a pressing need for a change of litigation culture and for judges and practitioners alike to adopt a more rigorous and disciplined approach to civil litigation. At the end of our first visit, the leader of the EU team wrote to me:

> I have worked for many years now in trying to lead reforms in Member States and help others do it. I have worked with many experts in doing so but I have very rarely met experts of your calibre. This, coming from a French man about an English man (or English Lord to be accurate) is not an easy confession to make!
>
> It was a real pleasure to see you handle meetings and people with finesse but in a very direct and straightforward manner. And with much humility and simplicity. 'Une main de fer dans un gant de velour' is how we put it back home, but it was even more than that.

This was praise indeed. I think I had learnt a great deal about how to lead and manage people during my years as a judge and in the various leadership roles that I had performed. As a fundamentally shy person, this is not a skill that I would ever have expected to possess.

At the time of writing (early 2019), I have become rather busy. I am enjoying the variety of the work that I am doing. I take delight in the fact that I can still attract work. Although I am fortunate in that I do not need to earn money, I confess that, after years of being paid so much less than I could have earned if I had stayed at the Bar, I do quite enjoy earning well. That is not to say that I regret for one minute leaving the Bar and being a judge for 23 years. I have no idea how long I will have the appetite or the ability to carry on. But, subject to my physical and mental health remaining intact, I would like to do so for some time yet if I am able to attract the work.

Having described by return to chambers, I now need to go back and turn to other aspects of my retirement. While I was still in office as Master of the Rolls, with the encouragement of Lord Judge, I had put my name forward for election as Deputy Treasurer of the Middle Temple in 2016. Election to this post would lead the following year to my election as Treasurer. Igor's advice was that it would not be wise to try to combine being Master of the Rolls with being Treasurer; but that to be Treasurer shortly after retirement would be a good bridge into the next phase of my life. And so it proved to be.

In the autumn of 2016, I relished being free of responsibilities. In October, Jacqueline and I walked the Cotswold Way from Chipping Camden to Bath.

It was long, but not too demanding. Walking down in to Bath was a wonderful way to enter that beautiful city. We had dinner with Tim and Teresa Lloyd in their flat in one of the sumptuous Georgian terraces for which Bath is rightly so famous. Tim had been a colleague during the first of my two periods in the Court of Appeal. The most appealing feature of the week was the fact that, for the first time since I was four years old, I was not working in the middle of October.

But I continued to give lectures from time to time. The first post-retirement lecture that I gave was at the Oxford Centre for Islamic Studies which was established in 1985 with the aim of encouraging the academic study of Islam. The Centre is in a huge new building which includes a mosque, a dome and minaret. At the time of our visit, it was an eerie place, largely empty of people and books. I spoke about Religion and the Law. The audience included many distinguished Oxford academics. Sitting in the front row was Sir Guenter Treitel QC whom I had never met before. He is a distinguished German-born academic contract lawyer and the retired Vinerian Professor of English Law at the University of Oxford. I had the great privilege of sitting next to him at the dinner that followed my lecture. I found that he wore his distinction with extraordinary modesty. He told me about his life in Berlin before he had to leave for England on the *Kindertransport* in 1938. He could still remember being required to give the Nazi salute in class at school. The family plan was that he would join the law firm of his father and uncle. I could have listened to him for hours. It was fascinating to have a tutorial on pre-war German history from a person who had lived through some of it, albeit as a child.

Early in November, we went to Israel. The main purpose of the visit was for me to deliver the Lionel Cohen lecture in Jerusalem. This is an annual lecture which has been delivered at the Law Faculty of the Hebrew University of Jerusalem since 1953 by many of the most distinguished jurists of the common law world. It is organised by the British Friends of the University. The title of my lecture was 'Protecting human rights in an age of terrorism'. We stayed for three nights in Jerusalem. For most of the time, we were in the company of Jonathan Cohen QC (now Mr Justice Cohen) and his wife Briony. Jonathan is the grandson of the eponymous Lord Lionel Cohen. We visited a Law Clinic in East Jerusalem where students give advice under professional supervision to some of the most deprived members of Israeli society, predominantly Arabs. We visited the Old City and the Supreme Court (both of which we had visited several times before, but which never cease to thrill). We had a guided tour of Talbiya, a residential part of pre-Second World War Jerusalem. And we had lunch with Professor Karayanni, the Dean of the Law Faculty, who is an Arab Israeli, and two of his predecessors.

From Jerusalem, we went to Tel-Aviv, a city which we hardly knew. We visited some of its excellent museums; walked along the front to Jaffa; and generally soaked up the atmosphere of this vibrant city. One evening we were entertained to dinner in an Arab restaurant in Jaffa by Justice Daphne Barak-Erez and her husband. She is one of the rising stars of the Supreme Court of Israel whom I had previously met in London at one of the legal exchanges in which we had participated. Like so many Israelis, she has a seriousness of purpose and a quest for knowledge that puts me to shame. On the following evening, we were entertained to dinner by Uzi and Liora Vogelman at the lovely Montefiore Hotel in the city centre. He too is a rising star of the Supreme Court whom I had previously met both in London and in Israel. It was a real joy to spend time with such delightful people. What united all the people we met during our visit to Israel was their sense of helplessness and frustration at the direction the country is being taken by its politicians.

In late November, we went to New York for several days. I had been invited to give a lecture and take a seminar at the Brooklyn Law School about civil justice. The visit had been arranged by Roberta Karmel, who is a professor of Securities Regulation at the School. She is the wife of David Harrison who was a good friend of Jacqueline's parents. We stayed in a large apartment which belongs to the School in Brooklyn. We had a very busy time, which is something that the feverish atmosphere of New York impels one to do. Amongst other things, we saw a production of *La Boheme* at the New York Met; went to the Neue Galerie which houses some splendid works by Klimt, Schiele and other early twentieth-century German and Austrian art; went to the spectacular New York Public Library; and had lunch at the Greenwich Village home of Fred and Barbara Newman, who are cousins of Jacqueline.

On 5 December, Fanny Waterman (then aged 96) hosted a musical soirée and supper in my honour at Woodgarth, her lovely home in Leeds. Splendid music was performed by the Gould Piano Trio whose pianist, Benjamin Frith, was one of Fanny's pupils. She had invited some very distinguished guests including Archbishop Sentamu, the Archbishop of York, Sir Alan Langlands, Vice-Chancellor of the University of Leeds, Sir Vernon Ellis, Chair of the Board of Trustees of the Leeds International Piano Competition, Mrs Sue Woodroofe, Principal of the Grammar School at Leeds and others. The evening was planned with flair and characteristic attention to detail. I was greatly touched to be honoured in this way.

To leap ahead to March 2018, Fanny had decided to present to the University of Leeds her archive comprising documents that she had accumulated over her long life: she celebrated her ninety-eighth birthday in March. They included correspondence and manuscripts from Benjamin Britten as well as minutes of meetings of the Leeds International Piano Competition and many other documents. To mark its gratitude, the University organised a celebration, which included a display of some of the archive, a piano recital by Leon McCawley and a conversation between Fanny and myself before a large audience. I was a little apprehensive about the conversation, because I wanted it to focus on her life and achievements and it could easily have been blown off course by her excitement.

I had gone up to Leeds a few days earlier for a dress rehearsal. The preparation paid off and the conversation was a triumph. Fanny was elated and performed magnificently.

2017 was my year as Treasurer of Middle Temple. The role of Treasurer is no longer largely ceremonial or presidential. The Inn combines many different functions. It owns a large estate of valuable property most of which is let to barristers' chambers; it is a degree awarding body, being responsible for calling student barristers to the Bar; it provides legal education; and is the professional home for approximately one quarter of the barristers of England and Wales. The Treasurer is involved in an executive capacity in the many issues that arise from these broad functions.

The panelled walls of the magnificent Elizabethan Hall and the corridors are covered with the coats of arms of past Treasurers and Readers of the Inn. The design of my coat of arms was largely based on a sketch drawn by Justin, one of our grandchildren. When he was about nine years old, he came to the Inn and was intrigued by the rows of coats of arms. We explained to him that they were meant to symbolise some key aspects or interests of the person concerned. Unasked, he drew a sketch on a scruffy piece of paper of white roses of Yorkshire, stars of David, piano keys and mountains. He had summed me up brilliantly. I retained the piece of paper and gave a copy to the College of Arms (the official heraldic authority of the United Kingdom) who used it as the basis for the design of my coat of arms which now hangs on the wall of the corridor that leads to the Prince's Room. I am very proud of the part Justin played in its genesis.

Although our own flat in Bloomsbury Square was only 15 minutes' walk away, we were persuaded to accept the offer of a charming seventeenth-century flat within the Inn. It was a good bolt hole to which to retreat for short periods during the day. It was also convenient to be able to flop into the flat after a long evening in the Inn. Access to the flat is by a steep wooden staircase which reminded me of the staircases of Wadham College. The nostalgic sentiment was reinforced by the wonderful sound of church bells that can be heard from the flat, especially in the quiet of the early morning.

My year as Treasurer started quite slowly. There were many members of staff to meet. By the end of the year, I recognised everybody, but regrettably I found some of the names elusive. A striking feature of the Inn was the friendliness of the staff. Nothing was too much trouble for them. Much of the credit for this must be accorded to Guy Perricone (the Under-Treasurer or Chief Executive) and the other senior members of staff.

It would be tedious to mention all the meetings that I attended during the year. I shall only describe a few of them in outline. I had to chair the periodic meetings of the Executive Committee, which is in effect the Cabinet and includes the chairs of the other principal committees. This is the powerhouse of the Inn where most of the important decisions are taken, although some of them are subject to the approval of Parliament. Parliament comprises the Benchers of the Inn who are the senior members who have been elected to be Benchers by Parliament. The Treasurer presides over meetings of Parliament which are held a few times each year. There are other meetings of various committees and bodies. I attended some, but by no means all, of these.

Five times each year, the Inn organises weekends for a group of approximately 50 students. Four were at Cumberland Lodge in Windsor Great Park and the fifth was at the Railway Hotel in York. These weekends are run by skilled practising barristers who have been trained in the art of advocacy teaching. The weekends start with a dinner on Friday evening and end after lunch on Sunday. The students take part in an intensive programme of advocacy training. Most of them make remarkable progress over the weekend. I always enjoyed these weekends. My task was to float around and talk to the students. I was also one of a number of senior members present who had to talk about their first case, preferably in a witty way. It was impossible to make my first case sound interesting, at any rate without totally misrepresenting what happened. So I talked about my experience as a juror instead. That always went down well.

As Treasurer, I had to go to services at the Temple Church from time to time. The Master of the Temple, Robin Griffith-Jones usually officiated. He has the most mellifluous bass baritone voice that I know. He uses it to good effect not only to impart his words of wisdom, but also to instil a sense of happiness in those who are lucky enough to be present to hear him. I found him almost supernaturally charming.

I attended meetings from time to time with the Treasurers of the other Inns, Lord Neuberger (Lincoln's Inn), Baroness Hale (Grays Inn) and David Pittaway QC (Inner Temple). I enjoyed good relations with all of them. All four of us periodically attended meetings of the Council of the Inns of Court (COIC), which was chaired by Desmond Browne QC. The big issue during 2017 was whether the four Inns should combine to provide a law course for Bar students (the Bar Professional Training Course) in competition with the private providers. The other three Inns were keen to do so. Middle Temple was split on the issue. A few objected on social grounds. They feared that such a course, which would not have the capacity to teach all students who wanted to go the Bar, would become the Oxbridge of the Bar and would further sharpen the divide between London and the Regions and disadvantage those who came from less affluent families. Others objected on the grounds that Middle Temple, which was less well off than the other Inns, did not have the financial muscle to fund the setting up of the course. Everyone agreed that, once established, the course would have to be self-financing. I strongly supported the proposal to establish the course for two reasons. First, it would provide a complete answer to those who believed that the Inns could no longer be justified in the public interest because, they argued, they were bastions of privilege and little more than glorified dining clubs. Secondly, the Inns would be able to charge their students fees that were significantly lower than the exorbitant fees that were being charged by the private sector providers. Towards the end of my year, Parliament voted in favour of incurring the expenditure necessary to work up the details of the proposal. I was relieved that the scheme was not strangled at birth as its opponents would have wished. In November 2018 during my successor's year, the detailed scheme was considered by Parliament and finally approved. I spoke at the debate and was greatly pleased by the outcome.

There was much to savour during my year as Treasurer. I had great pleasure in calling to the Bench the three distinguished people whom I had chosen as honorary benchers. They were my good friend Rosalie Abella, Justice of the Supreme Court of Canada; Sir Vernon Ellis, President of English National Opera, formerly Chair of the British Council and now Chair of the Board of the Leeds International Piano Competition; and Stephen Hough, pianist, composer and writer.

Early in May, a number of us went to Dublin for the annual Four Jurisdictions Conference. The four jurisdictions were England and Wales, Scotland, Northern Ireland and the Irish Republic. There were the usual panel discussions on various topics of current interest. I was on a panel which talked about the disclosure of documents in civil procedure. On the Saturday evening, we had an excellent dinner at the King's Inns which is the Irish counterpart of our four Inns of Court.

In May, together with a few other members of the Inn, Jacqueline and I went on a two-day visit to Gibraltar. Gibraltar has the highest density of Middle Temple members in the world. By courtesy of the Governor, Ed Davis CB, CBE, we stayed at The Convent, which was built as a convent in 1531 and has been the Governor's official residence since 1728. We met the Chief Minister, Fabian Picardo and the Chief Justice, Anthony Dudley. The small but lively Jewish community hosted a lavish lunch for all of us. The quantity of food that was served reminded me of meals at the many Bar-Mitzvahs and Jewish weddings that I had attended. Michael Bowsher, one of my fellow benchers, gave an excellent lecture on some of the problems that would arise from the UK decision to leave the European Union. We also had time for a guided tour of the Rock and an organ recital in the Cathedral by Roger Sayer, the Director of Music at the Temple Church. It was a surprisingly delightful and interesting visit.

In September, approximately 70 members of the Inn and 30 partners went on an Amity Visit to Washington DC. By courtesy of the Ambassador to the United States, Sir Kim Darroch, several of us were fortunate enough to spend five nights at the British Embassy. It was a huge privilege to stay in that beautiful Lutyens building. A number of us had a tour of the White House. This was followed by a two-hour White House Mess Lunch with Don McGahn, White House Counsel and Assistant to President Trump. Mr McGahn was charming, chatty and not too discreet about the President. He formally departed from the Trump administration in October 2018. We went to the Supreme Court for the Calling to the Middle Temple Bench of Justice Neil Gorsuch, Associate Justice of the US Supreme Court. Chief Justice Roberts, Justice Gorsuch and I were escorted into the magnificent courtroom where our group and others were assembled. Short speeches of welcome were made by the Chief Justice and me. Justice Gorsuch gave a witty speech in reply. This was a thrilling experience for me. I wonder what my parents and grandparents would have made of it. We then moved to the East and West Conference Rooms for a reception and into the Hall for dinner.

On the following two days, we had discussions with our American counterparts at the US Institute of Peace on topics which included Human Rights in the Age of Terrorism; Restrictions on Media Communications in the Interests of Truth or Privacy; Attorney-Client Privilege; and Climate Change and the Law. At the end of the first day of discussions, we were treated to a magnificent reception at the British Embassy. The Ambassador had spent the day visiting Florida following the recent floods. But he was back in time for the reception and he made a warm and witty speech. Other guests included many of the great and good of the political and legal world of Washington.

The two-day conference concluded with a comparative moot (mock appeal) in the court room of the US Court of Appeals for the Federal Circuit. The US moot was argued by US attorneys before three very garrulous US Appeal Court judges. The UK moot was argued by QCs and junior barristers before a rather more measured and less talkative court comprising senior English judges (one serving and two retired).

The end of the visit was marked by a reception generously hosted by a US firm on the roof terrace of their offices which has an uninterrupted view across to Capitol Hill. I made a short speech thanking William Hubbard, who had arranged the reception. This was one of several short speeches that I had to make during the visit. Making such speeches no longer held terrors for me.

In addition to the events that I have described, we had time to enjoy some of the sights of Washington. We visited a few of its wonderful museums. A particular delight was to explore Georgetown. The Washington visit was probably the highlight of my year.

Inevitably, I had to attend many Middle Temple and other dinners during my year. As Treasurer, I was able to choose the persons next to whom I was to sit. As a result, I met many interesting people from a wide range of backgrounds. The grandest dinner of the year is rather oddly called 'Grand Day'. The Treasurer is given a free hand to invite whoever he or she wishes to invite. Somewhat ambitiously, I invited some famous people whom I had never met. Some of them never bothered to reply; others sent polite apologies; but many others accepted. The result was a wonderful evening attended by members of my family, senior figures from the Law and famous people from various walks of life, as well as many members of the Inn. Lady Justice (Kate) Thirwall wrote to me after the dinner to say that it was quite the best Grand Day she had attended: 'You did look glamorous. Especially you Jacqui; when you came down the step from the High Table into the Hall after your dinner, your dress was shimmering: you looked fab.' That was quite the greatest compliment that anyone could have paid to Jacqueline.

Another memorable event was a dinner of the (Anthony) Trollope Society. It was attended by various members of the Trollope family, including the novelist Joanna Trollope and the QC Andrew Trollope. It was also attended by the actress Susan Hampshire, who had appeared in television adaptations of *The Pallisers* and *The Barchester Chronicles*. Baron (Julian) Fellowes, who had written an adaptation of *Dr Thorne*, was also present, as was Sir John Major, who is one of the vice-presidents of the Trollope Society. A speech was given by Steven Amarnick, an American academic. He described how over many years he had painstakingly restored and edited some 65,000 words that Trollope had excised from the first edition of *The Duke's Children*. It was a fascinating story.

We had a visit by our Royal Bencher, Prince William, the Duke of Cambridge. His main interest was in our students. The visit was meticulously choreographed as these things invariably are. A careful selection was made of students who were considered suitable for him to meet. There was a good mix of ethnicities and social backgrounds. It was my task to welcome him and act as his escort, as he flitted in that effortlessly royal way from group to group of students, and then accompany him out of the building. With a winning smile, he put everyone at their ease, making natural conversation which he interspersed with occasional gentle teasing. The students loved every minute of it. And I enjoyed talking to him too.

Inspired by my karaoke performance in Kuala Lumpur in 2014, I decided to have a karaoke evening in the Inn. Many of my colleagues wondered whether this was a wise thing to do. Our predecessors, some of whose severe portraits line the Inn's panelled walls, would have been incredulous and disapproving. But I thought it would be fun, especially for the staff and the younger members of the Inn. And so it proved to be. I started the proceedings by singing 'Hey Jude' again, and there were some outstanding performances by members and staff alike. Some of the senior members of the Inn peeled away the years and revealed themselves to be ageing rock stars, who had to be restrained from singing right through the night. The evening was considered to be a huge success. It was repeated by my successor in 2018 with increased numbers. It now seems to be a permanent feature of the Middle Temple calendar. This may turn out to be my most important and enduring legacy!

It is at this point that I should return to my love of music. I described in chapter three my exposure to classical music and my piano lessons as I was growing up. My passion for music has continued unabated throughout my life. My tastes are fairly catholic, both as to composer and type of music. But my deepest love is of the classical piano repertoire. Although I stopped having lessons at the age of 17, I have kept playing and occasionally practising ever since. For many years, I played regularly with a violinist friend who had played in the National Youth Orchestra in his youth. A little later, I played piano duets with Sir Michael Harris, who had been a fellow member of chambers and rose to become President of the Appeals Service.

On 31 January 2017, I presented 'A Musical Evening with John Dyson and Friends' in Middle Temple Hall. More than 200 people attended and I was very nervous. The programme consisted of piano duets played by me and Michael Harris (Schubert's Grand Rondeau in A major, movements from Faure's Dolly Suite and from Moskowski's Spanish Dances); and music for piano and clarinet played by me and Professor Gabriel Gorodetski (some of Schumann's Fantasiestucke and Romanze for piano and clarinet). In addition to being a gifted clarinettist, Gabriel is a distinguished Israeli historian, a fellow of All Souls College, Oxford and now well known for his editing of the diaries of Ivan Maisky. Despite the occasional glitch, I was fairly satisfied with our performances. However, if the success of the evening is to be measured by the number of requests I subsequently received to play, then it was a failure. But we did raise more than £21,000 for the Middle Temple Scholarship Fund and that gave me enormous satisfaction.

Spurred on by the excitement of this concert, I started having piano lessons again. My teacher, Yvonne Behar, is very good. I stopped after only six lessons owing to pressure of work. That may have been a mistake, but she helped me to improve my technique and I do now practise in a more disciplined way than I was doing before I had these lessons. In September 2018, I gave a short recital in St John's Church, Northwood. The audience was not more than about 40 people. Despite many hours of hard practice, I was very nervous. But I was reasonably pleased with my performance. I played J. S. Bach's second French suite and Schubert's Impromptus in G flat and A flat (Op 90 nos 3 and 4). I concluded with the arrangement by Myra Hess of Bach's 'Jesu Joy of Man's Desiring'. I have since been asked to play again and agreed to do so. I don't know why I put myself under such pressure. I believe that it all goes back to my mother's unrealistic insistence when I was a child that I try to achieve perfection in everything I did. As I said earlier, this attempt to achieve the impossible was reinforced, in the case of the piano, by Fanny Waterman's demand that I played every piece to concert standard. I never asked her to define what she meant by 'concert standard'. I suspect that she meant 'Wigmore Hall standard'.

My brother-in-law David Levy suggested to me sometime in 2017 that I publish a selection of some of my speeches and lectures. It had never occurred to me to do this but, encouraged by the suggestion, I approached Hart Publishing. I sent a selection to Sinead Moloney, the Publisher and General Manager. She agreed to publish them and proposed the title *Justice: Continuity and Change*. Choosing which speeches and lectures to publish was not too difficult but the process of eliminating duplication and then doing the proof-reading was more time-consuming than I would have expected. However, I was very pleased with the finished product. We had a well-attended book launch on 18 January 2018. Lord Briggs of Westbourne spoke. He described the book in embarrassingly glowing terms. He said that the speeches 'really do address the important, controversial issues of the day'. He concluded:

> There are lovely nuggets like John's speech at the Runnymede celebration of Magna Carta in 2015, his wonderful valedictory in Court 4 in July 2016 and his speech to his old school at Leeds Town Hall in 2011. All these give context to the heavier legal stuff, and a more rounded self-portrait of this remarkable man.

In 2018, I became free of the commitment of being Treasurer of Middle Temple. Jacqueline and I had a number of delightful (mainly walking) holidays during the year. These included a fortnight's tour of Sri Lanka. The holiday started with a reception hosted by His Excellency James Dauris, the British High Commissioner and Mrs Dauris to mark the seventieth anniversary of the independence of the state. It was for this event alone that I had to take a suit on the holiday. The reception was attended by the Earl and Countess of Wessex as well as many of the great and the good of Sri Lankan society. We were introduced to the Earl of Wessex (Prince Edward) who was very friendly and down to earth and seemed to be genuinely interested in talking to the guests. In April we walked from Viterbo to Rome and in May we walked the Lady Anne Way. This is a wonderful 100-mile trail from Skipton in Yorkshire to Penrith in Cumbria. The first part of the walk included a stretch in the Yorkshire Dales which I had walked many times in my youth. In July, we went to our apartment in Haute-Nendaz in Switzerland as usual.

We also had two trips to the United States. In June, we went on a brief visit to New York where I had been invited to take part in a panel discussion with US Associate Justice Stephen Breyer and the recently retired Chief Justice of Canada, Beverley McLachlin on 'the Independence of the Judiciary and the Rule of Law'. The discussion was moderated by Murray Hunt, the Director of the Bingham Centre for the Rule of Law. It was a great privilege to speak on a public platform with such distinguished jurists. But I felt that the event lacked sparkle because there was little, if any, disagreement between us on any of the issues that we discussed. We stayed at the Harvard Club which is in a magnificent late nineteenth-century building on 44th Street. It is redolent of New York Establishment. We also found time to walk the High Line and visit again the fabulous Frick Collection.

In August, we went to Colorado. I had been invited by Chief Judge Tymkovitch to speak at the biennial conference of the US Tenth Circuit which was attended by about 500 lawyers and their partners. I had offered him one of the speeches from my book. Politely, but firmly, he told me that, interesting though they would undoubtedly be, what they really wanted was a speech on Brexit. I had never delivered a speech on that subject. Moreover, although I was strongly opposed to Brexit, I had not mastered the intricacies of the arguments. So a lecture on Brexit would present me with quite a challenge. But it seemed churlish to refuse to accede to the judge's request. It was quite an effort to produce the speech. I was surprised that an American audience would be as interested in the subject as they plainly were. They seemed to be fascinated by the fact that Brexit has revealed a fundamental divide in UK society, similar in many ways to the schism that has been exposed in the United States by the election of President Trump.

We spent three days at the Broadmoor Hotel in Colorado Springs where the conference was held. The hotel was built in 1918 and is one of the great hotels of the United States. The participants in the conference included Associate Justices Sottomayor and Gorsuch, judges from opposite ends of the liberal/conservative spectrum of the US Supreme Court. We met many people who were strong supporters of President Trump. One said that she was angered by the way all of his supporters were dismissed by the elite of US society as ill-educated red-necks from the rust belt. Many, she said, were well-educated people who detested the policies of the Democrats and supported President Trump because they wished to see him dismantle most of what had been achieved by President Obama. They also had a visceral hatred of Hillary Clinton. When confronted with the appalling language and personal behaviour of President Trump, they shrugged their shoulders and said that this was a price worth paying in order to secure the benefit of his policies. There was much to savour at the conference. A highlight was a presentation by Bryan Stevenson, who is a black lawyer and professor of law at New York University Law School. He founded a practice dedicated to defending the disadvantaged in society and in particular representing wrongly convicted prisoners, some of them on death row. His speech was inspirational. At the end of the conference, I was presented with his bestselling book, *Just Mercy*.

Early in October, I attended an event that was organised by the Bonavero Institute of Human Rights at Mansfield College, Oxford to mark the seventieth anniversary of the Universal Declaration of Human Rights. Hillary Clinton unveiled a statue of Eleanor Roosevelt. She attended a dinner and stayed for a conference the following day. The theme of the conference was the rise of global illiberalism. Hillary Clinton gave a wide-ranging keynote address in which she expressed her concern about worldwide trends. She touched on President Trump, but if she was consumed with rancour and anger about her defeat in the 2016 presidential election and what was currently happening in the United States, she kept her feelings in check and maintained her dignity. I had spoken to her before the dinner the previous evening and found her unexpectedly warm and friendly. My impression of her did not fit the rather strident and severe persona that her television image had conveyed to me. And I was struck by how much time she spent talking to the many students who were present. During the panel discussions, there were excellent contributions from brilliant lawyers and journalists from repressive countries who fearlessly represent their clients and report on human rights abuses, often at great risk to their personal safety. I am pleased to be associated with the Institute as a member of its Advisory Board.

It could not have a better director than Professor Kate O'Regan, a former judge of the Constitutional Court of South Africa.

Later in October, I attended a one day seminar that was organised by the Supreme Court of Israel to mark the seventieth anniversary of the founding of the court. The theme of the seminar was 'the importance of the independence of the judiciary and how to secure it'. The particular *casus belli* for this subject was the perceived threat posed by the Israeli Government to the independence of the Supreme Court. I was on a panel which was asked to discuss the issue from an international point of view. My co-panellists were Justice Rosie Abella and Irving Cottler from Canada and Dorit Beinisch, a former President of the Israel Supreme Court. All three had participated in the conference in Krakow in 2016 which I have described in chapter eleven. The seminar was hosted by the President of Israel, Reuven Rivlin, in his official residence. Many current and former Justices of the Supreme Court were present as was the Minster of Justice, Ayelet Shaked who is seen by members of the court as leading the charge to curb the court's powers. After making a fairly conciliatory speech early in the seminar, the minister left without any explanation or expression of regret. It was as if she was not interested in hearing what anyone else had to say. Rosie Abella gave a powerful speech in praise of the Israeli court. I said that, on the whole, UK governments respect judicial independence and I described some of the measures that are in place to ensure that the independence of the judges is protected. In my closing remarks, I said that I was dismayed by the minister's early unexplained departure: it seemed to me to show great disrespect to the court and those attending the seminar. At the end of the proceedings, I was thanked by many of those present, including the current president of the court Esther Hayut, for saying what they felt unable to say, but I could.

After the seminar was over, we had supper in the garden of the residence. As usual, there was far too much food. And there had been an equally sumptuous feast the previous evening when a former president of the court, Mira Naor, hosted a small dinner party in her apartment. The guests at this party included Aharon and Elrika Barak. Aharon is a great jurist and most distinguished and influential former president of the court. He has been largely responsible for developing what we would call human rights law in Israel. I had not seen him for about 10 years. He looked thinner and frailer than when I had last met him, but there had been no apparent dimming of his intellectual powers. He greeted me with a great hug like a long lost friend. It was at this dinner party that I met Esther Hayut for the first time. She struck me as a strong and brave leader who was having to fight hard to maintain the independence of her court in difficult circumstances.

The first two years of my so-called retirement had been fulfilling and rewarding. I am a realist, if not a pessimist, and I know that this Indian summer of my life will be relatively short-lived. But I am making the most of it. I have to confess that I have been disappointed not to be given a life peerage. I understand that, during the negotiations between Lord Woolf (then Lord Chief Justice) and Lord Falconer (then Lord Chancellor), Lord Falconer made it clear that one of the consequences of the replacement of the Appellate Committee of the House of Lords by the new Supreme Court would be that Justices of the Supreme Court would be appointed to the House of Lords on retirement, where they would be expected to play a full part in scrutinising legislation. I also understand that shortly before David Cameron resigned as Prime Minister in July 2016 following the Brexit referendum, he had cleared the way for me to be given a peerage on my retirement in October. But his successor, Theresa May had other ideas. She did not like the idea of peerages being granted automatically to any group of people.

I understand that various members of the House of Lords, and perhaps others too, have been trying to intercede on my behalf, not least because, having been Master of the Rolls as well as a retired Justice of the Supreme Court, my cause may be thought to be even stronger than that of retired Supreme Court Justices. But nothing has happened and inevitably, as time goes by, the prospects of my going to the House of Lords are diminishing. So I have been getting on with my life doing other interesting things. If I were offered a peerage now, I would accept the offer, although Jacqueline would try to persuade me not to do so. Her view is that it is better to be a completely free agent in my final years of active life.

I have mentioned the peerage issue not because I am obsessed by it. This is far from the case. In fact, most of the time, I do not even think about it. But to sit in the House of Lords would have been a fitting end to my journey from the Jewish community of Leeds.

My retirement has been far more interesting and exciting than I had any reason to expect. After the intense heat of my high summer as Master of the Rolls, I am now enjoying the calmer beauty of my Indian summer. I want to carry on as long as I can.

15

A Jew in England

M Y JEWISHNESS HAS always been very important to me. It is a core part
of my identity. But the religious side of Judaism does not greatly
interest me, although I have belonged to a moderately orthodox
synagogue (*shul*) all my life. I go to *shul* on the principal holy days and occasionally on *Shabbat* (the Sabbath). These visits are not religious experiences for
me, although I quite enjoy the repeat rituals and reflecting on the fact that Jews
have been doing this kind of thing, with variations, for several thousand years.
I also relish the fact that one can go to a service in another country and be made
welcome despite local variations of practice. And I do enjoy reading in English
certain parts of the Old Testament. Sections or portions of the five books of
Moses tell stories which are of universal significance and describe profound
laws and precepts; and some passages in the books of the Prophets and the
Psalms contain poetry which is intensely moving and beautiful.

I have to confess, however, that for me the main attraction of going to *shul*
is to meet friends and catch up on the latest news. In a typical service, there is a
lot of noise interrupted by ineffectual shushing by those who purport to be in
charge. I imagine that visitors who are accustomed to the quiet and the air of
reverence that pervades typical church services are surprised, if not shocked, by
this but in my experience they are too polite to say so. Although I do not find
spiritual sustenance in *shul*, outstanding cantorial singing (*chazanut*) can move
me deeply. Much of it is packed with pain and sorrow, almost invariably in the
minor key.

However, my emotions are stirred more by some of the great non-Jewish
choral music by, for example, Bach, Handel, Haydn, Mozart and Brahms. I have
derived enormous pleasure from singing some of these great works in a local
choral society which I joined in 1974. I was chairman for many years and have
been president since I ceased to be chairman. We have sung many works which
have been inspired by the Christian faith. These have included various settings of
the requiem mass. I have never had a problem singing these works. The glory of
the music is what matters to me and I don't think too much about the words. The
only chorus that I recall causing me some difficulty was that of the Jews singing
'Crucify, Crucify him' in Bach's 'St John Passion'. The music is full of hate and
passion and singing it made me feel uncomfortable. But it is powerful and utterly
compelling. I have also sung many works celebrating Jesus and lamenting his
death and have enjoyed the music (if not some of the sentiments) hugely. I have

happily and lustily sung hymns, for example, at the service to mark the opening of the Legal Year in Westminster Abbey. Many observant Jews would deprecate such behaviour. But I have drawn the line at singing in a carol concert in church.

A highlight of the Jewish calendar for me is Passover (*Pesach*) and in particular the first night (*Seder* night). For almost the entirety of our married lives, we have held *Seder* at our home and for many years, our children and their families and Jacqueline's brother and his family have come for the traditional dinner. I preside over a rather abbreviated version of the service (partly in Hebrew and partly in English). The youngest present asks the four questions and the rest of the service provides the answers. We sing some songs. I try to conduct the service amidst a fair amount of chatter and involve everyone round the table. It is invariably a lovely family occasion which everyone enjoys.

My father had been brought up in a kosher household. Eating *traif* (non-kosher food) was not an option in his family and eating pork and shellfish would have been a cardinal sin, grossly offensive and unthinkable. My mother was intolerant of these restrictions as of the other many practices observed by traditional Jewish families. She had been reared on an unrestricted diet. As usual, she prevailed over my father. The result was that I was brought up in a non-kosher household where we routinely ate pork products (*schweinerei*) and shellfish. Jacqueline's upbringing was different in this respect. Although at some point, her family stopped keeping a kosher home, pork and shellfish were never to be seen at home or eaten outside their home. This is the approach that Jacqueline and I have adopted.

My strong sense of Jewish identity derives from a sense of belonging to a small community of people with whom I have a shared history. It is cultural rather than religious. That is not to say that I have an affinity with all Jews. I feel that I have little or nothing in common with ultra-orthodox Jews whose lives are totally dominated by their religion. I have more in common with my non-Jewish friends than I do with them. But I feel a close bond with Jews who have received a good liberal education and whose moral and cultural views are similar to my own. I know that my good non-Jewish friends are not anti-Semitic and, as I said earlier, I have had remarkably little direct experience of anti-Semitism: I describe such experiences as I have had in chapter three. But from time to time I have been in non-Jewish company when I have been on my guard against anti-Semitic remarks. So far as I am aware, no such remarks have ever been directed at me.

In recent decades, Israel has become a sensitive subject for Jews in our country. It has not always been like this. In 1948, when it looked as if the newly born state would be killed off at birth by its encircling Arab neighbours, and again in 1967 when the state's existence seemed for a time to be under threat, there was huge support for Israel from the British population. Perhaps this was because the Holocaust was still a recent event. But it may also have been because Israel was perceived as the underdog and, rather engagingly, the British people tend to support the underdog in any contest.

I regret the political direction that Israel has taken in recent years. It seems to me that it has made mistakes and can justifiably be criticised for these. But regrettably, many of the criticisms that are made are grossly unfair. For example, the accusation that Israel is an apartheid state is grotesque. What I find upsetting and frustrating is the treatment of Israel as compared with other countries some of which have appalling human rights records. Those who are on the left wing in our political system are particularly prone to this form of double standards. Whenever I have confronted critics of Israel with the fact that Israeli law provides strong human rights protection for everyone without discrimination (including Arabs) and that the laws are upheld by a fiercely independent judiciary, I have never been able to engage with them. I have often found that, when I mention Israel to non-Jews, I am greeted by a wall of silence. They do not respond, presumably because they do not want to reveal their true thoughts and upset me. This makes me feel uncomfortable, and I rapidly change the subject. There is obviously no such problem in Jewish company. Many Jews like me criticise the Israeli Government without inhibition just as they criticise the regimes of other countries too.

I have always been a Zionist in the sense that I support the existence of the state of Israel as a home for the Jewish people. The achievements of the state in no more than 70 years have been truly remarkable. The country is tiny and it has few resources except the talent and energy of its people. I rejoice and take great pride in its achievements. I have been a supporter of the Hebrew University, Jerusalem for many years. It is a fine liberal institution which enjoys a great international reputation. For many years I chaired the Legal Group of the Friends of the University and am now its president. I was very proud to be made an Honorary Fellow.

Although I have hardly ever encountered anti-Semitism myself, for much of my life I felt slightly awkward about revealing the fact that I was a Jew in non-Jewish company. In recent years since I have climbed to the top of the judicial ladder and the fact that I am a Jew has become well known, this feeling has largely evaporated. I am now rather ashamed to admit my previous sense of awkwardness. I can provide a graphic illustration of what I mean. I have described how I left my first chambers and became head of chambers at 2 Garden Court in 1986. During the discussions that took place before the final agreement was made, I did not reveal the fact that I was Jewish. Viewed objectively, it was plainly irrelevant. But I recall saying to the non-Jewish barristers with whom I was having my discussions just before we clinched the deal that they ought to know that I was Jewish. It was almost as if this was a dark secret which I felt that I had to disclose before the final commitment was made.

They thought that it was strange that I felt the need to make this revelation. I am sure that they were not conscious of my sense of awkwardness or the reason for it. I think it must have been borne of the sense of insecurity from which I suffer like many other Jews in this country. When I mention this to non-Jewish friends, they are incredulous. But I believe that insecurity is in the DNA of many, if not most of us. As has been said many times, the key lesson that history teaches Jews is that we always have to have our suitcases packed and be ready to move on. If that sounds paranoid, one only has to look at the fate of the Jews of Germany in the 1930s who regarded themselves as totally committed Germans, wholly cemented into German society. And although I feel very English and am proud to be English, my roots in this country, though strong, are not very deep. My mother came here in 1939 and members of her family suffered in the Holocaust. And my father's parents left Lithuania at the end of the nineteenth century, my grandfather escaping from decades of conscripted service in the Russian army and probably worse. It is likely that this explains why our suitcases are metaphorically packed. In recent times, with anti-Semitism becoming more overt and more widespread in this and many other countries, Jews are heard to ask: where would we go? Sadly, it is a shocking fact that, from talking to friends and acquaintances. I can say with confidence that such conversations are not uncommon. Jacqueline and I occasionally discuss this not as an issue for decision, but as something to have in the back of our minds. So where would we go? Perhaps more accurately, where would we try to go? New York? Canada? Israel? Of course, we don't want to go anywhere. We are British citizens and we belong here. I find it deeply upsetting that serious anti-Semitism (both in the right and left wings of our society) is on the rise. I think that the dark shadow of the Holocaust has provided a degree of protection against the malady during most of my life. But it seems to me that, with the passage of time, this protection is weakening. That is why I am firmly of the view that Holocaust Memorial Day and teaching the young about the Holocaust is so important, although I have been driven to the gloomy conclusion that anti-Semitism will not disappear until and unless the Jews cease to be identifiable as a distinct group.

Non-Jewish friends are shocked and incredulous when I tell them that synagogues organise security rotas to provide protection during services and other communal activities. For many years, I was on the rota at my synagogue. Similar protection is also often provided at secular Jewish events. This is not a hysterical overreaction. Measures of this kind, whose object is to deter anti-Semitic attacks, have the full support of the police.

The insecurity of Jews is well illustrated by what I call the 'Shipman factor'. In 2000, Dr Harold Shipman was convicted of the murder of 15 of his patients. When he was arrested, many Jews assumed that he was Jewish. He was a general practitioner from Manchester, which has a large Jewish population, and had a Jewish-sounding name. When it became clear that he wasn't Jewish, it was as if there was a collective sigh of relief in the whole Jewish community. Both Jacqueline and I felt this way and I know from conversations that many other Jews felt the same way too. Because we are a small community (approximately 250,000 of us in the United Kingdom), we feel responsible for each other's behaviour. Many of us feel collective embarrassment or shame when a high-profile Jew commits a criminal offence or even when he or she merely behaves badly. Bad behaviour includes bullying and gross flaunting of wealth.

The converse is that, like many other Jews, I take great pride in our successes and achievements. Sometimes, it is not clear whether a person is Jewish. Often, I want to know. 'Is he *unserer*?' ('Is he one of ours?') is a commonly heard question. That is why when I read obituaries (again like so many Jews), one of the points I look out for is whether the deceased person was Jewish. It is astonishing how many obituaries there are of Jews. The contribution that the tiny Jewish community has made to the public life of this country has been remarkable.

Anyone who is old enough will recall the cricket test propounded by the Conservative MP Norman Tebbit in 1990. It was directed at the suggested lack of loyalty to the England cricket team of South Asian and Caribbean immigrants and their children. Tebbit suggested that those immigrants who support their native countries rather than England in games of cricket were not significantly integrated into the United Kingdom. Some might apply the Tebbit test to Jews in relation to sporting contests between Israel and England. Who would a Jew support in a football match between England and Israel? I have never had to decide which country I would support. I think I might support Israel unless I thought Israel would win, because I have the very English habit of supporting the underdog. More seriously, regardless of which team I would support, I would utterly repudiate any suggestion that I have a greater loyalty to Israel than to England. I have lived all my life in this country. I have flourished here and given much of myself to this great country. If my first loyalty had been to Israel, I would have moved to that country and could still do so today. I refer to what I said in my Valedictory: see chapter eleven.

It is a curious fact that Jews are disproportionately well represented in the professions, particularly medicine and law. In the main, my parents' generation had no qualifications and limited formal education. Mostly, they ran their own businesses. They were desperately keen that their sons should have a good education and obtain professional qualifications. So many of my generation in Leeds were the first members of their families to go to university. In my experience, which is largely based on what happened in the Jewish community in Leeds, many of the girls were treated differently. They tended to be discouraged from going to university at all. If they insisted that they wanted to go, their parents would insist that they go to the University of Leeds and live at home. The prevailing culture was that girls needed to be protected from the wicked world. It is difficult to overstate the fear of pregnancy which drove much of this protective behaviour until the advent of the contraceptive pill and the liberal atmosphere heralded by the 1960s. A few parents were more enlightened than this. They allowed their daughters to go away to university. Jacqueline, who grew up in London, was fortunate to have such parents. She went to the University of Birmingham. Not only did she survive the experience, but she flourished there. I suspect that, if I had been a girl, the best that I could have hoped for was to live at home and go to the University of Leeds. To late twentieth- and early twenty-first-century eyes, it is extraordinary that, when

I was growing up, the traditional attitude that girls should marry early, raise a family and manage the home still held sway in many families.

So I joined the battalions of young Jews growing up in the post-Second World War world who went into the professions and especially into the Law. I have already described the rather disorganised way in which I stumbled into the profession. I have often wondered why so many Jews have been drawn to the Law. I have heard some say that it is because many of our ancestors spent their lives poring over difficult Talmudic texts and producing subtle interpretations and making fine and perhaps unconvincing distinctions. I wonder whether all that close study of the texts may be a reason why many of us are rather short-sighted. But I doubt whether it has much to do with why so many of us have taken to the Law.

Others give as the explanation for the large numbers of Jews in the Law the fact that Jews like to be independent. It is undoubtedly true that our ances-tors had to be able to pack their bags at short notice and take their skills with them when they fled from the Romans, the Spanish Christians, nineteenth-century pogroms, the Nazis and their many other persecutors, or when they were expelled from England in 1290. It is possible that these shared experiences have made many of us want to be independent. Or it may just be that Jews have had to learn to be independent, sharp-witted and to stand on their own feet and for that reason do not like to be answerable to anyone. And we do tend to love to argue.

A combination of these reasons may explain why there are so many Jewish barristers. After all, they are independent and their daily fare is the cut and thrust of argument. But it is odd that so many Jews have entered the Law, because, unlike medical skills or, say, those of a shoe-repairer, legal knowledge and skills are not readily transferable from one country to another. It is also a striking fact that many Jews have invested in property in this country. This is a surprising thing to do if your suitcase is packed for the move to the next country.

From the army of Jewish barristers has sprung a multitude of Jewish judges. Why is this? Is it because Jews have a love of justice? It would be nice to think so. But I have wondered whether there is another force at work here as well. Most of us are second or third generation Jews. We want to make our mark here and make a real contribution to society. Perhaps Jews want to be accepted and enjoy public recognition outside their community. Judges are criticised from time to time by government and the media for their decisions. But on the whole judges enjoy a prestige and are respected and trusted in this country in a way that politi-cians and journalists might envy. I think this is very important. I believe that it may explain why so many Jews have wanted to be judges. Although many of the Jews of my children's generation have entered the legal profession, many have preferred the world of financial services and the media. I think these are seen as more exciting, and perhaps more financially rewarding, than the Law. But that is not a subject for this memoir.

I feel that being a Jew has added a major dimension and a good deal of colour to my life. I enjoy belonging to the club. Although it is not one that I joined by choice, I have never had any desire to leave it. If I had tried, I would not have succeeded. Before the Second World War, many German Jews tried to leave by assimilation, but they failed. Although I am not particularly observant, I am a fully committed Jew and want to remain one.

16

My Family Life

I ENDED CHAPTER six with the birth of our son Steven in 1973. We now had two children and Jacqueline had stopped working as a lawyer with HM Inland Revenue (as HM Revenue and Customs was then called). For about five years she looked after the children full-time whilst also working at the local Citizens' Advice Bureau in Oxhey, Hertfordshire. Having started this memoir with a description of the families of my mother and father, it is now time to give a brief account of my life as a husband and father. It would be wrong to infer from the brevity of what follows and the fact that it appears towards the end of this memoir that my family has been an incidental adjunct and of little importance to me. Although I have worked very hard all my professional life, I have always recognised that what really matters is personal relationships. And for me, that means my family. As I said in my Valedictory speech in 2016, Jacqueline has been my rock and my life mate. She has boosted my morale when I have encountered difficulty, whether personally or professionally, as inevitably I have done from time to time. When I was a barrister, she listened uncomplainingly and with remarkable patience to my frequent lament that I had no practice. Her patience was all the more surprising because she is very quick both mentally and physically and not a naturally patient person.

She has made at least two sacrifices from which I have benefited. I have already mentioned her refusal of an offer by St Anne's College, Oxford in 1969 of a place to study for the BCL, choosing instead to study for an LLM at UCL so that we could spend more time together than would have been possible if she had been in Oxford. The second sacrifice was her decision not to have a career as a practising lawyer (probably a solicitor). She is an excellent lawyer and would unquestionably have had a successful career in practice if she had wanted to do so. But she decided that she preferred to be a full-time mother during our children's early years.

I can't now recall whether we had already reached a decision as to what she might do outside the home when in 1978 an advertisement appeared in the newspapers for a lectureship in tax law at UCL. Her application for the post was successful. If we had not had children, she would not have become an academic lawyer. She is far more interested in the practical side of life than examining its theoretical or philosophical underpinnings. I know from speaking to many of her former students that she was a superb teacher. Soon the authorities recognised her organisational and administrative skills as well.

Having become a senior lecturer, she was appointed successively Faculty Tutor at the Faculty of Laws; adviser to women students for the whole of UCL; and for six years Dean of Students for the whole of UCL. As Faculty Tutor, she was responsible for student admissions. As Dean of Students, she was responsible for the welfare and discipline of the entire student population of the university. The students presented her with a diverse range of problems. She had to deal with mental health issues and straightforward bad behaviour, some of which was criminal and most of which was attributable to excessive consumption of alcohol.

Eventually, when Jacqueline's mother Rita started to suffer from the devastating effects of Alzheimer's disease, Jacqueline became a part-time lecturer so that she could spend more time with her. In 2014 she retired altogether. Dame Hazel Genn QC, who was the Dean of the Faculty of Laws at UCL at the time, presided over a dinner at the Athenaeum Club to mark Jacqueline's retirement. It was a wonderful occasion. Hazel and several colleagues spoke warmly about her and she made a typically modest and charming speech in response. I was very proud that her achievements were recognised publicly in this way.

When I look back, I cannot believe that she managed to combine doing these demanding jobs with running our home, bringing up two children and supporting me. So far as I can remember, she never complained. She just got on with it. I have often reflected on how lucky I have been in my choice of life partner.

We did not really know each other when we became engaged. We did not live together before we married. There was no certainty that it would be a successful marriage. There never can be such certainty. We have been incredibly lucky that no external events put our relationship to the test. Although we had very little money at the beginning, we knew that we would be rescued by our parents if we became beset with financial problems. Neither we nor our children were struck down by some terrible illness or were permanently disabled as a result of an accident. Our children were both very bright and well-behaved. They did not break the law or fall into bad company. They found entirely suitable partners and even married them. And they produced five lovely grandchildren. In short, I have been greatly blessed.

Of course, there have been moments of difficulty. But there have been few of these. They have not remotely threatened the stability of our family. In the early years of our married life, the relationship between my mother and Jacqueline was quite difficult. I have had to contend with strong women all my life. My grandmother Malvine and my mother were both strong and determined. So too are Jacqueline and Michelle. My mother was used to getting her own way from the men in her life. It was rather a shock to her to encounter in Jacqueline a woman who also had strong views which she was not shy to express. She was not accustomed to criticism. So there were difficult clashes between the two women and I was caught in the cross-fire. This made me unhappy: I have always disliked conflict. Over time, their relationship improved and in her later years, my mother came to appreciate and love Jacqueline.

Michelle went a local private school, St Helen's Northwood. She was always studious and performed very well academically. At the age of 11, she went to North London Collegiate School, the school which Jacqueline had attended as had Sally, Steven's wife. This is an outstanding academic school from where Michelle went to study history at University College, Oxford in 1989. My father died in December 1988. He had been ill with a form of dementia for some time and in the last months of his life was being cared for in a mental hospital in York. The last time I saw him, he was heavily dosed with medication so that he was barely conscious. I found it very upsetting to see him in this state. I recall telling him that Michelle had been awarded a place at Oxford. It clearly registered, because his lips moved slightly and a hint of a smile fleetingly illuminated his impassive face. His passion for education stayed with him until the end.

My father was the first of our parents to die. He had been suffering from mini-strokes for some time. These had led to a loss of short-term memory and later to a complete change in personality and even some acts of violence. It was dreadful for all of us to see this degeneration and particularly unbearable for my mother. The main burden of coping with the practical problems that arose and of supporting my mother fell on Robert, who lives in Leeds to this day. He dealt with it magnificently. Although my father's death was a great relief, it was still very sad for us all. After he died, we started to go to Leeds to see my mother more frequently. For several years, she thrived on a combination of bridge and holidays. But gradually she declined and started to suffer from a form of dementia too. She spent the last period of her life in a nursing home. Towards the end, she said very little. She would smile feebly when I arrived to see her, but soon retreated into her private world. I would hold her hands and sing quietly to her some Bulgarian songs that she had taught me many years before. So far as I could tell, she enjoyed hearing them, but little else. She died in January 2005. Michelle was lovely with her and very caring during the final difficult years. Earlier, just as I had done as a child, she used to love listening to my mother describing her life in pre-war Europe.

After two years at Little Saints (the infant school for St Helen's), Steven went to St Martin's School in Northwood. This was an old-fashioned preparatory school from which boys were expected to move on to a public school. The headmaster wanted Steven to go to a boarding school, but we had other ideas. At the age of 13, he won a scholarship to Merchant Taylor's School, Northwood from where he went to study biochemistry at Magdalen College, Oxford. Naturally, I was thrilled that both of our children went to Oxford. My father would have been so proud of Steven who was his favourite grandchild.

We were fortunate that both children were academically very able. They did not need any additional coaching. We were not called on to spend much time helping them with their studies. I think I helped a little with Latin, but that was about the extent of it. Our children spend a huge amount of time helping our grandchildren with their studies and providing them with extra coaching. We would probably have done the same in today's world. The competition now is far greater than it was 30 years ago.

For most of our married lives we have lived in Metroland, which is served by the Metropolitan Line on the London Underground and was famously celebrated by the poet John Betjeman. It is not fashionable or chic or exciting. It does not attract literati or famous people. We have been living in what we still refer to as our family home for 35 years now. It is a detached house with a large garden. We love the garden and gardening. Trees and plants provide us both with a sense of calm and relaxation: what my mother used to call 'balsam'. We feel at home in this environment. Our suburban upbringings have left their mark. About 25 years ago, we bought a flat in Bloomsbury Square. This has been a perfect city pad. But we have never regarded it as 'home'.

As our children were growing up, we led an unexceptional and happy family life. Raising children is a challenge for anyone. Jacqueline was a brilliant mother. My parenting skills were less impressive but I tended to raise my game at the weekends. The four of us often went for walks in the nearby Chiltern Hills. We introduced the children to walking when they were very young. We used to keep their spirits up by feeding them with pieces of fruit and my telling them stories. When they were very young, they demanded to hear the same stories repeated over and over again and were upset if I tried something new. As they became older, they wanted novelty and more exciting stories. And eventually, they wanted no more stories.

Most of the time at weekends, we did things as a family. It was only occasionally that I spent time with the children on my own. I now regret this. There was one day when they were well into their teens and Jacqueline asked me to take them to some courses (one was a cycling proficiency course). When driving on our way to lunch, I managed to crash the car into the concrete wall of a multi-storey car park. Totally unreasonably, I lost my temper. The children insisted on taking me to a bookshop to buy me a book in the hope that this would help me to calm down. Not my finest hour, but perhaps one of theirs.

The one area of domestic life which was my domain was music. Jacqueline is not musical. Early in our married lives, she briefly had piano lessons, but to little effect. Unlike me, she was not brought up in a house full of music. Her mother Rita was tone deaf and, so far as I could tell, completely unresponsive to music. But she was an excellent wordsmith. On my twenty-seventh birthday (the first after our marriage), Rita gave me the *Shorter Oxford English Dictionary.* Her inscription read: 'To John. Our new son-in-law. To help us understand one another even better. Love and all good wishes. Rita'.

I had a very good relationship with Rita and Bobby. Rita was the perfect mother-in-law. I loved them both and I think that I was a good son-in-law. Whenever Jacqueline complained to her about me, she always said (however justified the complaint might be) 'Poor John, he works so hard'. Jacqueline soon realised that it was futile to complain. In 1983, when Rita finally persuaded Bobby to leave their family home in Mill Hill, with my encouragement they moved to a flat close to us in Northwood. They saw a great deal of our children as they were growing up. As a solicitor who had a real interest in the law, Bobby followed my career with great interest. He was not good at showing his emotions, but I know that he was proud of my achievements. He died in 1993 shortly after I was appointed as a High Court Judge. He attended my swearing in and engaged with Lord Chancellor Mackay in lively conversation. His cognitive functions survived intact until the end.

Rita was extremely outgoing. In the early 1970s, she entered local politics for the first time. She started as a Conservative councillor on the Greater London Council and then became a councillor of the London Borough of Barnet. By 1979, she was the Mayor of Barnet. Her meteoric rise brought her into contact with Mrs Thatcher who was the MP for Finchley and became Prime Minister for the first time in 1979. The two women got on well together. They would talk about clothes as well as more serious matters. Rita continued to thrive and enjoy her family until, like both my parents, she started to suffer from dementia: in her case, Alzheimer's disease. She spent her final months in Nightingale, a wonderful Jewish care home. Despite her illness, she did not suffer a personality change. She remained kind and optimistic to the end. She died in 2000, one week before Michelle was married to Jon.

Having been exposed to music for almost 50 years, Jacqueline does now enjoy it, although she does not share my passion for it. My passion continues unabated. Sadly, our children showed no real interest in music. Steven started to learn to play the piano and cello, but he would be the first to say that he had little musical talent, although, to my astonishment, he sang in a choir at Magdalen. He passed grade 1 on the piano and grade 3 on the cello and then gave both up instruments. Michelle was rather more persevering with the piano and clarinet. She passed grade 6 on the piano and grade 7 on the clarinet. But once she went to university, she dropped both. I spent many hours trying to help her with her practising, especially on the piano. The effort taxed the patience of both of us. There were occasional stormy sessions with one or both of us walking off the site. I did, however, enjoy accompanying her clarinet playing.

Three of our grandchildren play musical instruments. Sebastian (Michelle's older son) plays the piano and trombone; Justin (her younger son) plays the bassoon; and Edward (Steven's younger son) plays the piano. I have spent more time with Sebastian than with the other two. He has passed his grade 6 on the piano. I have enjoyed working with him and trying to pass on some of the discipline that was instilled into me by Fanny Waterman. We also play piano duets together to my delight and, I think, his too. In the summer of 2018, I accompanied him for his grade 1 trombone examination. Doing this gave me great pleasure.

But I must return to the early life of our children. Birthday parties became more of a challenge as they grew up. We devised and organised these parties ourselves without the assistance of professional entertainers. Perhaps the most memorable party was one which involved a murder mystery. Two teams of children had to go into the local woods and, following clues which we had buried in the undergrowth, to search for a dead body which we had wrapped in a pair of my pyjamas. The pyjamas were copiously smeared with tomato ketchup. We all enjoyed this home-made entertainment very much.

Holidays were an important part of our family life. When the children were small, we used to go to Woolacombe, Devon. We then started to go abroad. In 1976, we went to a very basic holiday camp in St Aygulf on the Cote d'Azur. One day, we were invited to the nearby luxurious flat of Jacqueline's uncle Gerald. He insisted on driving us back to our camp in his Rolls Royce. We managed to persuade him not to inspect the tiny wooden huts which comprised our sleeping accommodation. Gerald was a warm, generous man who had made a great deal of money from selling high quality china. Throughout his life, we felt like the poor relations. He always said that his sister Rita and her family were clever but lacked common sense. In his lexicon, lack of common sense meant lack of real wealth.

From 1976 onwards, we went abroad every summer. All my adult life, I have been drawn to Europe. For several years we went on camping holidays with a company called Canvas Holidays. The tents were erected by the company and were well-appointed. Although our children later learned the art of erecting a tent, we never did. Canvas Holidays was as close to camping as the two of us ever got. We loved the first few of these holidays, which were all in France. But after a while, the toilet facilities began to take their toll as did the sound of small rodents racing round in the kitchen and in the space between the inner and outer lining of the tent.

In the late 1970s and early 1980s, we used to make a point of going to Vevey to see Malvine. She was still sprightly and active both physically and mentally. She had moved out of her flat overlooking the Lake of Geneva and was living in the Hotel de Famille. She was still able to walk along her beloved *quai* taking the children by the arm and swinging them as she went.

As I have described in chapter 1, she came to Leeds for her ninetieth birthday in 1982. There was quite a gathering. The four of us drove up from London together with Uncle Emil, one of Malvine's siblings. He regaled us with some of his memories of life in Sofia before the First World War. I deeply regret not having recorded what he told us. Others who were present at the party were my parents, Robert and his family, my aunt Margit and my cousins James and Janet, and their children. Michelle made a speech on behalf of all the great-grandchildren. Malvine died in 1983.

In 1981, we bought a one-bedroom flat in Haute-Nendaz which was then quite a small resort in the Swiss canton of Valais. I had been vaguely thinking of buying a property in the Alps. A love of the mountains of Switzerland was deeply embedded in my psyche. Those early holidays which I have described in chapter three had left an indelible mark. We had never even heard of Haute-Nendaz. Foolishly, we agreed to go out for an inspection weekend with an agent who was selling property in Switzerland. My father wisely warned me to be careful and to look at a range of properties in several resorts. The agent only showed us some flats in one block in Haute-Nendaz. We (or more precisely, I) fell for a flat which had a large balcony overlooking the Rhone Valley. We agreed to pay the asking price then and there. We were seduced by some brilliant salesmanship and paid far too much. I can only say in mitigation that the agent also seduced an English estate agent, a Professor of Law from Cambridge University and various other apparently wise and intelligent people into buying flats in the same block at similarly inflated prices. It was an embarrassingly bad investment which was only partially rescued by the fall in sterling against the Swiss franc since 1981. Jacqueline was more circumspect than I was and altogether more doubtful about the enterprise. But she agreed to the purchase, although she insisted that she would do no cooking. She said: 'Either you take me out or you do the cooking'. She has held me to this ever since. As the local restaurants are poor and expensive, I do all the cooking even when we entertain friends for dinner. My repertoire has not expanded over the years.

We still own the flat. For many years, we went there every winter to ski and every summer to walk. We had many lovely holidays, first with the children and later on our own. The children both loved the skiing. I believe that Steven liked the walking, but Michelle did not. In retrospect, I can say that perhaps we should have done more exciting things in the summer than walking in the same mountain resort every year. But both of our children are now serious walkers and take their children along with them. We no longer ski, but we still walk enthusiastically in the mountains.

On graduating, Michelle decided that she wanted to qualify as a solicitor. This came as a complete surprise to us, since she had never shown any interest in the Law. In fact, her intelligence and analytical skills equipped her well to be an excellent lawyer. But she soon found that she did not enjoy the life of a solicitor in a large commercial City firm. So she became a government lawyer in the Treasury Solicitor's Office where she prospered. Politics and government policy appealed to her more than commercial life. After a while, she decided to move to the mainstream Civil Service because she felt that in this way she could make a real contribution to the development and delivery of government policies. And this she has done with great success in the various departments in which she has worked. She is now near the top of the Senior Civil Service ladder.

After reading biochemistry at Oxford, Steven studied for a PhD in cell biology at Gonville and Caius College, Cambridge. His supervisor was Professor John Gurdon (a Nobel Prize winner) who was very enthusiastic about Steven's ability and disappointed that he did not stay on and continue with his research. But Steven did not want to spend his life in a laboratory. He had always shown an interest in economics and business, unlike the rest of the immediate family.

He joined McKinseys and did management consultancy for a short time. After that, he joined the healthcare section of Apax Partners, a private equity firm, and flies around the world (principally to the United States) doing hair-raising deals which involve enormous sums of money. He is now a full partner and I am looking to him to support us in our dotage if that becomes necessary.

Jacqueline and I are both proud of our children and their achievements in their very different worlds. They seem to have inherited the work ethic with which I have been imbued since my earliest years. Despite their hectic lives, both professionally and domestically, we are still in close contact with them.

One can give one's children a good education and, one hopes, set an example by leading a good life and instilling in them good moral values. But there are limits to parental influence. There was no certainty that our children would find partners, still less suitable partners, with whom to share their lives. Our own experience had shown the overwhelming power of sexual love and the impetuosity of youth. Michelle fell in love with Jonathan Hall (now a QC). From our point of view, it was a pity that he was not Jewish. But we liked him and his family. Michelle and Jon are extremely well-suited to each other. They struck a deal whereby any children would bear his name and be brought up as Jews. He has been fascinated by the exotic background of Michelle's family. Although as an atheist he understandably has never converted to Judaism, he has joined our Jewish family with gusto. He has learnt some Hebrew; fasts on the Day of Atonement as a gesture of solidarity with Michelle; and performs security duties at the Reform synagogue to which they belong. He is proud of Michelle's achievements and has encouraged her greatly. He has had a meteoric career as a barrister and has been instructed by government and other public bodies in many high-profile cases. Despite the stress imposed by his work, he has always found time to be an excellent full-time family man.

We never expected Steven to marry a Jewish girl. Most of his girlfriends were not Jewish. Ever the deal-maker, he agreed with us to try for one year to find a suitable Jewish girl. I think it was during this year that he met Sally. She is unquestionably a suitable Jewish girl. We knew her parents and two of her grandparents were friends of Rita and Bobby. Sally is a solicitor who no longer practises. She has established a consultancy called Firm Sense Limited and advises professionals on how to enhance their effectiveness. She is now also on the board of the University of East London and the Haberdashers' Livery Company. Sally and Steven are mutually supportive and are proud of each other's achievements. When Steven is in the country, he devotes himself to his family with great energy.

The birth of our first grandchild was a great moment in our lives. Rosalind (Rosi) was born in 2002. As the only girl, she occupies a special place among our five grandchildren. She was followed by four noisy boys Sebastian (2004), Oliver (2005), Justin (2006) and Edward (2007). They are all very different and all continue to give us great pleasure. In the early years, Michelle's three and Steven's two used to spend weekends with us from time to time. It was always a pleasure to have them come to stay but something of a relief when they returned to the bosom of their families. Now they can defeat us at any sport in which we still dare to engage with them, even Edward the youngest. And Sebastian can now beat me at chess too. They all know far more than we do about all manner of things. We take great delight in this. It is, of course, how it should be. This is not the place to describe the details of their lives. I hope that they will find this memoir of some interest. I know that the cricket fanatic Oliver will enjoy reading of my failures on the cricket field and comparing them with his own successes.

For most of our married lives, Jacqueline and I have been keen walkers. As I said in my Valedictory speech, I have been happiest when in her company, just doing the simplest of things. Among the things to which I was referring was walking in the countryside, preferably hilly or mountainous countryside. My early years of walking in the hills of the North of England have left their mark. Flat featureless landscape has no attraction for me. Since about 1990, we have been on walking holidays, usually in France or Italy, with a group of friends led by Sir Ivor Crewe (Master of University College, Oxford). Ivor plans these holidays with great skill and enthusiasm and selflessly makes all the travel arrangements and chooses and books the hotels.

Apart from this, the two of us have particularly enjoyed holidays walking from place to place alone with our bags transported by a travel company. We have done many such walks both in the United Kingdom and in Europe. There is something wonderfully wholesome and restorative about a long walk through beautiful countryside with one's life companion. I have always loved maps, particularly the UK Ordnance Survey maps. They are so informative about landscape and man's influence on it. I view with dismay the prospect that the arrival of the GPS may well sound the death knell of maps. The accommodation on these holidays has never approached the five star level. Sometimes it is uncomfortably small. This is usually because tiny en suite facilities have been carved out of bedrooms which were often quite small in the first place. But this does not trouble us. We have spacious facilities at home. Five star hotels with their uniform marble floors and mirrors hold little attraction for us. I suspect that, if Jacqueline had married a man who loved expensive cars and smart hotels in fashionable places, she might have been more attracted by them than she is now. But that is a pointless speculation.

We shall continue walking as long as we can, enjoying each other's company. And I hope to live long enough to see our grandchildren mature into happy and fulfilled adults.

17

Epilogue

FOR MANY YEARS, I had to overcome a natural shyness and endure the embarrassment of blushes sweeping across my face. I did not regard myself as a leader. I was happy to be an obedient follower and enjoy the praise of those who were leaders. It was only when I was well into middle age that I discovered that I could be an effective leader.

I have described earlier how Lord Taylor asked me to take over as chairman of the Ethnic Minorities Advisory Committee from Mr Justice Brooke. He said that, after the zealous and almost Messianic Brooke, he wanted someone to calm things down and steady the ship. He thought that my combination of firmness and emollience was what was needed. This is a theme that was picked up in the letter I received from the leader of the EU team engaged in the modernisation of the Cypriot civil justice system which I have quoted in chapter fourteen. And in his speech for my swearing-in as Master of the Rolls, Lord Wilson said:

> It is the mildness, sometimes almost gentleness, of your manner in and out of court. It can mislead people. For behind it there lies a steely determination.

Although my father thought that the thunderstorm which accompanied my birth was a sign of something portentous, I am sure that neither he nor my mother could have envisaged that I would have the kind of life that I have been fortunate enough to enjoy. I owe my strong work ethic to my parents, especially my mother. Even in my retirement, I am unhappy if I am not stretched and under pressure. I was lucky to have loving parents who were devoted to their children and determined that they should succeed to the limits of their ability. But they were rather protective and controlling. They did not encourage me to spread my wings. Even when I went to Paris at the age of 17, I stayed in the extremely comfortable apartment of one of my mother's school friends. I would have matured and benefited greatly from two years of National Service (a period of peacetime compulsory service in the armed forces away from home). But National Service was phased out at about the time of my eighteenth birthday. I might have rebelled against my parents' protectiveness and quest for obedience and conformity. Fortunately for them, I didn't do so.

I have been lucky in so many ways. I never had to fight in a war. My generation has taken for granted the fact that there has been peace in Western Europe since the Second World War. It now seems unthinkable that there might be another war between the countries of Western Europe. But nothing is certain. I firmly believe that the EU has played a part in cementing the relationship between the countries of Western Europe. That is why I view Brexit with such dismay. It is perhaps not surprising in view of my background that I feel a strong affinity with Europe. I still love taking the cross-Channel ferry and driving through France and into Switzerland. I love hearing spoken French and Italian and eating French and Italian food.

But like anyone, I have had my reverses and disappointments. I was disappointed not to get a first class degree in Greats at Oxford despite the fact that there were very good reasons for my near miss and I had the consolation of a good first in Mods. Setting myself on fire when attempting to light a barbeque in 1990 was horrific and could easily have led to an early death. Perhaps most difficult of all was the ME or post-viral fatigue and the resulting depression from which I suffered between about 2008 and 2010 which I have described in chapter nine.

I gradually acquired a certain toughness and independence of spirit over many years. But I have always sought consensus where possible. That is why I enjoy chairing committees. I gain a great deal of satisfaction from allowing people of differing views a reasonable opportunity to have their say and then helping them reach a decision to which all or most of them can subscribe. I dislike extremes. When I hear a person propounding strong right-wing views, I tend to move firmly to the left. And when I hear a person advocating strong left-wing views, I lurch to the right. The middle ground is my natural habitat. The motto I chose for my coat of arms which now hangs in a corridor in Middle Temple reads '*in media via*'.

In most legal disputes, there is a winner and a loser and the judge has to choose. Unless the losing party was a villain, I tried to let him or her down as gently as possible, explaining carefully my reasons for doing so. I felt it important to lessen the pain of losing so far as I could. But I have learnt not only as a judge, but more generally, that it is impossible to please everyone all the time. Sometimes, plain speaking is necessary.

Although I have always strived to avoid conflict, I have not been afraid to speak my mind and stand up to people if I disagree with them. From time to time, I have had to criticise people or confront them. Occasions when I have had to do this range from renegotiating the terms of remuneration of the senior clerk at 2 Garden Court; expressing my disagreement with government ministers over aspects of their policy and expressing my disagreement publicly and without mincing my words when giving evidence to the Justice Committee in Parliament; and disagreeing with the opinions expressed by colleagues in the Court of Appeal and Supreme Court. But I have not sought out or relished such disagreements or confrontations.

I am proud that I have generally been regarded as a progressive judge. As Lord Wilson put it: 'You are, by nature, a progressive. But a cautious one'. I like to be as well prepared as the circumstances will allow. I am prepared to be bold and innovative, but only when I am sure of my ground.

In describing this journey through my life, I have been struck by how rich, varied and exciting it has been. It is most unlikely that I would have had such a life if I had played safe and stayed in Leeds to practise at the local Bar. I am grateful to my parents for encouraging me to accept the offer from Chambers in London from which so much else in my life has flowed. Not least has been the chance meeting with Jacqueline in 1969. My decision to ask her to marry me was by far the most momentous event in my life and our lifelong partnership a source of joy and comfort to me.

Index

A v B plc (Flitcroft) v MGN Ltd, 117–18
AAA v Associated Newspapers Ltd, 187
Administrative Court, 98–99, 198
adjudicators:
  appointing, 108
advocacy, 199
  bad advocacy, 203
  oral advocacy, 202–3
  training, 212
Al Rawi v Security Service, 134–35
Appellate Committee of the House of Lords,
        119, 123–24, 131, 135
appellate judging process, 148
  Court of Appeal, 202
  Supreme Court, 201–2
appointing adjudicators, 108
appointing judges, 88, 107–8, 123, 127
  appellate judges, 148
articles programme, 61
Assange v Swedish Prosecution Authority, 134
Assistant Recorder, 85–86, 91, 196, 203

Bar:
  applying for silk, 78
  appointment to High Court, 87–88
  Assistant Recorder, 85–86, 91, 196, 203
  civil law, 76
    clinical negligence, 79
    construction cases, 76–79, 84
    non-construction cases, 81–84
  criminal cases, 75–76, 86–87
  diversification of practice, 81–84
  family law, 75
  Recorder, 86
Bar Professional Training Course, 212
barristers:
  judges compared, 198–99
  Queen's Counsels, 78–79
Being a Jew
  anti-Semitism, 223–24
  Bar-Mitzvah, 36–37
  Jewish identity, 222, 227
  Israel, 222–23
  legal profession, 225–26
  religion, 30–31, 48, 221–22

Belhaj and another v Straw and others, 194–95
Bencher of the Middle Temple, 211–12
  appointment, 84–85
Bingham, Tom (Baron Bingham of Cornhill):
  appointment as Lord Chief Justice, 93
  Court of Appeal Criminal Division, 92
  *R v Secretary of State for the Home
        Department, ex parte Amin,* 118
Black v Wilkinson, 189
*BPP Holdings Ltd v Revenue and Customs
        Commissioners,* 159
Bull v Hall, 189

chambers, 66–67
  2 Garden Court, 80–81
  11 King's Bench Walk, 67–68
children, *see* Dyson, Steven; Hall, Michelle
Civil Justice Council, 122–23, 143, 146,
        151, 152
civil procedure reforms, 119–22
Clarke, Anthony (Lord Clarke
        of Stone-cum-Ebony), 120, 127,
        134–35, 116
conversion course, 61–62
courtship, 70–71
Court of Appeal, 113–14
  A v B plc (Flitcroft) v MGN Ltd,
        117–18
  civil appeals, 114–19
  criminal appeals, 124–25
  diversity of cases, 114
  *Inland Revenue Commissioners v John
        Lewis Properties Plc,* 114–15
  invitation to apply, 112
  judgments, 114–15
  *Mbasogo, president of Equatorial Guinea
        v Logo Ltd and others,* 116–17
  Paragon Finance Plc v Nash, 115
  *R (Wood) v Commissioner of Police
        of the Metropolis,* 119
  *R v Secretary of State for the Home
        Department, ex parte Amin,* 118
  swearing in, 113
Court of Appeal Criminal Division (CACD),
        90–93, 124

cricket, 27–28, 35, 38
criminal cases, 75–76, 95–98
    appeals, 124–25

Denning, Tom (Baron Denning), 77, 153, 164,
        176, 179
Denton v T H White Ltd, 159, 204
Deputy Head of Civil Justice, 120–21
    Civil Justice Council, 122–23, 143
    Designated Civil Judges, 121–22
    "judicial family", 123–24
    retirement, 124
    Rule Committee, 122–23
Designated Civil Judges, 121–22, 158, 183
divorce:
    divorce cases, 65, 75
    mother's divorce from first husband, 4
Dyson, Jacqueline (*née* Levy) (wife), 228
    education, 70–71
    employment, 74, 228–29
    married life:
        children, 228, 230–31
        work, 228–29
    meeting, 68–69
    parents, 70–71, 229
Dyson, Gisella (*née* Kremsier) (mother), 1–6, 224
    arrival in Leeds, 6, 19–21
    influence of, 45, 216
    marriage to Richard, 6–7, 8
    relationship with Jacqueline, 229
    religion, 36–37, 48, 222
Dyson, Richard (father), 14–18
    death, 230
    family name, 20–21
    marriage, 6–7, 8, 19–21
    travel, 18–19
Dyson, Steven (son), 74, 89, 164, 230, 232
    career, 234–35
    marriage, 235
Dytch, Freda (paternal grandmother), 14–17,
        20–21
Dytch, Louis (paternal grandfather), 14–18, 21

education:
    Classics, 35–36, 40–42
    Leeds Grammar School:
        A'Levels, 42–43
        Junior School, 25–32
        Main School, 33–45
        O'Levels, 38
    prep school, 23–25
    see also Wadham College, Oxford

engagement, 72–73
European Convention on Human Rights, 92,
        99, 117–18, 119, 133–34, 152–53,
        165, 178, 186–87

father, *see* Dyson, Richard

Garland, Patrick, 64–65, 76–77
grandchildren, 232, 235–36

Hall, Michelle (*née* Dyson) (daughter), 89,
        184, 229, 230
    death of Malvine, 232–33
    marriage, 235
    solicitor, 234
*Harb v HRH Prince Abdul Aziz bin Fahd bin
        Abdul Aziz*, 193–94
hearings by telephone, 121
High Court judge:
    appointment, 87–88
    Circuit Judge, 93–106
    Court of Appeal Criminal Division, 90–93
    head of the Official Referees, 106–8
    knighthood, 89–90
    swearing in, 89
    Technology and Construction Court, 107–8
Hillsborough Stadium Disaster
        Inquiry, 81–82, 207
holidays:
    adulthood, 167, 217–19, 233–34
    childhood, 12–13, 32–33, 37
    honeymoon, 73–74
    retirement, 217–19
    student, as a, 60–61, 62
Human Rights Act 1998, 92, 99, 117, 119, 149
Hyamson, Derek, 64–66
*HJ (Iran) v Secretary of State for the Home
        Department*, 133

*Inland Revenue Commissioners v John Lewis
        Properties Plc*, 114–15
Irvine, Derry (Baron Irvine of Lairg), 93,
        106–7, 111, 113
Israel (visits to), 59–60, 209–10, 224

Judge, Igor (Baron Judge), 139–40,
        141–43, 155
judges:
    appointing judges, 88, 107–8, 123, 127
    appellate judges, 148
    barristers compared, 198–99
    pressures, 199–200

public criticism, 203–4
risk of desensitisation, 198
Judicial Appointment Commission (JAC), 88,
    127, 147–48, 181
Judicial Committee of the Privy Council
    (JCPC), 136–37
"judicial family", 123–24
judicial appointments, 125
judicial review cases, 93, 98–99
    importance of, 179
    proposed reforms, 151, 163
    R v Home Secretary ex p Norney, 99–101
    *R v North Derbyshire Health Authority ex
        p Kenneth Graeme Fisher*, 101
Judicial Studies Board (JSB), 109–110
    Equal Treatment Advisory Committee,
        110–11
    Ethnic Minorities Advisory Committee,
        110–11
jury service, 125–26
jury trials, 63, 76, 91–92, 96, 126, 196–97,
    198, 204

Keating, Donald, 64–65, 76–77, 79–80, 81,
    172–73
Kremsier, Malvine (*nee* Goldstein)
    (grandmother), 1–13
    holidays with, 32, 233
    influence of, 90, 229
    ninetieth birthday, 9, 233
Kremsier, Jenö (grandfather), 1–9, 15

Lamb v Camden London Borough Council,
    77, 172
Legal Group of the Friends of the Hebrew
    University, Jerusalem (FHU), 111–12
Levy, Bobby (father-in-law), 71–72, 89, 231–32
Levy, Rita (mother-in-law), 70–73, 89, 229,
    231–32
*Locabail (UK) Limited v Bayfield Properties
    Limited*, 106
Lord Chancellor v Detention Action,
    191–92
*Lubenham Fidelities v South Pembrokeshire
    District Council*, 80
*Lumba v Secretary of State for the Home
    Department*, 131–32

McCann v UK, 99
*Macob Civil Engineering Ltd v Morrison
    Construction*, 108, 163
Malvine, *see* Kremsier, Malvine

marriage:
    honeymoon, 73–74
    wedding, 73
Master of the Rolls
    application, 140
    diary, activities and meetings, 141–85
    interview, 140
    invitation, 139
    memorable cases:
        AAA v Associated Newspapers Ltd, 187
        Belhaj and another v Straw and others,
            194–95
        Black v Wilkinson, 189
        *Harb v HRH Prince Abdul Aziz bin Fahd
            bin Abdul Aziz*, 193–94
        Lord Chancellor v Detention Action,
            191–92
        *Othman (Abu Qatada) v Secretary
            of State for the Home Department*,
            186–87
        *R (David Tracey) v Cambridge University
            Hospitals NHS Trust and Secretary
            of State for Health*, 190–91
        R (Evans) v Attorney General,
            189–90
        *R (Gudanaviciene and others) v Director
            of Legal Aid Casework and the
            Lord Chancellor*, 191, 192
        *R (Long) v Secretary of State for
            Defence*, 192–93
        *R (Miranda) v Secretary of State for the
            Home Department*, 193
        R (Nicklinson) v Ministry of Justice, 188
        *R (on the application of AM) v Director
            of Public Prosecution*, 188–89
        *R (T) v Greater Manchester Chief
            Constable*, 186
    origins of the position, 141
    swearing in, 141
maternal grandparents, *see* Kremsier, Malvine;
        Kremsier, Jenö
*Mbasogo, President of Equatorial Guinea v
    Logo Ltd and others*, 116–17
Middle Temple, 62–63, 79, 212, 214–16,
    238
    Bencher of the Middle Temple, 84–85
    Deputy Treasurer of Middle Temple,
        208, 211
    Treasurer of Middle Temple, 157, 211–217
Mitchell v News Group Newspapers Ltd,
    159, 204
mother, *see* Dyson, Gisella

music, 47–48, 50, 59, 91, 215–16, 221, 231–32
  Dame Fanny Waterman, 31, 38–39, 45, 94,
       105, 167, 210, 232
  piano lessons, 30–31, 39–40, 45, 216

Neuberger, David (Baron Neuberger
       of Abbotsbury), 68, 127, 139,
       154–55, 166, 171, 184, 212

oral advocacy, 202–3
*Othman (Abu Qatada) v Secretary of State
       for the Home Department*, 186–87
over-turned/reversed judgments, 100–1, 128,
       140, 200–1
Oxford:
  arrival, 52–53
  Union debates, 54–55
  see also Wadham College, Oxford

Paragon Finance Plc v Nash, 115
Paris, 8, 48–50, 175, 237
  mother, 5
paternal grandparents, *see* Dytch, Freda;
       Dytch Louis
Phillips, Nicholas (Baron Phillips of Worth
       Matravers), 120, 122–23, 127, 129,
       132, 134, 135–36, 139–40, 143
Privy Council, 113, 136–37
pupillages:
  Derek Hyamson, under, 65–66
  Patrick Garland, under, 64–65

*R (David Tracey) v Cambridge University
       Hospitals NHS Trust and Secretary
       of State for Health*, 190–91
R (Evans) v Attorney General, 189–90
*R (Gudanaviciene and others) v Director
       of Legal Aid Casework and the
       Lord Chancellor*, 191, 192
R (Long) v Secretary of State for Defence,
       192–93
*R (Miller) c Secretary of State for Exiting the
       European Union*, 174
*R (Miranda) v Secretary of State for the Home
       Department*, 193
R (Nicklinson) v Ministry of Justice, 188
*R (on the application of AM) v Director
       of Public Prosecution*, 188–89
R (T) v Greater Manchester Chief Constable,
       186
*R (Wood) v Commissioner of Police of the
       Metropolis*, 119

R v Home Secretary ex p Norney, 99–101
*R v North Derbyshire Health Authority ex
       parte Kenneth Graeme Fisher*, 101
*R v Secretary of State for the Home
       Department ex parte Amin*, 118
*R v Secretary of State for the Home
       Department ex parte Hardial
       Singh*, 132
Rabone v Pennine Care NHS Trust, 133–34
Rance v Mid-Downs Health Authority, 84
re Lehman Bros International (Europe), 134
Recorder, 86–87
religion, 30–31, 48, 221–22
  Bar-Mitzvah, 36–37
  maternal grandparents, 3
  see also Being a Jew
retirement:
  arbitral appointments, 206–7
  advisory work, 207
  London Borough of Lewisham inquiry
       into redevelopment of New
       Bermondsey, 207
  Republic of Cyprus reform of civil
       procedure rules, 207–8
  Treasurer of the Middle Temple, 208,
       211–17
  time with family, 208–9
  lecturing, 209
  Israel, 209–10
  travel, 209–10
  music, 210–11
  mediation, 207
Rodger, Alan (Baron Rodger
       of Earlsferry), 130
*RT (Zimbabwe) v Secretary of State
       for the Home Department*, 133

Smith v Ministry of Defence, 165
sports:
  athletics, 37–38
  cricket, 27–28, 35, 38
  football, 28–29
  rowing, 51–52
  rugby, 35
  Wadham College, Oxford, 51–52, 58
Supreme Court Judge:
  appointment, 127, 129
  interview, 127
  judgments, 131–32, 135
  lecturing, 137
  praise for role as, 135–36
  privileges associated with position, 137–39

speaking, 137
swearing in, 129
sentencing tariff periods, 98–99

Taylor, Peter (Baron Taylor of Gosforth), 81,
91–93, 96, 98, 109, 111–12, 207, 237
Technology and Construction Court (TCC), 107–8
telephone, hearings by, 121
Thomas, John (Baron Thomas of Cwmgiedd),
141, 144, 155, 161, 183
title, 129, 219–20
peerage, lack of, 219–20
training:
Assistant Recorder, 85, 196–97
Bar Professional Training Course, 212
Ethnic Minorities Advisory Committee, 109–11
Judicial Studies Board, 109–10

Von Hannover v Germany, 118

Wadham College, Oxford, 43–44
accommodation, 53–54
final year, 61
Honorary Fellow, 113–14
music, 58–59
sporting activities, 58
studies, 56–58
tutorial system, 52–53
Waterman, Dame Fanny, 31, 38–39, 45, 94,
105, 167, 210–11, 232
Woolf, Harry (Baron Woolf), 126, 132,
219–20
Civil Justice Council, 122–23
civil procedure reforms, 119–20
Designated Civil Judges, 121–22